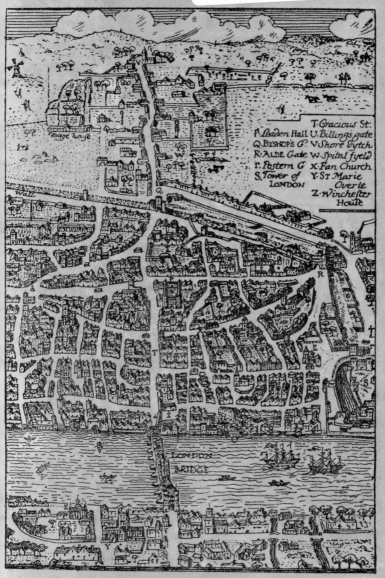

Bridge House

P. Leaden Hall
Q. Byshop's G.
R. Alde Gate
Γ. Postern G.
S. Tower of
LONDON

T. Gracious St.
U. Billings gate
V. Shore Dytch
W. Spital fyeld
X. Fan Church
Y. St Marie
   Overie
Z. Winchester
   House

Wall

LONDON
BRIDGE

Pleasance

from J. A. B.

29th March, 1924.

A WANDERER IN LONDON

THE TOWER AND THE TOWER BRIDGE

A WANDERER IN LONDON

BY

E. V. LUCAS

WITH SIXTEEN ILLUSTRATIONS IN COLOUR BY

NELSON DAWSON

AND THIRTY-SIX OTHER ILLUSTRATIONS

TWENTIETH EDITION

METHUEN & CO. LTD.
36 ESSEX STREET W.C.
LONDON

First Published	.	.	.	September	1906
Second Edition	.	.	.	October	1906
Third Edition	.	.	.	December	1906
Fourth Edition	.	.	.	January	1907
Fifth Edition	.	.	.	June	1907
Sixth Edition	.	.	.	January	1908
Seventh Edition	.	.	.	July	1909
Eighth Edition	.	.	.	January	1910
Ninth Edition	.	.	.	November	1910
Tenth Edition	.	.	.	May	1911
Eleventh Edition	.	.	.	November	1911
Twelfth Edition	.	.	.	February	1912
Thirteenth Edition	.	.	December	1912
Fourteenth Edition	.	.	May	1913
Fifteenth Edition	.	.	.	August	1913
Sixteenth Edition	.	.	.	January	1914
Seventeenth Edition	.	.	March	1915
Eighteenth Edition	.	.	August	1917
Nineteenth Edition	.	.	June	1919
Twentieth Edition	.	.		1920

CONTENTS

CHAPTER I.

v

CONTENTS

LIST OF ILLUSTRATIONS

IN COLOUR

LIST OF ILLUSTRATIONS

IN MONOTONE

viii

LIST OF ILLUSTRATIONS

ix

NOTE

The reproduction of "The Holy Family" by Leonardo da Vinci has
been made by permission of Mr. F. Hollyer, 9 Pembroke Square, W.,
from whom carbon prints can be obtained.

PREFACE TO FIFTEENTH EDITION

SINCE this book was written, in 1905-6, London has undergone many and vast changes. She has added to her treasures a museum wholly devoted to the illustration of her wondrous past; the National Gallery has been enlarged and is being re-arranged; South Kensington Museum has been re-built; the Tate Gallery has been extended and enriched; the Victoria Memorial has been erected; the Edward Memorial has been ordained; the decision to beautify Buckingham Palace has at last been reached; a new and superb opera house has been built and has failed; taxi-cabs have multiplied by thousands; picture theatres by hundreds; and the Underground has lost its smoke for ever. These are but a few of those changes which any writer who sets out to enumerate the charms of London has to take into consideration.

When I came to the task of revision it almost

seemed as if to write a new book—London Revisited—were best.   But perhaps wiser counsels prevailed, and I have retained the old title and done what I could to bring the text into line with 1913. A perfect reviser, however, would be at work almost daily, and as an example of the necessity for such vigilance and persistence, I may remark that very soon after this edition goes to press the priceless Layard collection of Old Masters will arrive at the National Gallery.

June, 1913.

A WANDERER IN LONDON

CHAPTER I

NO. 1 LONDON AND PICCADILLY

LONDON, whichever way we turn, is so vast and
varied, so rich in what is interesting, that to one
who would wander with a plastic mind irresponsibly day
after day in its streets and among its treasures there is not
a little difficulty in deciding where to begin, and there is
even greater difficulty in knowing where to end. Indeed,
to a book on London—to a thousand books on London—
there is no end.

But a beginning one can always make, whether it is
appropriate or otherwise, and since I chance to live in
Kensington and thus enter London by Kensington Gore
and Knightsbridge, there is some fitness in beginning at

1

Hyde Park Corner, by that square, taciturn, grey house just to the east of it which we call Apsley House, but which I have always been told is really No. 1 London— if any No. 1 London there be. Let us then begin at No. 1 London—just as a Frenchman bent upon discovering the English capital would begin at Charing Cross : Charing Cross, one of the meeting places of East and West, whose platform William the Conqueror would surely have kissed had he waited for the Channel steam-boat service.

To take a walk down Fleet Street—the cure for ennui invented by the most dogmatic of Londoners—is no longer an amusing recreation, the bustle is too great ; but to take a walk down Piccadilly on a fine day remains one of the pleasures of life : another reason for beginning with No. 1 London. Piccadilly between Hyde Park Corner and Devonshire House is still eminently a promenade. But only as far as Devonshire House. Once Berkeley Street is crossed and the shops begin, the saunterer is jostled ; while the Green Park having vanished behind the Ritz Hotel, the sun and the freshness are lost too. But between those two ducal houses on a smiling day one may enjoy as fair a walk as in any city in the world.

No. 1 London enjoys its priority only I think in verbal tradition. To the postman such an address might mean nothing, although the London postman has a reputation for tracking any trail, however elusive. The official address of Apsley House is, I fancy, 149 Piccadilly. Be that as it may, it is No. 1 to us, and a gloomy abode to boot, still wearing a dark frown of resentment for those broken windows, although the famous iron shutters have gone.

The London rough rarely mobilises now, and when he does he breaks no windows; but those were stormier days. Opposite is the Duke himself, in bronze, on his charger, looking steadfastly for ever at his old home, where the Waterloo survivors' dinner used to be held every year, with lessening numbers and lessening, until the victor himself was called away.

An earlier equestrian statue of Wellington once dominated the triumphal arch now at the head of Constitution Hill (where Captain Adrian Jones, that rare thing, a soldier sculptor, has set up a spirited quadriga), but this, I know not why, was taken down and erected afresh at Aldershot. A third Wellington trophy is the Achilles statue, at the back of Apsley House, in the Park, just across the roadway. This giant figure was cast from cannon taken at Salamanca and Vittoria, Toulouse and Waterloo, and was set up here by the women of England in honour of the great and invincible soldier. There is a coloured print which one may now and then see in the old shops (the last time I saw it was in the parlour of a Duke of Wellington inn at a little village in Wiltshire), of the hero of Waterloo riding beneath the Achilles on his little white horse, with his hand to the salute: one of the pleasantest pictures of the stern old man that I know, with the undulations of Hyde Park rolling away like a Surrey common in the distance.

We have no Iron Duke in these days, and Apsley House is desolate, almost sinister. Albeit within its walls are four of Jan Steen's pictures, to say nothing of one of the finest Correggios in England and Velasquez' portrait of himself.

And so we leave No. 1 London frowning behind us, and

come instantly to smiling wealth, for the little terrace of
mansions between Apsley House and Hamilton Place is a
stronghold of that powerful family which moved Heinrich
Heine to sarcasm and Hans Christian Andersen to sentiment, and is still the greatest force in European finance.

Never in the recent history of London have so many
changes come so rapidly as in the past few years, to which
belong not only the rise of the motor and the loss of
horse 'buses and cabs, but the elimination of hundreds of
landmarks and the sweeping away of whole streets drenched
with human associations.   Such is the ruthless march of
utilitarianism and luxury (some of the most conspicuous
new buildings being expensive hotels) that one has come to
entertain the uneasy feeling that nothing is safe.   Certainly
nothing is sacred.   A garage being required for the motor
cars of the Stock Exchange, what, one asks oneself, is there
to prevent the demolition of the Charterhouse ?   Since
Christ's Hospital could be moved bodily to Sussex in order
that more offices might rise in Newgate Street, why should
not the Brothers be sent to Bournemouth ?   The demand
for another vast caravanserai for American visitors on the
banks of the Thames may become acute any day : why
should not the Temple site be utilised ?   One lives in fear.

I never look at the Adelphi Terrace without a misgiv-
ing that when next I pass it will have vanished.   Nothing
but its comparative distance from the main stream of
commerce can have saved Gray's Inn.   There is an architect
round the corner ready with a florid terra-cotta tombstone
for every beautiful, quiet, old-world building in London.
Bedford Row is undoubtedly doomed : Queen Anne's Gate
trembles : Barton Street knows no repose.   Clifford's Inn is
going : Holywell Street has gone.   He who would see London
before London becomes unrecognisable must hasten his

A DUTCH LADY

AFTER THE PICTURE BY FRANS VAN MIEREVELT IN THE WALLACE COLLECTION

steps. The modern spirit can forgive everything except age.

The modern London architect dislikes large, restful, unworried spaces and long unbroken lines : hence many of our new buildings have been for the most part fussy and ornamental—and not at all, I think, representative of the national character. Somerset House (save for its fiddling little cupola) is perhaps London architecture at its simplest , the Law Courts, with all their amazing intricacy and elaboration, are London's public architecture at its most complex and unsuitable. One of the most satisfying buildings in London is the Adelphi Terrace ; one of the most charming, the little row of dependencies to the north of Kensington Palace. St. James's Palace is beautiful, but Buckingham Palace could hardly be more commonplace. It is, however, to be beautified soon.

To Somerset House, the Adelphi, St. James's Palace and the Tower Bridge, different though they are, the epithet English can be confidently applied ; but Buckingham Palace is French, and it would be difficult to use the word English of many of the great structures now rising in London. We seem to have no national school of urban architecture any longer, no steady ideals. The new London that is emerging so rapidly lacks any governing principle. The Ritz Hotel, for example, is Parisian, the Carlton and His Majesty's Theatre are Parisian, and in Russell Square there is a new hotel that has walked straight from Germany at its most German and grotesque.

But if London's completed new buildings are not satisfactory, their preparations are. There is nothing out of Méryon's etchings more impressive than our contractors' giant cranes can be—fixed high above the houses on their

scaffolding, with sixty vertical yards of chain hanging from
their great arms.   Against an evening sky, with a little
smoke from the engine purpling in the dying sun's rays,
and the mist beginning to blur or submerge the surrounding houses, these cranes and scaffoldings have an effect of
curious unreality, a hint even of Babylon or Nineveh, a
suggestion at any rate of all majestic building and builders
in history.   London has no more interesting or picturesque
sight than this.

Among the best public buildings of recent days are the
National Portrait Gallery, seen as one walks down the
Charing Cross Road, and the Institute of Painters in Water
Colours in Piccadilly, and the Record Office in Chancery
Lane.   The South Kensington School of Science is good, so
square and solid and grave is it, albeit perhaps a little too
foreign with its long and (in London) quite useless but
superbly decorative and beautiful loggia ; but what can
we say of the Imperial Institute and the Natural History
Museum and the Victoria and Albert Museum close by,
except that they are ambitious and symmetrical—the ideal
of the Kindergarten box of bricks carried out to its highest
power ?

It is as though London had been to a feast of architecture and stolen the scraps.   She has everything.   She has
Queen Anne's Mansions, that hideous barracks, and she has
Standen's in Jermyn Street, which is a Florentine palazzo ;
she has St. John's, Westminster, with its four unsightly
bell-towers, and St. Dunstan's-in-the-East with its indescribably graceful spire ; she has Charing's Eleanor Cross
and the Albert Memorial ; she has Westminster Hall and
the new Roman Catholic Cathedral ; she has Cannon Street
Station and the Heralds' College ; she has the terra cotta

Prudential Office in Holborn and within a few yards of it the medieval façade of Staple Inn; she has Euston Station and the new Ecclesiastical Commissioners' offices at Westminster; she has Park Lane and Bedford Row; she has the Astor Estate Office and Frascati's; she has Chelsea Hospital and Whitehall Court; she has the Gaiety Theatre and Spence's in St. Paul's Churchyard with its plain stone gables; she has the white severity of the Athenæum Club and Waring and Gillow's premises in Oxford Street, a gay enough building, but one that requires the spectator to be a hundred yards in front of it—which he cannot be.

London has learnt nothing from Philadelphia or Paris of the value of regularity, and if she can help it she never will. I suppose that Regent Street and Park Crescent were her last efforts on a large scale to get unity into herself, and now she has allowed the Regent Street curve to be broken by the Piccadilly Hotel. But since the glory of London is her disorder, it does not matter. Nothing will change that.

The narrowness and awkwardness of London streets are a perpetual reminder of the Englishman's incapacity or unwillingness to look ahead. In no other city in the world would it have been permitted to build recently two theatres and the Coliseum in a street so narrow as St. Martin's Lane. Nowhere else is traffic allowed to be so continuously and expensively congested at the whim of private companies. In the city itself, in the busy lanes off Cheapside for instance, where waggons are sometimes kept eight hours before they can be extricated, this narrowness means the daily loss of thousands of pounds. London's chance to become a civilised city was probably lost for ever at Waterloo. Had Wellington been defeated, carriages might now be running four abreast down Fleet Street. Yet as neither Napoleon nor Baron Haussman ever came our way, we must act accordingly; and the railway companies are still building on their branch lines arches wide enough to carry only a single pair of rails.

But in spite of architectural whimsies, there are in no city of the world so many houses in which one would like to live as in London. In spite of our studious efforts to arrange that every room shall have one or more draughts in it : in spite of our hostility to hot water pipes and our affection for dark and dreary basements; it is generally agreed that the English house can come nearer to the idea of home than that of any other people, and there can be no doubt that the English home is to be found in its perfection in London. Even as I write the memory of friendly houses, modern and Georgian and of even earlier date, in various parts of England, rises before me : houses over which the spirit of welcome broods, and within which are abundant fires, and lavender-scented sheets, and radiant almost laughing cleanliness, and that sense of quiet efficient order that is perhaps not the least charming characteristic of an English country house. Yet it is without treachery to these homes that one commends the comfortable London house as the most attractive habitation in the world ; for a house, I take it, should be in the midst of men, and in spite of so many blemishes which no one feels so much as the mistress of a country house—and the greatest of which is dirt—the London home is the homeliest of all. Perhaps a touch of grime is not unnecessary. Perhaps houses can be too clean for the truest human dailiness.

While walking about London I have noticed so many houses in which I could live happily ; and indeed to look for these is not a bad device to make walking in London

THE PARABLE OF THE UNMERCIFUL SERVANT

AFTER THE PICTURE BY REMBRANDT IN THE WALLACE COLLECTION

tolerable—to take the place of the thousand and one distractions and allurements of the walk in the country. One becomes a house-collector: marking down those houses which possibly by some unexpected turn of Fortune's wheel one might take, or which one wants to enter on friendly terms, or which one ought once to have lived in when needs were simpler.

Holland House is, of course, too splendid : one could never live there; but there is, for example, at 16, South Audley Street, a corner house where one would be quite happy, with double windows very prettily placed and paned, and a front door with glass panels quite as if it were in the country and within its own grounds, through which may be seen the hall and a few paintings and some old black oak. I expect that Captain Guest's house in Park Lane is fairly comfortable, although that also is too large ; and the low white house standing back in Curzon Street is probably too ambitious too; but there is a house at the corner of Cheyne Walk and Beaufort Street, in whose top windows over-looking the grey and pearl river one could be very serene. Other Cheyne Walk houses are very appealing too : No. 15, with a sundial, and No. 6, square and grave, and No. 2, with its little loggia, and Old Swan House, that riparian palace. If however I was to overlook the Thames I think I would choose one of the venerable residences on the walls of the Tower, from which one could observe not only the river but, at only one remove, the sea itself.

I have sometimes amused myself by jotting down the addresses of the houses I have liked, intending to find out who lived in them ; but the *London Directory* seems to be hopelessly beyond the reach of anyone not in an office or a public-house. But I do happen to know who it is that owns some of the most desirable houses in my bag. I know, for example, that Aubrey House, Kensington, belongs to Mr. W. C. Alexander; I know that the little low house facing St. James's Park by Queen Anne's Gate once belonged to the late Sir James Knowles; and there is Kingston House, a beautiful white house on the south side of Hyde Park, in Kensington Gore, an old house within its own gates, with a garden behind it, which I have discovered to belong to a certain Lord. Everyone that I know seems to want that.

If ever I were found in these houses it would not be for theft, but to see if their Chippendale was really worthy of them, and how blue their china was, and if they had any good pictures. Perhaps many a burglar has begun purely as an amateur in furniture and decoration. And there are still so many pictures in London houses, in spite of the temptation to sell offered by American gold. I must not enumerate any of the private collections here, as it might mean vexation to the owners; but I could. I could even give the number of the spacious Kensington road where Tom Girtin's epoch-making London water colour "The White House at Chelsea" hangs. . . .

I rather think it is Charles Kingsley who says, in one of the grown-up digressions in *Water Babies*, that the beauty of the house opposite is of more consequence than that of the house one lives in: because one rarely sees the house one is in, but is always conscious of the other. Kingsley (if it was Kingsley) was good at that kind of hard practical remark; but I fancy that this one means nothing, because the kind of person who would like to live in an ugly house would not care whether the house opposite was beautiful or not. I, who always want too much, would choose above all things to live in a beautiful house with no house opposite; yet since that is hardly likely to be, I would choose to live in a beautiful house with long white blinds that shut out the house opposite (beautiful or ugly) and yet did not exclude what it amuses us in London to call light.

Not that the house opposite would really bother me very much. In fact, the usual charge that is brought against it in this city—that it encourages organ-grinders—is to my mind a virtue. London without organ-grinders would not be London; and one likes a city to be true to its character, good or bad. Also there is hardly any tune except our National Anthem of which I can honestly say I am tired; and as often as one comes to the conclusion that one can endure even that no longer, it justifies itself and recovers its popularity by bringing some tiresome evening to an end.

In naming desirable houses I am thinking chiefly of the houses with individual charm: old houses, for the most part, which have been made modern in their accessories by their owners, but which retain externally their ancient gravity or beauty—such as you see in Queen Anne's Gate, or the Master of the Temple's house, or Aubrey House on Campden Hill. I am thinking chiefly of these old comely houses, and of the very few new houses by architects of taste, such as Mr. Astor's exquisite offices on the Embankment—one of the most satisfying of London's recent edifices, with thought and care and patience and beauty in every inch of it, whether in the stone or the wood or the iron: possessing indeed not a little of the thoroughness and single-mindedness that Ruskin looked for in the cathedrals of France.

But a few desirable houses of the middle or early-nineteenth century one has marked approvingly too—such as Thackeray's house in Kensington Palace Gardens, that discreet and almost private avenue of vast mansions, each large enough and imposing enough to stand in its own park in the country: but here packed close together— not quite in the Park Lane huddle, but very nearly so— and therefore conveying only an impaired impression of their true amplitude. (It is of course the houses of a city that give one the most rapid impression of its prosperity or poverty. To walk in the richer residential quarters of London—in Mayfair and Belgravia, South Kensington and Bayswater and Regent's Park, is to receive an over- whelming proof of the gigantic wealth of this people. Take Queen's Gate alone: the houses in it mount to the skies and every one represents an income of five figures. The only one of them, however, that I covet is at the corner of Imperial Institute Road—a modern Queen Anne mansion of the best type.)

Thackeray's old house in Young Street spreads its bow windows even more alluringly than the new one; but there is a little house next to that, hiding shyly behind ever- greens, where I am sure I could be comfortable. This house—it is only a cottage, really—has one of London's few wet, bird-haunted lawns. It is so retiring and whisper- ing that the speculative builder has utterly overlooked it all these years. Another retiring house that I should like to have is that barred and deserted house in Upper Cheyne Row, Chelsea, and I could be happy in Swan Walk, Chelsea, too, and at No. 14 or 15 Great College Street, Westminster.

Of the exceedingly little houses which one could really inhabit there are several on Campden Hill. There is one in Aubrey Walk which once I could have been very happy in: I am afraid it is too small now. It could be moved bodily one night anywhere: a wheelbarrow would be enough —a wheelbarrow and a pair of strong arms. It is so small

THE LADY WITH A FAN

AFTER THE PICTURE BY VELASQUEZ IN THE WALLACE COLLECTION

and compact that it might be transferred to the stage of
Peter Pan as a present for Wendy. I go that way continually just to look at it. And there is the white house
with a verandah at Kensington Gate which has been so
built in by new mansions as to be almost invisible; and,
best of all perhaps—certainly so in spring—there is the
secluded keeper's lodge in Kensington Gardens overlooking
the Serpentine, and the more spacious Ranger's home in
Hyde Park.

The most outrageously unreal new miniature house in
London is not on the outskirts at all but in the city itself
—in Fetter Lane, in fact. I mean the lodge in the garden
of the Record Office. This little architectural whimsy
might be the abode of an urban fairy or gnome, some
minute relation of Gog or Magog, or even a cousin of the
Griffin at Temple Bar. It is charming enough to have
such a tenant; and whoever lives there believes nobly in
heat, for the chimney is immense. South Lodge, near
Rutland Gate, has a near relation to it. The quaintest of
the old miniature London houses is that residence for the
sexton which is built against the wall of St. Bartholomew
the Great in Smithfield—a very Elizabethan doll's house;
the oddest of the new miniature London houses is a
tobacconist's shop in Sherwood Street—like the slice of
ham in a sandwich.

But this architectural digression has taken us far from
Piccadilly and the crossing at Hamilton Place where we
were standing when my pen ran away. After Hamilton
Place the clubs begin, one of the first being the largest of
those for women of which London now has so many, with
their smoking rooms all complete. One would like to
hear the Iron Duke on this development of modern life.
"Smoke and be——" would he say?

To me a more interesting structure than any Piccadilly club, whether it be for men or women, is the curious raised platform on the Green Park side of the road at this point, which was set there by a kindly observer some years ago, who noticed that porters walking west with parcels were a good deal distressed after the hill, and so provided them with a resting place for their burdens while they recovered breath. The time has gone by for its use, no one in these parts now bearing anything on the shoulder, omnibuses being so many and so cheap: but the platform remains as a monument to pretty thoughtfulness.

When I first came to London, Piccadilly still had its goat. I remember meeting it on the pavement one day in 1892, opposite Hamilton Terrace, and wondering how it got there and why the people, usually so curious about the unusual, were taking so little notice of such a phenomenon, as it seemed to me. It must have been soon after that it died and, with true London carelessness, was not replaced. London never replaces anything.

Were it not for the traffic—omnibuses, carriages and cabs all day and until long after midnight, and in the small hours traction engines rumbling into Covent Garden with waggon loads of cabbages and vegetables from the Thames valley—Piccadilly opposite the Green Park would be the perfect place for a house. But it is too noisy. None the less residences there are, between the clubs, many of them either having interesting associations of their own, or standing upon historic sites: such as Gloucester House, at the east corner of Hamilton Place, where the Elgin marbles, which are now in the British Museum, first dwelt after their ravishment from the Acropolis; and Nos. 138 and 139, next it, which stand upon the site of the abode of the disreputable "Old Q" who posed to three genera-

tions as the model debauchee, and by dint of receiving
9,340 visits of two hours each from his doctor during the
last seven years of his life, and a bath of milk every morning, contrived to keep alive and in fairly good condition
until he was eighty-six. It was in the half of Old Q's
house which afterwards was called No. 139, and was pulled
down in 1839 and rebuilt, that Byron was living in 1816
when his wife left him for ever. Lord Palmerston for
some years occupied what is now the Naval and Military
(or "In and Out") club; and Miss Mellon the actress,
who married Mr. Coutts the banker, lived at No. 1 Stratton
Street, which was for so long the residence of the Baroness
Burdett-Coutts. In the good old knifeboard days one
had the history of these houses from communicative and
perhaps imaginative 'bus drivers. Their successors, the
chauffeurs, cannot tell any one anything, partly because
they are men at the wheel, and partly because they are
not within speaking distance of any of their fares, and
partly because they are engineers and moderns, and therefore not interested in the interesting. The iron law of
utilitarianism which called them into being is the foe of
so many of the little amenities of life.

And so, passing Devonshire House's rampart, we come
to Berkeley Street, and the strolling part of the walk is
over. Any one who is run over at this corner—and that
is no difficult matter—will have the satisfaction of knowing
that he shares his fate with the author of *The Pleasures
of Memory*. Being only a little past eighty at the time,
Rogers survived the shock many years.

This reminds me that the infrequency with which Londoners are run over is one of the most amazing things in
this city. To ride in a taxi in any busy street, is, after
a short time, to be convinced that the vehicle has some

such power of attraction over human beings as a magnet has over needles. Men rise up from nowhere apparently with no other purpose but to court death, and yet all seem to view the advancing danger with something of the same air of astonishment as they would be entitled to assume were they to meet a railway train in Kensington Gardens. It seems to be a perpetual surprise to the Londoner that vehicles are making any use of his roadways.

PICCADILLY LOOKING EAST

CHAPTER II

ROMANCE AND THE WALLACE PICTURES

Dull Streets—London and London—The Rebuilder again—Old Paris—
The Heart of the Matter—A Haunt of Men—External Romance—
Dickens and Stevenson—The True Wandering Knight—The Beauti-
ful Serpentine—London Fogs—Whistler—The Look-out down the
River—Park Lane—Tyburn—Famous Malefactors—The Fortunate
John Smith—The Wallace Collection—Rembrandt and Velasquez—
Andrea del Sarto—Heresies about the Fête Champêtre School—Our
Dutch Masters—Metsu's Favourite Sitter—Guardi and Bonington—
Miniatures and Sèvres.

THE more I wander about London the less wanderable
in, for a stranger, does it seem to be. We who
live in it and necessarily must pass through one street in
order to get to another are not troubled by squalor and
monotony ; but what can the traveller make of it who
comes to London bent upon seeing interesting things ?
What can he make of the wealthy deserts of Bayswater ?
of the grimy Vauxhall Bridge Road ? of the respectable
aridity of the Cromwell Road, which goes on for ever ? of
the grey monotony of Gower Street ? What can he make
of the hundreds of square miles of the East End ? And
what, most of all, of the interminable districts of small
houses which his train will bi-sect on every line by which he
can re-enter London after one of his excursions to the
country ? Nothing. He will not try twice.

And yet these poorer districts are London in the fullest sense of the word, although for the most part when we say London we mean the Strand and Piccadilly. But the Strand and Piccadilly might go and it would not really matter: few persons would suffer extremely; whereas were Poplar or Bermondsey, Kentish Town or Homerton, to fall in ruins or be burnt, thousands and thousands of Londoners would have lost all and be utterly destitute.

It perhaps comes to this, that there is no one London at all. London is a country containing many towns, of which a little central area of theatres and music halls, restaurants and shops, historic buildings and hotels, is the capital; and it is this capital that strangers come to see. For the most part it is this capital with which the present pages are concerned. London for our purposes dwindles down to a very small area where most of her visitors spend all their time—the Embankment, Trafalgar Square, and Piccadilly, Regent Street and the British Museum, the Strand and Ludgate Hill, the Bank and the Tower. That is London to the ordinary inquisitive traveller. Almost everything that English provincials, Americans and other foreigners come to London to see, is there.

It is not as if leaving the beaten paths were likely to lead to the discovery of any profusion of curious or picturesque corners. A few years ago this might have been so, but as I have said, a tidal wave of utilitarianism has lately rolled over the city and done irreparable mischief. London no longer offers much harvest for the gleaner of odds and ends of old architecture, quaint gateways, unexpected gables. Such treasures as she still retains in the teeth of the re-builder are well known: such as Staple Inn and the York Water Gate, a house or two in Chelsea (mostly doomed),

SAN GIORGIO MAGGIORE, VENICE

AFTER THE PICTURE BY GUARDI IN THE WALLACE COLLECTION

the city churches, a corner or two near Smithfield,
Butcher's Row, Aldgate, and so forth. She has nothing,
for example, comparable with the Faubourg St. Antoine
in Paris, where one may be rewarded every minute by
some beautiful relic of the past. London, one would say,
should be first among cities where symbols of the past
are held sacred; but in reality it is the last.

Hence I am only too conscious as we walk up Park Lane
(having returned to No. 1 London to begin again), that we
shall be wandering in streets that present little or no
attraction to the stranger from the shires or the pilgrim
from over seas. For beyond some mildly interesting architecture Mayfair streets can offer nothing to any one that is
not interested in their past inhabitants. Better to have
stuck to Piccadilly or Oxford Street, with their busy pavements: much better, perhaps, and at the same time to have
accepted the fact that London is before all things a city of
living men and women.

That is what the traveller must come to see—London's
men and women, her millions of men and women. If he
would eat, drink and be merry, he must go elsewhere; if he
would move in beautiful and spacious thoroughfares, he
must go elsewhere; if he would see crumbling architecture
or stately palaces, he must go elsewhere; but if he has any
interest in the human hive, this is the place. He can study
it here day and night for a year, and there will still be vast
tracts unknown to him.

For a great city of great age and a history of extraordinary picturesqueness and importance, London is nearly destitute of the external properties of romance. But although,
except here and there—and those in the more placid and
law-abiding quarters, such as the Inns of Court—the dark

gateway and the medieval gable are no more, I suppose
that no city has so appealed to the imagination of the
romantic novelist. The very contrast between the dull
prosaic exterior of a London street and the passions that
may be at work within is part of the allurement.

It was undoubtedly Dickens who first introduced Englishmen to London as a capital of mystery and fun, tragedy
and eccentricity: it was Dickens who discovered London's
melodramatic wealth. But Dickens did not invent anything. It was Stevenson in his *New Arabian Nights* who
may be said to have invented the romantic possibilities of
new streets. Dickens needed an odd corner before he set
an odd figure in it; the Wilderness, for instance, came
before Quilp, the Barbican before Sim Tappertit; but
Stevenson, by simply transferring the Baghdad formula to
London, in an instant transformed, say, Campden Hill and
Hampstead, even Bedford Park and Sydenham Hill, into
regions of daring and delightful possibilities. After reading the *New Arabian Nights* the tamest residence holds
potentialities; and not a tobacconist but may be a prince
in disguise, not a hansom cabman but may bear a roving
commission to inveigle you to an adventure.

In ordinary life to-day, even in London among her
millions, adventures are, I must admit, singularly few, and
such as occur mostly follow rather familiar lines; but since
the *New Arabian Nights* there has always been hope, and
that is not a little in this world.

Even without Stevenson I should, I trust, have realised
something of the London cab driver's romantic quality.
He is the true Wandering Knight of this city. He does
not in the old way exactly hang the reins over his horse's

neck—or, rather, to be modern, he does not permit his steering wheel to turn itself—but he is as vacant of personal impulse as if he did. His promptings come all from without. There he sits, careless, motionless (save for quick eyes), apathetic. He may sit thus for an hour, for two, for three, unnoticed ; he may be hailed the next moment. A distant whistle, an umbrella raised a hundred yards away, and he is transformed into life. He may be wanted to drive only to a near station—or to a distant suburb. One minute he has no purpose in his brain : the next he is informed by one and one only—to get to St. Pancras or Notting Hill, the theatre or the Bank, the Houses of Parliament or Scotland Yard, in the shortest space of time. And this romantic is the servant of every one who has a shilling—bishop or coiner, actress or M.P.

I want to say one other word about romantic London before we really enter Park Lane. Beneath one of her mists or light fogs London can become the most mysterious and beautiful city in the world. I know of nothing more bewitchingly lovely than the Serpentine on a still misty evening—when it is an unruffled lake of dim pearl-grey liquid, such stuff as sleep is made of. St. James's Park at dusk on a winter's afternoon, seen from the suspension bridge, with all the lights of the Government offices reflected in its water, has less mystery but more romance. It might be the lake before an enchanted castle. And while speaking of evening effects I must not forget the steam which escapes in fairy clouds from the huge chimney off Davies Street, just behind the Bond Street Tube Station. On the evening of a clear day this vapour can be the most exquisite violet and purple, transfiguring Oxford Street.

To artists the fog is London's best friend. Not the black fog, but the other. For there are two distinct London fogs—the fog that chokes and blinds, and the fog that shrouds. The fog that enters into every corner of the house and coats all the metal work with a dark slime, and sets us coughing and rubbing our eyes—for that there is nothing to say. It brings with it too much dirt, too much unhealthiness, for any kind of welcome to be possible. "Hell is a city much like London" I quoted to myself in one of the worst of such fogs, as I groped by the railings of the Park in the Bayswater Road. The traffic, which I could not see, was rumbling past, and every now and then a man, close by but invisible, would call out a word of warning, or some one would ask in startled tones where he was. The hellishness of it consisted in being of life and yet not in it —a stranger in a muffled land. It is bad enough for ordinary wayfarers in such a fog as that; but one has only to imagine what it is to be in charge of a horse and cart, to see how much worse one's lot might be.

But the other fog—the fog that veils but does not obliterate, the fog that softens but does not soil, the fog whose beautifying properties Whistler may be said to have discovered—that can be a delight and a joy. Seen through this gentle mist London becomes a city of romance. All that is ugly and hard in her architecture, all that is dingy and repellent in her colour, disappears. "Poor buildings," wrote Whistler, who watched their transformation so often from his Chelsea home, "lose themselves in the dim sky, and the tall chimneys become *campanili*, and the warehouses are palaces in the night, and the whole city hangs in the heavens."

I have said that it was Dickens who discovered the London of eccentricity, London as the abode of the

SUZANNE VAN COLLEN AND HER DAUGHTER
AFTER THE PICTURE BY REMBRANDT IN THE WALLACE COLLECTION

odd and the quaint, and Stevenson who discovered London
as a home of romance. It was Whistler who discovered
London as a city of fugitive, mysterious beauty. For
decades the London fog had been a theme for vituperation
and sarcasm : it needed this sensitive American-Parisian
to show us that what to the commonplace man was a foe
and a matter for rage, to the artist was a friend. Every
one knows about it now.

Fogs have never been quite the same to me since I was
shown a huge chimney on the south side of the Thames,
and was told that it belonged to the furnaces that supply
London offices with electric light; and that whenever
the weather seems to suggest a fog, a man is sent to the
top of this chimney to look down the river and give notice
of the first signs of the enemy rolling up. Then, as his
news is communicated, the furnaces are re-stoked, and
extra pressure is obtained that the coming darkness may
be fought and the work of counting-houses not interrupted.
All sentinels, all men on the look-out, belong to romance ;
and from his great height this man peering over the river
shipping and the myriad roofs for a thickening of the
horizon has touched even a black London fog with romance
for me. I think of his straining eyes, his call of warning,
those roaring fires. . . .

Park Lane is the Mecca of the successful financier. A
house in Park Lane is a London audience's symbol for
ostentatious wealth, just as supper with an actress is its
symbol for gilt-edged depravity ; yet it is just as possible
to live in Park Lane without being either a plutocrat or
a vulgarian, as it is to be dull and virtuous in the few
minutes after the play that are allowed for supper at a
restaurant before the light is switched off—to plunge his
guests in darkness being the London restaurateur's tactful
reminder that closing time has arrived.

Park Lane is interesting in that every house in it has personal character; while a few are beautiful. Of Captain Guest's I have already spoken. It might have been built to stand among trees in its own deer park : a remark that applies with even more propriety to Dorchester House (the home of the American Embassy, with a spread eagle over the door), and to Londonderry House, and to Grosvenor House, all of which quietly take their place in this street almost as submissively as the component parts of a suburban terrace. Such natural meetings of architectural incompatibles is one of London's most curious characteristics. There are, I believe, in Park Lane no two houses alike; but now and then one comes upon one more unlike the others than one would have thought possible—as for example that richly carved stone façade at the end of Tilney Street, a gem in its way, but very, very unexpected here.

Before it was Park Lane and wealthy this pleasant thoroughfare—half-town and half-country, catching all the sun that London can offer in summer and winter—was known as Tyburn Lane, Tyburn Tree, where highwaymen and other malefactors danced upon air, being at the north end of it, near the Marble Arch, now so foolishly isolated —a gateway leading to nowhere—at the south end of Edgware Road, as a triangle let into the roadway now indicates, with particulars on a tablet on the adjacent Capital and Counties Bank. The last hanging at Tyburn was in 1783, after which the scene was moved to the front of Newgate (now also no more). We have the grace to do such deeds in secret to-day; but nothing in our social history is more astonishing than the deliberateness with which such grace came upon us.

Tyburn was the end of a few brave fellows, and many

others. Perkin Warbeck, who claimed the throne, died here, and Fenton, who killed Buckingham; Jack Sheppard very properly had a crowd numbering 200,000, but Jonathan Wild, who picked the parson's pocket on the way to the gallows, had more; Mrs. Brownrigg's hanging was very popular, but among the masses through whom Sixteen-stringed Jack wended his way, with a bouquet from a lady friend in his hand, were probably more sympathisers than censors. The notorious Dr. Dodd, in 1777, also drew an immense concourse.

These curious Londoners (Hogarth has drawn them) once at any rate had more (or less) than they were expecting, when, in 1705, John Smith, a burglar, was reprieved after he had been hanging for full fifteen minutes, and being immediately cut down, came to himself "to the great admiration of the spectators" (although baulked of their legitimate entertainment), and was quickly removed by his friends, enraptured or otherwise, to begin a second, if not a new, life.

And here, having come to Oxford Street before I intended, let us forget malefactors and the gallows in walking through the Wallace Collection at Hertford House, which is close by, and gain at the same time some idea of London's wealth of great painting: deflecting just for a moment to look at the very charming raised garden in the Italian manner which has just been ingeniously built over a subterranean electric light station in Duke Street. This is quite one of the happiest of new architectural fancies in London, with its two domed gateways, its stone terraces and its cypresses. One might almost be on Isola Bella.

Opinions would necessarily differ as to what is the greatest picture on the walls of Hertford House, but I suppose that from the same half dozen or so most of the good critics would select that one. It is not in me to support my choice with professional reasons, but I should be inclined to name Rembrandt's "Parable of the Unmerciful Servant". Near it come the same painter's portraits of Jan Pellicorne and his wife, and Velasquez' "Portrait of a Spanish Lady," sometimes called "La Femme a l' Eventail," of which I for one never tire, whether I think of it as a piece of marvellous painting or as a sad and fascinating personality.

But there are also such masterpieces as Andrea del Sarto's "Virgin and Child with St. John the Baptist and two Angels," notable for the beauty of it and the maternal sweetness and kindliness of it, and the quiet ease of the brush. It is not perhaps quite so lovely as a rather similar picture belonging to Lord Battersea, which was exhibited in London some ten years ago, and which, after the same painter's portrait of the young sculptor in the National Gallery, is the most exquisite of his paintings that I have seen in England; but it is very beautiful. And in the largest of the Wallace rooms may also be seen Frans Hals' "Laughing Cavalier" who does not really laugh at all but smiles a faint mischievous smile that I dare swear worked more havoc than any laughter could. Here also is Murillo's "Charity of St. Thomas of Villanueva" (No. 97), with its suggestion of Andrea del Sarto in the beautiful painting of the mother and children to the right of it; and two charming Nicolas Maes': wistful, delicate, smiling boys with hawks on their wrists; and several other glorious Velasquez'; and Vandyck's superb "Philippe le Roy, Seigneur de Ravels" (No. 94), with his Lady (No. 79); and one of Rubens' spreading landscapes; and two of Luini's exquisite Madonnas; and some feathery Hobbemas; and Gainsborough's "'Perdita' Robinson"; and a number of Reynolds at his best, of which I would carry away either

"Mrs. Hoare with her Infant Son," or "Mrs. Nesbitt with a Dove"; and two of the best portraits by Cornelius de Vos I have seen; and the sweet and subtle Mierevelt that is reproduced opposite page 4. I name these only, but there is not one picture in the large room that does not repay individual study.

Before leaving it, I would say that, without going into any kind of rapture, I have always been very fond of Adrian Van der Velde's "Departure of Jacob into Egypt" (No. 80), partly for the interesting drama and reality of it all, and partly for its noble cumulus cloud, since no picture with a cumulus cloud painted at all like life ever fails to catch and hold my eye; and with this picture I associate in memory the Berchem on the opposite wall, "Coast Scene with Figures" (No. 25), for a kind of relationship which they bear the one to the other.

In Room XVII, which unites the great gallery with the Fête Galante school, I would mention the magnificent Claude—"Italian Landscape" (No. 114)—and the absolutely lovely Cuyp on the opposite wall (No. 138) "River Scene with View of Dort," only more beautiful than the "River Scene" (No. 54) of the same master in the large room. The Dort picture has an evening quietude approached only by William Van der Velde the younger, in his "Ships in a Calm," in Room XIV, and by Berchem, in his "Landscape with Figures" (No. 183), all misty gold and glamour, in the same room.

Among the pictures in Room XV that I make a point of returning to again and again, one of the first is "A Fountain at Constantinople" (No. 312) by Narcisse Virgile Diaz de la Pēna, commonly called Diaz, who lived at Barbizon, and was the dear friend of Theodore Rousseau, the painter of No. 283, and of Jean François Millet, who is

not represented either here or at the National Gallery.
Exactly what the fascination of this Turkish scene is I
cannot define, but it affects me curiously and deeply, and
always in the same way. This room is given up to French
painters, Decamps being represented here better, I believe,
than in any collection, if not so numerously as in the
Thomy-Thierry gallery at the Louvre. Personally I could
wish for more of Corot and Rousseau and Diaz, and less of
Decamps, although his "Villa Doria Pamfili" (No. 267)
always draws me to it and keeps me there. Meissonier too
I could exchange for something more romantic. One Corot
there is, and one Rousseau, both very fine, both inhabited
by their own light; but there is no Millet. Having seen
the Fête Galante School in all its luxuriance in Rooms
XVIII, XIX and XX and on the staircase, one can perhaps understand why the peasants of Barbizon's greatest
and simplest son have been excluded.

As to the Fête Galante school, there is a word to be
said. If one has any feeling but one of intense satisfaction
in connection with the Wallace treasure house, it is a hint
of regret that the collectors were so catholic. I would
have had them display a narrower sympathy. I resent
this interest in the art of Boucher and Lancret, Pater and,
although not to the same extent, Watteau and Greuze.
After Rembrandt and Velasquez, Andrea del Sarto and
Reynolds, such artificialities almost hurt one. Each to
his taste, of course, and I am merely recording mine; but
as a general proposition it may be remarked that great art
should not be too closely companioned by great artfulness.
On the other hand there is much to be said for catholicity;
and I would include one Fragonard in every gallery if only
for the sound of his exquisite name. But at Hertford
House he is wholly charming in his work too, especially
in "The Schoolmistress"

THE "LAUGHING" CAVALIER

AFTER THE PICTURE BY FRANS HALS IN THE WALLACE COLLECTION

Rooms XIV and XIII belong to the Dutch, and are hung with small pictures by great craftsmen—Rembrandt, with a curiously fascinating yellow landscape (No. 229); Terburg, who is at his happiest in the "Lady Reading a Letter" (No. 236), reproduced opposite page 36; William Van der Velde; Gerard Dou; Van der Heyden, with "The Margin of a Canal" (No. 225), so clear and solemn; Paul Potter, at his best in a small canvas; Caspar Netscher, with a "Lace Maker" (No. 237), one of the simplest and most attractive works of this artificer that I have seen, and notable for the absence of that satin which he seems to have lived to reproduce in paint; and Gabriel Metsu, represented by several little masterpieces, all faithful to that womanly figure whom he painted so often, and who, I imagine, in return did so much for the painter's material well-being: for she is always busy in such pleasant domestic offices as bringing enough wine, or preparing enough dinner, or playing an air upon the harpsichord; and is always smiling, and always the same (as the clever wife notoriously has to be), with her light hair smoothed back from her shining brow, and her fair nose with the dip where one looks for the bridge, and her red jacket and white cap. One seems to know few women in real life better than this kindly Dutch friend of Gabriel Metsu. Lastly I would name Jan Steen, who in this collection is not at his greatest, although, as always with him, he gives a sign of it somewhere in every picture. In the "Merry Making in a Tavern" (No. 158), for example, the mother and child in the foreground are set down perfectly, as only his touch could have contrived; and in the "Harpsichord Lesson" (No. 154), the girl's hands on the keys are unmistakably the hands of a learner.

In Room XII are the Guardis for which the Wallace Collection is famous—soft and benign scenes in Venice, gondolas that are really moving, oars from which you can hear the silver drops splashing into the water, beautiful fairy architecture: Venice, in fact, floating on her Adriatic like a swan. The best Guardis ever brought together are here, hung side by side with the more severe and architectural Canaletto, to show how much more human and southern and romantic Venice may be made by pupil than by master. For the water colours you seek Rooms XXI and XXII, notable above all for their examples of Richard Parkes Bonington, that great and sensitive colourist, who, like Keats, had done his work and was dead before ordinary men have made up their minds as to what they will attempt. In two or three of these tiny drawings Bonington is at his best—particularly in No. 700, "Fishing Boats"; No. 714, "The Church of Sant' Ambrogio, Milan," and, above all, No. 708, "Sunset in the Pays de Caux" which might be placed beside Turner's greatest effects of light and lose nothing, although it is only seven and a half inches by ten.

On the ground floor are a few more pictures, among them two or three which one would like to see in the great gallery, properly lighted, such as Bramantino's charming fresco of "The Youthful Gian Galeazzo Sforza reading Cicero," which should be reproduced for all boys' schools; Pieter Pourbus' very interesting "Allegorical Love Feast" —this painter's work being rare in England; and Bronzino's portrait of Eleanora de Toledo. In the room where these pictures hang are the cases devoted to coloured wax reliefs, a very amusing collection. In the great hall at the back is the armour, and elsewhere are statuary, furniture and a priceless company of miniatures, many of them very naked, but all dainty and smiling. I am no judge of such confectionery, but I recall one or two that seem to stand out as peculiarly dexterous or charming: I remember

in particular a portrait wrongfully described as " The Two
Miss Gunnings," by Adolphe-Hall, and Samuel Cooper's
Charles II. I have said nothing of the Sèvres porcelain
and enamelled snuff boxes, the bronzes and ecclesiastical
jewels. I may indeed almost be said to have said nothing
of the collection at all ; for it defies description. Amazing
however you consider it, when you realise that it was all
the work of two connoisseurs it becomes incredible. Certainly its acquisition is the best thing that has happened
to London in my time. Second to it is that wonderful
assemblage of beautiful things brought together by George
Salting, now also the nation's.

CHAPTER III

MAYFAIR AND THE GEORGIANS

OF the vast tracts of wealthy residential streets in Bayswater and Belgravia and South Kensington there is nothing to say, because they are not interesting. They are too new to have a history (I find myself instinctively refusing to loiter in any streets built since Georgian days), and for the most part too regular to compel attention as architecture. But Mayfair is different: Mayfair's bricks and stones are eloquent.

Mayfair, whose oldest houses date from the early years of the eighteenth century, is strictly speaking only a very small district; but we have come to consider its boundaries Piccadilly on the south, on the north Oxford Street, on the east Bond Street, and on the west Park Lane. Since most of the people who live there have one or more other houses, in England or Scotland, Mayfair out of the season is a very desolate land; but that is all to the good from the point of view of the wanderer. It is still one of the most difficult districts to learn, and so many are its *culs de sac*

THE SHRIMP GIRL
AFTER THE PICTURE BY HOGARTH IN THE NATIONAL GALLERY

—often a mews, for from almost every Mayfair house may be heard a horse stamping—and so capricious its streets, that one may lose one's way in Mayfair very easily. I can still do so, and still make a discovery every time ; whether, as on my last visit, the little very green oasis between South Street and Mount Street with the children in an upper room of a school singing a grave hymn, or, on the visit before, an old ramifying stable-yard in Shepherd Street, absolutely untouched since the coaching days.

In Shepherd's Market, just here, which is one of the least modernised parts of London, it is still possible to feel in the eighteenth century. It lies just to the south of Curzon Street, in the democratic way in which in London poor neighbourhoods jostle wealthy ones, and it is a narrow street or two filled with bustling little shops and busy shopkeepers. Many of the houses have hardly been touched since they were built two hundred years ago, nor have the manners of the place altered to any serious degree. Gentlemen's gentlemen, such as one meets about here, remain very much the same: the coachmen and butlers and footmen who to-day emerge from the ancient Sun inn, wiping their mouths, are not, save for costume, very different from those that emerged wiping their mouths from the same inn in the days of Walpole and Charles James Fox. Edward Shepherd, the architect who built Shepherd's Market, lived in Wharncliff House, the low white house in its own grounds with a little lodge, opposite the Duke of Marlborough's square white palace, and it still looks to be one of the pleasantest houses in London.

A thought that is continually coming to mind as one walks about older London and meditates on its past is how modern that past is—how recently civilization as we understand it came upon the town. Superficially much is

3

changed, but materially nothing. Half an hour spent on the old *Spectator* or *Tatler*, or with Walpole's *Letters* or Boswell's *Johnson*, shows you that. The London of Gay's *Trivia*, that pleasant guide to the art of walking in the streets of this city, is at heart our own London—with trifling modifications. The Bully has gone, the Nicker (the gentleman who broke windows with halfpence) has gone, the fop is no longer offensive with scent, wigs have become approximately a matter of secrecy, and the conditions of life are less simple; but Londoners are the same, and always will be, I suppose, and the precincts of St. James still have their milkmaids. It is too late in the day to quote from the poem (which some artist with a genial backward look, like Mr. Hugh Thomson, ought to illustrate), but my little edition has an index, and I might quote a little from that, partly because it is interesting in itself, and partly because it transforms the reader into his own poet. Here are some entries :—

Alley, the pleasure of walking in one
Bookseller skilled in the weather
Barber, by whom to be shunned
Butchers, to be avoided
Cane, the convenience of one
Coat, how to chuse one for the winter
Countryman perplexed to find the way
Coachman, his whip dangerous
Crowd parted by a coach
Cellar, the misfortunes of falling into one
Dustman, to whom offensive
Fop, the ill consequence of passing too near one
Father, the happiness of a child who knows his own
Ladies dress neither by reason nor instinct
Milkman of the city unlike a rural one

Overton the print seller
Oyster, the courage of him that first ate one
Prentices not to be relied on
Perriwigs, how stolen off the head
Playhouse, a caution when you lead a lady out of it
Shoes, what most proper for walkers
Stockings, how to prevent their being spattered
Schoolboys mischievous in frosty weather
Umbrella, its use
Wig, what to be worn in a mist
Way, of whom to be inquired
Wall, when to keep it

From these heads one ought—given a knack of rhyme—to be able to make a *Trivia* for oneself; and they show that the London life of Gay's day—*Trivia* was published in 1712—was very much what it is now. There were no Music Halls, no cricket matches, no railway stations; but I doubt if they lacked much else that we have.

From No. 1 London the best way to Shepherd's Market is by Hamilton Place and Hertford Street, or it may be gained from Piccadilly by the narrow White Horse Street. Hertford Street is a street of grave houses where many interesting men and women have lived, only one of whom, however—Dr. Jenner, the vaccinator, at No. 14—has a tablet. The erection of tablets in historic London—a duty shared by the County Council and the Society of Arts—is very capriciously managed, owing to a great extent to the reluctance of owners or occupiers to have their walls thus distinguished for gapers. Mayfair, so rich in residents of eminence, has hardly any tablets. Upon Hertford Street's roll of fame is also Capability Brown, who invented the shrubbery, or at any rate made it his ambition to make shrubberies grow where none had grown before, and was employed on this task, and on the laying out of gardens, by gentlemen all over England. Sheridan lived at No. 10 during four of his more prosperous years, in the house where General Burgoyne (who was also a playwright) died. Bulwer Lytton was at No. 36 in the eighteen-thirties.

Mayfair proper, which takes its name from the fair which was held there every May until the middle of the eighteenth century, on ground covered now by a part of Curzon Street and Hertford Street, has changed its character as completely as any London district. In those days it was notorious. Not only was the fair something of a scandal, but the Rev. Alexander Keith, in a little chapel of his own, with a church porch, close to Curzon Chapel, was in the habit of joining in matrimony more convenient than holy as many as six thousand couples a year, on the easiest terms then procurable south of Gretna Green. Among those that took advantage of the simplicities and incuriousness of Keith's Chapel was James, fourth Duke of Hamilton, in his curtain-ring marriage with the younger of the beautiful Miss Gunnings. Curtain-ring and Keith notwithstanding, this lady became the mother of two Dukes of Hamilton, and, in her second marriage, of two Dukes of Argyle. Keith meanwhile died in the Fleet prison. Not only is his chapel no more, but Curzon Chapel, its authorised neighbour and scandalised rival, is no more ; for a year or so ago the Duke of Marlborough, wishing a new town house, used its site.

Curzon Street, of which this mansion is one of the most striking buildings, might be called the most interesting street in Mayfair. Although it has new houses and newly-fronted houses, it retains much of its old character, and it is still at each end a *cul de sac* for carriages, and that is always a preservative condition. Now and then one comes

LADY READING A LETTER

AFTER THE PICTURE BY TERBURG IN THE WALLACE COLLECTION

to a house which must be as it was from the first—No. 35, for example—which has the old windows with white frames almost flush with the façade (a certain aid to picturesqueness, as Bedford Row eminently shows), and the old tiled roof. Like so many houses in this neighbourhood, No. 21 retains its extinguishers for the torches of the link boys. To give a list of Curzon Street's famous inhabitants would not be easy; but it was at No. 19 that Lord Beaconsfield died, and at No. 8 died the Miss Berrys, of whom Walpole has so much that is delightful to say.

Curzon Street's tributaries have also preserved much of their early character: Half Moon Street, Clarges Street, the north part of which has the quaintest little lodgings, Bolton Street, and so forth. In Half Moon Street, named, like many other London streets and omnibus destinations, after a public house, lived for a while such very different contemporaries as Hazlitt, Shelley and Madame d'Arblay. I like the picture of Shelley there a hundred years ago: "There was," says Hogg in his life of his friend, "a little projecting window in Half Moon Street in which Shelley might be seen from the street all day long, book in hand, with lively gestures and bright eyes; so that Mrs. N. said he wanted only a pan of clear water and a fresh turf to look like some young lady's lark hanging outside for air and song." Mrs. N. might walk through Half Moon Street to-day till her legs ached, and see no poet. Our poets are for the most part at the British Museum or the Board of Trade, and are not at all like larks.

Clarges Street, which is next Half Moon Street on the east, has its roll of fame too. Dr. Johnson's blue-stockinged friend Mrs. Elizabeth Carter died at a great age at No. 21, and Nelson's warm-hearted friend Lady Hamilton occupied

No. 11, from 1804 to 1806. Edmund Kean lived at No. 12 for eight years, and Macaulay lodged at No. 3 on his return from India. No. 32, in Mr. Kinnaird the banker's days, was one of Byron's haunts. Bolton Street, near by, which just two hundred years ago was the most westerly street in London, was the home of Pope's friend Martha Blount, who inspired some of his most exquisite compliments; and it was there that Madame d'Arblay moved in 1818 and was visited by Sir Walter Scott and Samuel Rogers.

At its east end Curzon Street narrows to a passage between the gardens of Devonshire House and Lansdowne House, which takes the foot passenger into Berkeley Street. Once, however, a horseman made the journey too: a highwayman, who after a successful coup in Piccadilly, evaded his pursuers by dashing down the steps and along this passage—a feat which led to the vertical iron bars now to be seen at either end.

Berkeley Square is smaller than Grosvenor Square but it has more character. Many of the wealthy inhabitants of Grosvenor Square are willing to take houses as they find them; but in Berkeley Square they make them peculiarly their own. At No. 11 Horace Walpole lived for eighteen years (with alternations at Strawberry Hill), and here he died in 1797. At No. 45 Clive committed suicide. "Auld Robin Gray" was written at No. 21.

To the task of tracing the past of this fashionable quarter there would of course be no end, and indeed one could not have a much more interesting occupation; but this is not that kind of book, and I have perhaps said enough to send readers independently to Wheatley and Cunningham,[1] who have been so useful to me and to whom

[1] *London Past and Present. Its Histories, Associations and Traditions*, by H. B. Wheatley, based upon Peter Cunningham's *Handbook of London*. Three volumes. Murray.

INTERIOR OF A DUTCH HOUSE

AFTER THE PICTURE BY PETER DE HOOCH IN THE NATIONAL GALLERY

old London is more familiar than new London. For any one bent on this pleasant enterprise of re-peopling Mayfair, Berkeley Square is a very good starting point. Charles Street, Bruton Street, and Mount Street all lead from it, of which Charles Street perhaps retains most of its ancient peace and opulent gravity. One of its newer houses, with three dormer windows, has some of the best wrought-iron in London. At No. 42 lived, in 1792, Beau Brummell; while another Charles Street dandy—but only half a one, since he smirched his escutcheon by writing books and legislating —was the first Lord Lytton. Here also Mr. Burke flirted with Fanny Burney, before Mrs. Burke's face too. Later, Beau Brummell moved to 4 Chesterfield Street, where he had for neighbour George Selwyn, who made the best jokes of his day and dearly loved a hanging. In Bruton Street—at No. 24—lived in 1809 another George who was also a wit, but of deeper quality, George Canning.

Through Bruton Street we gain Bond Street, London's Rue de la Paix, which only a golden key can unlock; but into Bond Street we will not now stray, but return to Berkeley Square and climb Hay Hill,—where the Prince of Wales, afterwards George IV, with a party, was once way-laid by footpads; but to little profit, for they could muster only half a crown between them—and so come to Dover Street, where once lived statesmen and now are modistes. Among its old inhabitants were John Evelyn, who died in the ninth house on the east side from Piccadilly, and Harley, Earl of Oxford, in whose house, the second from Piccadilly on the west side, Pope and Swift and Arbuthnot used to meet in what Arbuthnot called Martin's office— Martin being Scriblerus, master of the art of sinking. In another Dover Street house lived Sir Joshua Reynolds' sister, whose guests often included Johnson and his satellite.

Albemarle Street, which also is no longer residential and has been given up to business, also has great traditions. Lord Bute lived here, and here Zoffany painted the portrait of John Wilkes; Charles James Fox lived here for a little while, and Robert Adam and James Adam, who with their brothers built the Adelphi, both died here. Louis XVIII stayed at Grillion's Hotel when in exile in 1814. But the most famous house is John Murray's, at No. 50, where the *Quarterly Review*, so savage and tartarly, was founded, and whence so much that is best in literature emerged, whose walls are a portrait gallery of English men of letters. Byron's is of course the greatest name in this house, but Borrow's belongs to it also. Scott and Byron first met beneath this roof.

It was at the Mount Coffee House in Mount Street, which takes one from Berkeley Square to Grosvenor Square, that Shelley's first wife Harriet Westbrook, about whom there has been too much chatter, lived, her father being the landlord; but Mount Street bears few if any traces of that time, for the rebuilder has been very busy there. And so leaving on the left Farm Street, where Mayfair's Roman Catholics worship, we turn into Grosvenor Square. Grosvenor Square is two hundred years old and has had many famous residents. It was in an ante-room of the Earl of Chesterfield's house here that Johnson cooled his heels and warmed his temper. Mr. Thrale died in Grosvenor Square, and so did John Wilkes, at No. 30. At No. 22 lived Sir William and Lady Hamilton, with "Vathek" Beckford, and thither went Nelson after the battle of the Nile. When gas came in as the new illuminant, Grosvenor Square was sceptical and contemptuous, and it clung to oil and candles for some years longer than its neighbours.

The two Grosvenor Streets, Upper and Lower, have rich

PORTRAIT OF A TAILOR

AFTER THE PICTURE BY MORONI IN THE NATIONAL GALLERY

associations too. Mrs. Oldfield died at No. 60 Upper Grosvenor Street in 1730; at No. 13 Scott and Coleridge had a memorable meeting in 1809. The two Brook Streets, and indeed all the Grosvenor Square tributaries, are also worth studying by the light of Wheatley and Cunningham; while South Audley Street, although it is now principally shops, is rich in sites that have historic interest. At 77, for instance, lived Alderman Wood, the champion of Caroline of Brunswick, who was his guest there on her return from Italy in 1820. Many notable persons were buried in Grosvenor Chapel, among them Lady Mary Wortley Montagu and John Wilkes.

The house within its own walls and gates at the south-east corner of South Audley Street is Chesterfield House, built in the middle of the eighteenth century for the famous fourth Earl of Chesterfield, who wrote the *Letters*, and who by his want of generosity (but that was in Grosvenor Square) stimulated Dr. Johnson to a better letter than any of his own. And at this point we enter Curzon Street again.

CHAPTER IV

ST. JAMES'S AND PICCADILLY EAST

The other Park Lane—High Politics—Samuel Rogers—St. James's Place
—Male streets—Hoby the Bootmaker—Carlyle's feet—St. James's
Street—St. James's Palace—Blücher in London—Pall Mall and Nell
Gwynn—The Clubs—St. James's Square—Dr. Johnson's Night
Walk—Jermyn Street—St. James's Church—Piccadilly again—The
Albany—Burlington House—The Diploma Gallery—A Leonardo
—Christy Minstrels and Maskelyne and Cook—Georgian London
once more—Bond Street and Socrates—Shopping—Tobacconists—
Chemists—The Demon Distributor—Bond Street's Past—Regent
Street—The Flower Girls.

FROM Mayfair it is a pleasant walk for one still interested in the very core of aristocratic life to that
other Park Lane, Queen's Walk, lined also with its palaces
looking westward over grass and trees—these, however,
being the grass and trees of Green Park. Some of London's
most distinguished houses are here—among them Hamilton
House and Stafford House, where are pictures beyond
price. Arlington Street, where the upper Queen's Walk
houses have their doors, has long been dedicated to high
politics. Every brick in it has some political association
from Sir Robert Walpole to the late Lord Salisbury.
Horace Walpole lived long at No. 5, and was born opposite.
At No. 4 lived Charles James Fox; and it was at lodging
in Arlington Street in 1801 that Lady Nelson parted

PORTRAIT OF A YOUNG SCULPTOR

AFTER THE PAINTING BY ANDREA DEL SARTO IN THE NATIONAL GALLERY

for ever from her husband, being "sick of hearing of ' Dear Lady Hamilton ' ".

St. James's Place also has political associations, but is more tinged with literature than Arlington Street. Addison lived here, and here lived Pope's fair Lepel. Fox, who seems to have lodged or lived everywhere, was here in 1783. "Perdita" Robinson was at No. 13 ; Mrs. Delany died here ; and Byron was lodging at No. 8 when *English Bards and Scotch Reviewers* burst on the town. But the king of St. James's Place was Samuel Rogers, who lived at No. 22 from 1803 until 1855, when he died aged ninety-five, and in that time entertained every one who was already distinguished and distinguished the others by entertaining them.

St. James's Place is the quietest part of aristocratic London. I have been there even in mid afternoon in the season and literally have seen no sign of life in any of its odd ramifications. Every house is staid ; every house, one feels, has had its history and perhaps is making history now, wealth and birth and breeding and taste are as evident here as they can be absent elsewhere. One doubts if any Cockney child, even the most audacious, venturing up the narrowest of narrow passages from the Green Park into this Debrettian backwater, ever dared to do more than peep at its blue-blooded gravity and precipitately withdraw. I would go to St. James's Place for a rest cure: it is the last sanctuary in London which the motor-bus will desecrate.

Arlington Street and St. James's Place have kept their residential character; but St. James's Street and Pall Mall have lost theirs. They are now the principal male streets of London. Women are the exception there, and there are no London streets so given up to women as these to men.

The buildings are clubs and a few men's shops, most famous of which in the past was Hoby's, the bootmaker. Hoby claimed to have won Vittoria, and indeed all Wellington's battles, by virtue of the boots he had made for him in St. James's Street and the prayers he had offered for him in Islington, where he was a Methodist preacher. I suppose there are still characters among London tradesmen; but one does not hear much about them. Interest in character seems to have died out, the popular ambition to-day being for every man to be as much like every other man as he can. Hoby was splendid. When Ensign Horace Churchill of the Guards burst into his shop in a fury, vowing never to employ him again, the bootmaker quietly called to one of his assistants, "John, put up the shutters. It's all over with us. Ensign Churchill has withdrawn his custom." Hoby kept all the Iron Duke's orders for boots; I wonder where they are now. I know personally of only one great man's letter to his bootmaker, and that is on the walls of a shop near Charing Cross, and in it Thomas Carlyle says that there at last, after many years, have his feet found comfort.

Before St. James's Street was given up to clubs—White's with its famous bow window, Boodle's, Brooks's, the Thatched House, to mention the old rather than the new —it had its famous inhabitants, among them Edmund Waller, Gillray the caricaturist, who committed suicide by throwing himself from a window at No. 29, Campbell the poet, and James Maclean the gentleman highwayman.

St. James's Street has the great scenic merit of terminating in the gateway of St. James's Palace, a beautiful, grave, Tudor structure of brick. The palace, now the home of court officials, was the royal abode from the reign of William III, in whose day Whitehall was burnt, to

George IV. Queen Mary died there. Charles I was imprisoned there before his execution and walked to Whitehall on the fatal morning from this place—to bow his comely head down as upon a bed. General Monk lived in the palace for a while, and Verrio, the Italian mural painter, who covered fair white ceilings with sprawling goddesses and cupids, had his home here in the reign of James II. In 1912-13 the delegates met here in the hope of bringing the Balkan War to a satisfactory end. In 1814 Blücher lodged in Ambassador's Yard, and, settled in his window with his pipe, bowed to the admiring crowds—an agreeable picture to think upon. Ambassadors' Yard is still one of the quietest spots in London, and indeed the Palace is a very pleasant place in which to retire from the streets, for those who prefer the repose of masonry to the repose of nature, such as St. James's Park offers. Levées are still held at St. James's; but the old practice of hearing the Laureates declaim their state poems has been abandoned without any particular wrench. Every morning at eleven the lover of military music may enjoy the Guards' band.

And so we come to the Park, of whose beauty I have already said something, and to the splendours of the new Mall, which is London's Champs Elysées, and to the monotonous opulence of Carlton House Terrace, the new home of ambassadors. The new gateway at Whitehall, and the Victoria Statue opposite Buckingham Palace, that dreariest of royal homes, which, however, is to be soon refaced, and I hope kept white, are part of the memorial to the great queen; the Edward memorial is to be at the foot of Regent Street, opposite the Athenæum Club.

Pall Mall is not only more sombre in mien but has more seriousness than St. James's Street. The War Office is here, and here are the Carlton and the Athenæum. Marlborough House is here too. But it was not always thus, for at the house which is now No. 79, but has been rebuilt and rebuilt, once lived Mistress Elinor Gwynn, over whose garden wall she leaned to exchange badinage with Charles II. The impostor Psalmanazar lodged in Pall Mall, and so did Gibbon, greatest of ironists. Gainsborough painted there, and Cosway, and there was the house of John Julius Angerstein, whose collection of old masters formed the nucleus of our National Gallery.

Captain Thomas Morris's pleasant song about the charms of the sweet shady side of Pall Mall over all the allurements of the country has never found any echo in me. I find Pall Mall equally forbidding in wet weather or fine. There is something chilling about these huge, sombre, material monasteries called clubs, solemn temples of the best masculine form, compounded of gentlemen and waiters, dignity and servility. They oppress me. Pall Mall has no sweet shade ; its shade is gloomy.

Turning up between the Army and Navy and the Junior Carlton clubs one comes to St. James's Square, once another abode of the rich and powerful, and now a square of clubs and annexes of the War Office, with a few private houses only. In 1695, when it was already built round, the square was a venue for duellists, and in 1773 a mounted highwayman could still carry on his profession there. At Norfolk House, No. 31, George III was born. The iron posts at No. 2 were cannon captured off Finisterre by Admiral Boscawen. At No. 15 lived Thurlow. At the north corner of King Street was Lord Castlereagh's, and here his body was brought after his suicide in 1822. It was round this square that Johnson and Savage, being out of money, walked and walked for hours one night, "in high spirits and brimful of patriotism," inveighing against the

ST. JAMES'S STREET AND ST. JAMES'S PALACE

ministry and vowing to stand by their country. Later
Johnson used often to quote the stanza about the Duchess
of Leeds—

> She shall have all that's fine and fair,
> And the best of silk and satin shall wear,
> And live in a coach to take the air,
> And have a house in St. James's Square,—

saying that it "comprised nearly all the advantages that
wealth can give." But King Street's chief interest for
me is centred in Christie's rooms, for here one may see
during the season so many beautiful pictures—better often
than our National Gallery examples—and even if one may
not buy one can attend the private views or even the sales
themselves, provided that one has no awkward nervous
affection which might be mistaken by the auctioneer for
the frenzied nods of the millionaire collector. In course
of time nearly every privately owned picture finds its way
to Christie's, and I advise all visitors to London in the season
to get into the habit of dropping into the rooms on the
chance of finding a masterpiece. At Shepherd's Gallery
opposite are the best British painters to be seen; but for
the chief dealers Bond Street must be sought.

All the streets in this neighbourhood have their pasts:
Bury Street, where Swift had lodgings when he was in
London, and Steele, after his marriage, and Moore and
Crabbe; Duke Street, where, at No. 67, Burke had
rooms; and Jermyn Street, home of bachelors whose
clubs are their father and their mother, where in its palmy
residential days lived great men and women, even Marlborough himself and Sir Isaac Newton. Gray lodged here
regularly, over Roberts the hosier's or Frisby the oilman's;
and in 1832, in a house where the Hammam Turkish Bath
now is, Sir Walter Scott lay very near his end.

To the end of all, in the case of many illustrious persons, we come at St. James's Church, between this street and Piccadilly, one of Wren's red brick buildings and a very beautiful one too, with a font and other work by Grinling Gibbons and a Jacobean organ. Here lie cheerful Master Cotton, who helped with the *Compleat Angler*, and Van der Velde the painter of sea-fights, and the ingenious but reprehensible Tom d'Urfey, and Dr. Arbuthnot, friend of Pope and Swift and Gay and wit. Mrs. Delany is also here, and Dodsley the bookseller, and the dissolute Old Q, and Gillray; and here was baptised the great Earl of Chatham. And so we come to Piccadilly again—the business part of it—with its crowded pavements, its tea rooms and picture galleries and restaurants.

St. James's Church is Piccadilly's most beautiful old building; the Institute of Water Colour Painters its most impressive new one; Burlington House is its principal lion, and the Albany its quietest tributary. Many famous men made their home in this mundane cloister, where all is well-ordered, still and discreet—like a valet in list slippers. Monk Lewis had his cell at No. 1 A; Canning was at 5 A; Byron at 2 A, in rooms that afterwards passed to Lytton; Macaulay was at 1 E for fifteen years—in the eighteen-forties and fifties. Mr. Gladstone also was a brother of the Albany for a while. Only by the expedient of pretending to have a friend here (whose name one must first ascertain) can a stranger get past the janitor into the Albany.

Of Burlington House, since it changes its exhibitions twice a year, there is little to say in a book of this character. As a preliminary step for the full enjoyment of the Bond Street tea shops there is nothing like the summer Academy, where four thousand pictures wet from the easel

HOLY FAMILY

AFTER THE DRAWING BY LEONARDO DA VINCI IN THE DIPLOMA GALLERY,
BURLINGTON HOUSE

touch each other; but the winter exhibitions of Old Masters are among the first intellectual pleasures that London offers, and are a recurring reminder of the fine taste and generosity of the English collector, and the country's wealth of great art.

Few people find their way to the permanent Diploma Gallery at the top of Burlington House, where hang the pictures with which in a way every Royal Academician pays his footing, together with a few greater works. But to climb the stairs is important, for the Diploma Gallery contains what might be called without extravagance the most beautiful drawing in London—a Holy Family by Leonardo da Vinci, reproduced on the opposite page. The picture being in monochrome the reproduction does it less injustice than usual, preserving much of its benign sweetness, and the lovely maternity of it. A bas-relief of Michael Angelo and a figure of Temperance by Giorgione are other treasures of this gallery. Reynolds' sitter's chair and easel and three or four fine portraits are also here; Maclise's vast charcoal cartoon of the meeting of Wellington and Blücher: sixty-six designs for Homer by Flaxman; Watts' Death of Cain; and a number of impressionistic oil sketches by Constable, some of them the most vivid presentments of English weather that exist. The rest is strictly diploma work and not too interesting. The sculpture room, full of diploma casts, yellow with paint or London grime, is, I think, the most depressing chamber I ever hurried from; but a few of the pictures stand out —Reynolds' portrait of Sir William Chambers, and Raeburn's "Boy and Rabbit," and Sargent's "Venetian Interior," for example. But it is Leonardo and Michael Angelo and Constable that make the ascent necessary.

A few years ago it was to Piccadilly that every fortunate

4

child was taken, to hear the Christy Minstrels; but this form of entertainment having been killed in England, within doors at any rate, that famous troupe is no more. The St. James's Hall has been razed to the ground, and a vast and imposing hotel has risen on its site; yet twenty years ago the names of Moore and Burgess were as well known and as inextricably associated with London's fun as any have ever been. But the red ochre of the Music Hall comedian's nose now reigns where once burnt cork had sway: and Brother Bones asks no more conundrums of Mr. Johnson—"Can you tole me?"—and Mr. Johnson no more sends the question ricochetting back for Brother Bones triumphantly to supply its answer. A thousand humorous possibilities have been discovered and developed since then, from tramp cyclism to the farces of the cinematoscope, and faces are blacked now only on the sands.

Gone too is the Egyptian Hall, that other Piccadilly Mecca of happy childhood, where incredible illusions held the audience a-gape twice daily. Maskelyne still remains, but there is no Cook any more, and the new Home of Mystery is elsewhere; while every Music Hall occasionally has its mysteries too. Change! Change! But the Burlington Arcade remains, through which, half stifled by heat and patchouli, one may if one likes regain the quietude of Georgian London: for one comes that way to Cork Street and Old Burlington Street and Boyle Street and Savile Row, which have been left pretty much as they were. In Old Burlington Street lived General Wolfe as a youth; and here lived and died the poet Akenside. Pope's friend Arbuthnot lived in Cork Street. Savile Row being the headquarters of tailoring is now almost exclusively a masculine street, save for the little messenger girls who run

THE NATIVITY

AFTER THE PICTURE BY PIERO DELLA FRANCESCA IN THE NATIONAL GALLERY

between the cutters and the sewing rooms; but once it was a street of family mansions, many of which are not much altered except in occupants since they were built in the seventeen-thirties. Poor Sheridan, who once lived at No. 14, died at No. 17 in great distress—just before assistance came to him from the Regent, who had been postponing it for weeks and weeks, a failure of duty which led to Moore's most scathing poem. George Tierney, who fought a duel with Pitt, lived at No. 11, which previously was tenanted by Cowper's friend Joseph Hill, to whom he wrote rhyming epistles. Grote's house is marked by a tablet.

One of Piccadilly's claims to notice I must not overlook —its shops. Though not so wholly given up to shops as Regent Street or Bond Street, where everything can be bought, Piccadilly contains certain shops of world-wide fame, whose windows I for one never tire of studying. One of these is that condiment house on the south side where, according to Sydney Smith, the gourmets of England will make their last stand when their country is under invasion. It is still as wonderful as in the days of the witty Canon : the ends of the earth still combine to fill it with exotic delicacies. Close by is I suppose the best known taxidermist and naturalist's in the world, where you may see rhinoceroses' heads and hartebeests' horns, tiger skin rugs and coiled boa-constrictors, all ready for the English halls of great hunters. These shops are unique, and so also is that on the north side whose window is filled with varnished chickens and enamelled tongues, all ready for Goodwood or Henley or Lord's, where it is the rule that food shall be decorative and expensive.

Bond Street, which Socrates would find more than filled with articles that he could do without, is more complete as a shopping centre. You may buy there anything from a muff-warmer to a tiara, from caravan-borne tea to an Albert Cuyp; for old and new picture dealers have made it their own, and I shall never forget that it was at Lawrie's in 1893 that I first saw Corot at his best—in four great pictures from a Scotch collection. Next to the picture dealers I like Bond Street's jewellers, although far behind the Rue de la Paix's both in taste and experimental daring. In the matter of jewels London is still faithful to its old specialising habit—the best jewellers being still in Bond Street and close by, and its diamond merchants still congregating almost exclusively in Hatton Garden; but a decentralising tendency is steadily coming upon the town. Not so very long ago, for example, Wardour Street stood for old furniture, and Holywell Street for old books. But to-day Holywell Street does not exist, and old book and old furniture shops have sprung up all over London. Longacre, once wholly in the hands of carriage-makers, is now a centre also for motor cars, which may, however, be bought elsewhere too. The publishers, once faithful to Paternoster Row, have (following John Murray) now spread to the west. Departmental London, so far as retail trade is concerned, is practically no more.

The saddest change in the shops of London is in the chemists: the greatest, in the tobacconists. There must now be a tobacconist to every ten men of the population, or something near it, and many of these already save the purchaser such a huge percentage that a time must be coming when they will pay us to buy tobacco at all. The new tobacconists are in every way unworthy of the old: they know no repose, as a tobacconist should; they serve you with incredible despatch and turn to the next customer.

To loiter in one of their shops is beyond consideration and
no Prince Florizel could be a tobacconist to-day, unless he
was prepared for bankruptcy. Of course there are still a few
old-fashioned firms on secure foundations where a certain
leisure may be observed ; but it is superficial leisure. I
feel convinced that below stairs there is a seething activity.
And even in these shops one cannot really waste time,
although to enable one to do that with grace and a sense
of virtue is of course the principal duty of the leaf. It
will prove our decadence, our want of right feeling, of
reverence, when I say that in all London I know to-day
of only one tobacconist with enough piety to retain the
wooden Highlander who once was as necessary and important to the dealer in Returns and Rappee as is the figure
of Buddha to a joss house.

Sadder still is the decay of the chemist. There are
here and there the real old chemist's windows, with a
row of coloured jars such as poor Rosamund lost an
excursion for; but how rare these are! Our new business habits, imported chiefly from America, have in no
respect done so much injury—aesthetically—as in sub-
stituting the new store-druggist's crowded window for
the old chromatic display. In the modern stress of competition there is no room to spare for pure decoration;
and so the purple jars have gone. And within all is
changed too. An element of bustle has come into the
chemist's life. Of old he was quiet and sympathetic and
whispering : now his attitude is one best described by the
words "Next please." I wonder that the sealing wax remains. Surely there is some American device to improve
upon sealing wax? A few of the good old shops may still
be seen, if one is quick. There is one in Norton Folgate
with a row of coloured jars; and, best of all, there is that

wonderful herbalist's in Aldgate, opposite Butchers' Row, buy Dr. Lettsom's pills and the famous Nine Oils.

Another commercial sign of the times in London is the increase of news-agents (in addition to the kerb-stone salesmen), and with them the rise of the demon distributor. No recent London street type is more noticeable than he: a large-boned centaur, half-hooligan, half-bicycle, who, bent double beneath his knapsack of news, dashes on his wheel between the legs of horses, under wagons and through policemen, in the feverish enterprise of spreading the tidings of winner and starting price. A few years ago London knew him not; to-day we should not know London without him.

But I am forgetting that we are in Bond Street, where these rough-riding Mercuries do not penetrate. The past of this thoroughfare has been almost wholly buried beneath modern commerce, but it is interesting to recollect that it was at No. 41, which was then a silk-bag shop, on March 18, 1768, that the creator of Uncle Toby and Corporal Trim died. It was at No. 141 New Bond Street that in 1797 Lord Nelson lay for three months after the battle of Cape St. Vincent, where his arm was shot.

From Bond Street one is quickly in Regent Street, once more among the shops and in the present day; but Regent Street is not interesting except as part of a great but futile scheme to plan out a stately and symmetrical London in honour of a blackguard prince. Of this, Portland Place, Park Crescent and Regent's Park are the other portions. The project was noble, as the width of Portland Place testifies, but it was not in character with London, and it failed. No second attempt to provide London with a Parisian thoroughfare—with anything approaching French width and luxury—occurred until the Mall was taken in hand and the space in front of Buckingham Palace was made symmetrical.

Regent Street in its turn leads to Oxford Street, where the great drapery shops—I should say, emporiums—are: paradises of mannequins and super-mannequins. More attractive to me is the little, almost Venetian, knot of flower-sellers who have made the island in Oxford Circus their own, in summer adding to its southern air by large red umbrellas. Of such women one should buy one's flowers.

CHAPTER V

TRAFALGAR SQUARE AND GREAT ENGLISHMEN

London's finest site—Nelson—The French salutes—Trafalgar Day—
The Steeple-jack—St. Martin's-in-the-Fields—The Gymnast—
"Screevers"—Sentimental Patriotism—Partisan loyalty—A peril of
predominance—London's statues—The National Portrait Gallery—
A recruiting ground.

OF Trafalgar Square London has every right to be proud. Here at any rate, one feels, is a genuinely national attempt at a grandiose effect. The National Gallery façade is satisfactory in its British plainness and seriousness; St. Martin's Church, with its whiteness emerging from its grime, is pure London; the houses on the east and west sides of the square are commendably rectangular and sturdy; the lions (although occupied only in guarding policemen's waterproofs) are imposing and very British: while the Nelson column is as tall and as commanding as any people, however artistic or passionately patriotic, could have made it. It is right. I am not sure but it touches sublimity. Apart, I mean, altogether from the crowning figure and all that he stands for in personal valour, melancholy and charm, and all that he symbolises: conquest itself —more than conquest, deliverance. Indeed with the idea of Nelson added, there is no question at all of sublimity; it is absolute. I like the story of the French sailors who visited London in 1905 rising to salute it as they were driving

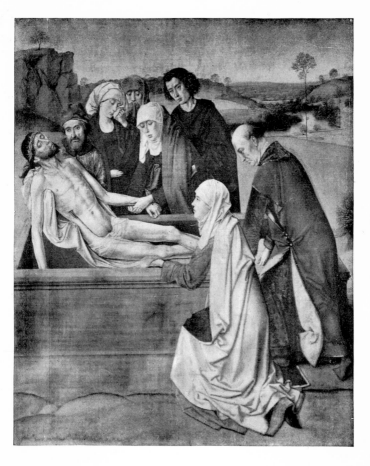

THE ENTOMBMENT

AFTER THE PICTURE BY ROGIER VAN DER WEYDEN IN THE NATIONAL GALLERY

past on their way to the West End. Would they have saluted Wellington's statue at Hyde Park Corner, I wonder? May be; but certainly not with the involuntary spontaneity that marked the Trafalgar Square demonstration. (Fortunately, exhaustive as was our hospitality, they were not taken to the grave of Sir Hudson Lowe at St. Mark's in North Audley Street.)

Every now and then the Nelson column is festooned in honour of Trafalgar Day, and for a while its impressiveness is lost. Wreaths at the foot were better. Patriotism and hero-worship, however, do not resent broken lines; and the ropes of evergreens that twine about the pillar draw thousands of people to Trafalgar Square every day. I remember the first time I saw the preparations in progress. Turning into the square from Spring Gardens, I was aware of a crowd of upturned faces watching a little black spot travelling up the pillar. It reached the top, disappeared and appeared again, waving something. It was a Steeple-jack, an intrepid gentleman from the north of England, if I recollect aright, who had the contract for the decorations, and with whom, on his descent, it was the privilege of several newspaper men to have interviews.

I was tempted after reading one of these to seek him myself, and either induce him to take me to the top with him, or hand him a commission to describe the extent of Nelson's view from that altitude, which, under the title "What Nelson Sees," would, I thought, make a seasonable and novel Trafalgar Day article. But I dared neither to converse with the living hero nor climb to the dead one, and that article is still unwritten. On a clear day Nelson must have a fine prospect to the south—not quite to his ancient element, of course, but away to the Surrey hills, and east and west along the winding river.

St. Martin's Church—the real name of which is St.
Martin's-in-the-Fields (how far from fields to-day!) stands
upon its hill as proudly almost as St. Paul's, and has not a
little of St. Paul's grave dignity.   From its steps many
Londoners get their impression of State pageants: I was
standing there when the Shah drove by some years ago on
a visit to the City fathers.   Among those who lie beneath
this church is Nell Gwynn, and Francis Bacon was christened
there.

St. Martin's spire was once used for a strictly secular purpose, when, in 1727, Violanti, an Italian acrobat, fastened
one end of a rope three hundred yards long to its summit,
and the other to a support in the Royal Mews beyond St.
Martin's Lane, and descended upon it head foremost with
his arms and legs outstretched, among the crowd being
"the young princesses with several of the nobility."
The pavement to the north and south used to be the
canvas of two very superior "screevers"—as the men are
called who make pastel drawings on paving stones.   London
has fewer "screevers" than it used, and latterly I have
noticed among such of these artists as remain a growing
tendency to bring oil paintings (which may or may not be
their own work) and lean them against the wall, supplying
themselves only the minimum of scroll work beneath.   To
such go no pennies of mine—unless of course the day is
dripping wet.   On a dry pavement the "screever" must
show us his pictures in the making: they must, like hot
rolls, be new every day.   We will have no scamping in
this art.

Trafalgar Square, with Nelson and the surrounding
figures of stone, notable among them the beautifully easy
presentment of Gordon, brings us to the general consideration of London statues, of which there are many here and

there, although, since we are not naturally a statue-erecting or statue-valuing people, as the French are, for the most part they escape notice. Among the French, indeed, wherever you go, a livelier love of country and a more personal pride in it are to be found.

The old gibe against that nation that it has no word for home, and no true sense of home, might be met by the reminder that France itself is the home of the French in a way that England can never be called the home of the English. An Englishman's home is the world; a French-man's France; and he is never wearied in beautifying that home, and praising it, and keeping it homely. Such pride has he in it that there is hardly a place in the whole country without its group of statuary in honour of some brave or wise enfant of the State, which is decorated at regular intervals and whose presence is never forgotten. It is impossible to do anything for France and escape recognition and tribute. With the English, patriotism is taken for granted; but the French nourish it, tend it like a favourite flower, enjoy every fresh blossom.

It is true that on certain anniversaries we also decorate some of our statues—Beaconsfield's, Gordon's, Nelson's; but we do so, I fear, less as a people than as a party. Charles the First's statue facing Whitehall has its wreaths once a year, but they come from a small body of "Legiti-mists"; the new Gladstone statue in the Strand will no doubt be decorated too for a few years, but it will not be a national duty, and none of those who take primroses to Parliament Square on April 19 will be represented.

It is the manner of an Englishman not to remember—except as a partisan. Even the unveiling of the Gladstone statue in 1905, even the unveiling of a memorial to an Englishman of so commanding a personality and intellectual power (apart from politics) as he, was unattended by any member of the Conservative Government, although he had been dead long enough, one would have said, to permit them to be present without confusion or loss of dignity. The incident is significant. We are all for or against.

To look neither back nor forward, to care nothing for the past and even less for the future, and to accept all benefits as one's due and hardly as a matter for thanks, is a hard habit of mind that must, I suppose, come to a dominant pre-eminent race that has for so long known no hardship or reverse or any dangerous rival. Patriotically we are like the man in the American story who had a prayer written out on the wall and made his devotions every morning by jerking his thumb at it and remarking "Them's my sentiments". Our patriotism for the most part consists in being British as much as possible, rather than in individually assisting Britain or glorying in Britain.

The danger of being at the top is that one gets into the habit of thinking of it as the only position ; and that thought brings atrophy. A nation that wants to be at the top must necessarily work harder and think more and view itself more humbly than one that has long occupied that dizzy altitude. Also it must be careful to add some reward to virtue beyond virtue. In the rarefied atmosphere of success one forgets the little things : certainly one forgets the necessity of celebrating the stages of one's painful climb. Hence, I think, much of our British carelessness about statues of great men. Given a loss of naval or military prestige, and relegation to a lower rank among the powers, and perhaps we should very quickly begin to be interested in our country again : a new national poetry

VIRGIN AND CHILD

AFTER THE PICTURE BY BELLINI IN THE NATIONAL GALLERY

would emerge, new heroes would be discovered, and nothing fine would be taken for granted. I wonder. I hope so.

I have I think named all of London's statues that ever receive any attention. The others are chiefly statesmen, soldiers and kings, and may be said hardly to exist. I recall as I write Queen Anne in front of St. Paul's and again at her beautiful gate by St. James's Park ; George I on the top of the spire in Bloomsbury ; George II in Golden Square ; George III in a little scratch wig on a prancing horse at the east end of Pall Mall ; George IV, riding without stirrups, and visibly uncomfortable, in Trafalgar Square ; James II (looking too much like Mr. Forbes Robertson the actor) behind the Admiralty ; Queen Elizabeth on the wall of St. Dunstan's-in-the-West ; Mary Queen of Scots for some reason or other on a new façade in Fleet Street ; Queen Victoria, by Blackfriars Bridge, standing, and in Kensington Gardens, seated ; Cromwell in the shelter of Westminster Hall, very nigh the replaced bauble ; Richard Cœur-de-Lion, splendidly warlike, on his horse, by the House of Lords ; the Duke of York of discreditable memory on his column in Waterloo Place, doing all he can by his sheer existence to depreciate the value of the national tribute to Nelson close by ; Wellington at Hyde Park Corner and again before the Royal Exchange ; Havelock in Trafalgar Square ; Captain Coram by his Foundling Hospital ; Shakespeare in the middle of Leicester Square, within hail of the Empire and the Alhambra, and again, with Chaucer and Milton, in Hamilton Place ; Milton outside St. Giles's, Cripplegate ; Lord Strathnairn at Knightsbridge ; Boadicea, in her chariot, on Westminster Bridge ; Darwin, Huxley, Owen and Banks in the Natural History Museum ; William Pitt, a gigantic figure, in Hanover Square ; Charles

James Fox in Bloomsbury Square and at Holland House; Carlyle in Chelsea; Sir Hugh Myddelton in Islington Green; Canning (who has a sparrow's nest under his arm every spring) in Parliament Square; Cobden in Camden Town; Sir Robert Peel (in profile very like Lamb) in Cheapside; Lord Herbert of Lea opposite the War Office; Cardinal Newman by the Brompton Oratory; John Wesley opposite Bunhill Fields; George Stephenson at Euston; Sir John Franklin in Waterloo Place, near several Crimean heroes; Byron, seated, in Hamilton Gardens and in relief in St. James's Street and again in Holles Street; Robert Burns, Robert Parkes and Sir Arthur Sullivan in the Embankment Gardens; Sir Wilfred Lawson there too, looking thirstily at the Thames; the Duke of Cambridge in Whitehall; Sir Henry Irving in the Charing Cross Road; and Prince Albert, unnamed and unrecognised in Holborn Circus, and again, all gold, in Kensington Gardens, seated beneath a canopy not without ornamentation. This, though far from complete, may be called a good list; and I doubt if there are many Londoners who could have supplied from memory half of it.

Indoor collections of statues and busts are to be seen in the Abbey, in St. Paul's, in the National Portrait Gallery and the Tate Gallery, in the Houses of Parliament and the British Museum; while the long façade of the Institute of Royal Painters in Water Colours in Piccadilly has a fine row of the masters in that medium— De Wint and David Cox, Girtin and Turner, for example; and the Birkbeck Bank, off Chancery Lane, has a rich assortment of reliefs of illustrious intellects, including Hazlitt and Besssmer, Leonardo da Vinci and Charles Lamb. On the roof of Burlington House, again, are many artists.

To the National Gallery in Trafalgar Square we shall return later; but after my digression on statues and the English pride or want of pride in their great men, this is the time to enter the National Portrait Gallery, hard by, where pictures of most of the nation's principal sons since the days when painters first got to work among us (less than a poor four hundred years ago, so modern is our culture,) may be studied. In masterpieces the gallery is not rich—nor need it be, for the interest is rather in the sitter than in the artist—yet it has many very fine portraits (quite a number of Reynolds', for example), a few superlatively fine, and not many wholly bad. Taken as a whole it is a very worthy collection, and one of which England has every reason to be proud. A composite photograph of each group of men here would make an interesting study, and it might have significance to a Lavater—unless, of course, the painters have lied.

Some of the best and most interesting portraits are in Room XXV, which is the first room to take seriously as one climbs the building, where sailors, soldiers and authors grace the walls. Here is Füger's unfinished head of Nelson, doomed and sad and lovable; Danloux's Viscount Duncan on the bridge of his vessel; Sir Joshua's Admiral Keppel; a flaming Lord Heathfield by Copley; Wolfe as a youth, and again, with his odd lean face, as a general; Landseer's sketch of Walter Scott without a dog, and Allan's Walter Scott in his study with his dog asleep; Laurence's large full face of Thackeray, above the ingratiating bust of the great novelist as a schoolboy; Romney's Cowper; and Sargent's Coventry Patmore, that astonishingly vital and distinguished work. Here also, still in Room XXV, are a number of George Frederick Watts's great contemporaries painted by himself and pre-

sented by him to the nation; but these I have never been
able to admire or believe in quite as I should like to.

Among the famous portraits in the first floor rooms—
Nos. XIV-XXI—are Barry's unfinished sketch of Dr. Johnson, so grim and mad; Reynolds' Goldsmith and Burke;
Hickel's vast and rural Charles James Fox; Arthur Pond's
Peg Woffington in bed; Phillips' rapt Blake; Stuart's Wool-
lett the engraver; Romney's family of Adam Walker, and
Lady Hamilton (one of how many?); Rossetti's chalk
drawing of his mother and sister; and some magnificent
self-painted portraits of great artists not inferior to many
in the Uffizi—notably Romney, very sad; Sir Joshua,
in the grand manner; Joseph Wright; and that very interesting craftsman, John Hamilton Mortimer, in a picture
that might hang as a pendant to one recently presented to
the Diploma Gallery at Burlington House. Elsewhere is
a fine Van Dyck by himself.

Ascending to the top floor we recede to Augustan,
Stuart and Tudor periods. Here are Hogarth's Lord
Lovat; Kneller's Sarah Jennings, Duchess of Marlborough;
Van Ceulen's William III as a boy, very sweet and pensive,
and the same artist's Earl of Portland; Gheeraedts' Queen
Elizabeth and the famous Countess who was Sidney's
sister, Pembroke's mother; Zucchero's James VI of Scotland and I of England, as a child with a hawk; Van Dyck's
children of Charles I; Mierevelt's Queen of Bohemia ("Ye
meaner beauties of the night"); Sadler's Bunyan in middle
age, with dangerous little red eyes; Lefebvre's Isaac
Barrow, that lean divine; Lely's Flaxman; and a putative
but very interesting Mary Queen of Scots. I mention
these because they seem to stand out; because technically
they catch the eye; but the most interesting men often
are the worst painted, as for example the author of

"Hamlet" and "Love's Labour's Lost," who in his portrait here, the "Chandos" as it is called, looks incapable of writing either work, or indeed of doing anything more subtle than acquiring wealth as a sober unambitious merchant, sitting on the bench among the unpaid, or propping the Establishment in the capacity of church-warden.

On the ground floor are some very interesting electro-types of recumbent figures of Kings and Queens from the tombs in the Abbey. Here also is Bacon seated in his chair, from the great chancellor's tomb at St. Albans, and a little Darnley kneeling to his ill-fated queen. The two death masks of Cromwell, more unlike than they ought to be, should be noticed, and one of Thomas Carlyle, very different from Boehm's bust which stands near it.

The pavement between the corner of Trafalgar Square and the National Portrait Gallery has long been appropri-ated by the War Office as London's chief recruiting ground; and here you may see the recruiting sergeants peacocking up and down, flicking their legs with their little canes, throwing out their fine chests, and personifying with all their might the allurements of the lordliest life on earth. One has to watch but a very short time to see a shy youth, tired of being an errand boy or grocer's assistant, grab at the bait; when off they go to the barracks behind the National Gallery to complete the business. Is it, one wonders, another Silas Tomkyns Comberbatch? Not often.

CHAPTER VI

THE NATIONAL GALLERY AND THE BRITISH MASTERS

I ONCE startled and embarrassed a dinner table of artists and art critics by asking which was the best picture in the National Gallery. On my modifying this terrible question to the more human form, "Which picture would you choose if you might have but one?" and limiting the choice to the Italian masters, the most distinguished mind present named at once Tintoretto's "Origin of the Milky Way". One could understand the selection, so splendid in vigour and colouring and large audacity is this wonderful work; but it would never be my choice to live with. Another, an artist, also without hesitation, chose Titian's "Bacchus and Ariadne"; and I can understand that too, but that also would not be my choice. After very long consideration I have come to the conclusion that mine would be Francesca's "Nativity". Take it for all in all I am disposed to think that Francesca's "Nativity" appeals to me as a work of companionable beauty and charm before any Italian picture in the National Collection.

Piero della Francesca was born about 1415, and died in 1492, and we may assume him to have painted this picture in the height of his powers—say about 1450. It is thus four and a half centuries old. In other words it was in existence, exercising its sweet spell on those that saw it, while Henry VI was on our throne, a hundred years before Shakespeare

MOUSEHOLD HEATH

AFTER THE PICTURE BY OLD CROME IN THE NATIONAL GALLERY

was born. The picture is unfinished and in not the best preservation, but its simplicity and sincerity and beauty are unharmed. The reproduction of it in this volume is necessarily small and, as in the case of all process blocks of great works, only a reminder of the original; but it conveys the exquisite grace of Mary's attitude. The little birds which Francesca's sweet thoughtfulness painted in must be looked for in the picture itself.

But all this talk of one's favourite picture is futile : because there are so many others that one could not really do without. Perhaps no picture is steadily one's favourite. Better to confess to a favourite in each room, or a favourite for every mood. There are Italian days and there are Dutch days, French days and English days. The National Gallery has a picture for each, all the year round.

The National Gallery, I hope, will never be crystallised. Something will always be happening owing to the acquisition of new works by purchase or bequest. I write these words in May, 1913, and in August there may be a dozen new pictures of which this edition takes no account. I hope so, as I say, but it is awkward for compilers of guide books.

At the Tate Gallery we shall take the rooms in their numerical order. But here, let us begin with Room XX at the head of the left hand stairs, because that is the first of the British rooms and it is well, in a British National Gallery to let curiosity begin at home. Moreover, we do know practically for a certainty, that, although new British pictures may arrive from time to time, these rooms are fixed for many years to come.

Room XX is particularly interesting, because there Sir Charles Holroyd, the Director, has hung not only the earliest British pictures, but works by certain of those foreigners, settled here at the invitation of royalty, whose influence for many years determined the trend of our national art. Here, for example, are Holbein's "Ambassadors" and that lovely full-length of Christina of Denmark which we so nearly lost when the Duke of Norfolk, a little while ago, decided to sell it. And here are many Hogarths, chief among them, for interest, the "Marriage à la Mode" series, and for beauty "The Shrimp Girl". "The Shrimp Girl," and the portrait of Mrs. Salter (No. 1663), and one or two of the heads of his servants (No. 1374), exhibit a Hogarth whose fine free vivid way with paint interests me far more than his delineation of interiors, where technically he seems to me to come far below Jan Steen. But Jan Steen could not have painted the Mrs. Salter : rather indeed does that, in its easy cool liquid colouring, suggest Vermeer of Delft.

Room XXI is dedicated to landscape. Crome is its presiding genius with his increasingly lovely "Mousehold Heath," and his not much less lovely "Windmill" on the same open space, so near his Norwich home, and certain other pictures, among which are two recently bequeathed by George Salting—the profoundly still and impressive "Moonrise" (No. 2645) and a "Heath Scene" (No. 2644) with its joyous atmosphere. Here too is the "Poringland Oak," a recent purchase, one of the noblest pictures of a tree painted since Crome's own adored Hobbema laid down the brush. But "Mousehold Heath" is *the* picture here. When I enter Room XXI it becomes the abode of "Mousehold Heath" and "Mousehold Heath" only. It is that, I realise, which I came to see; and when I go away it is with the golden light of it, the scented air of it, in my very system. Not all Turner's Titanic miracles, not all Constable's mighty transcriptions of English weald and weather, not all Wilson's memories of the age of gold, affect me as Crome does in this great and beautiful picture. I do not say that he is greater than they; but upon me he exerts a greater influence, to me he is more of a magician.

Gainsborough is here too with his "Musidora," his superb "Watering Place," and other landscapes, notable among which is No. 1783, the "View of Dedham"; while the Salting bequest made us the richer by the charming small portrait, filled with vivacity, of Miss Elizabeth Single-ton. Some little beautiful Wilsons also hang in this room.

We now enter the Turner Room, but here it is un-profitable to say much, because the pictures are from time to time changed. The two Turners—and in some ways the best—that can never change are in Room XXVI, beside two Claudes, as Turner insisted in his will.

To me, to whom art is never so appealing as when it is still and reposeful, shipwrecks and tempests are merely amazing; and so I always seek first, and return to again and again, two Turners of a quietness equal to the quietude of any landscape I know, in which perhaps the quietude is the more noticeable by the absence of any external aid. It is the essential quietude of the country. I refer to the "Chichester Canal," No. 560, which is reproduced on the page opposite 126, and to No. 492, "A Frosty Morning: Sunrise," which conveys a sense of still cold more com-pletely than any other winter picture, however it may be loaded with corroborative snow flakes or figures blowing on their nails. These are my favourites—these and "The Sun Rising in a Mist," next the Claude, which enters a region of which Claude knew nothing. Having seen these, there is still before one the exquisite delight of the Turner water colours in the basement, and after that all the other great Turners at the Tate.

The little Room XXIII should be peeped into for certain little Constables by way of preparation for his more important works in Room XXIV, particularly "The Hay Wain" and the new Salting examples—the green "Spetchley" (No. 2653) and the boisterously modern "Weymouth Bay" with its glorious sky. In the "Stoke-by-Nayland, Suffolk," No. 1819, "The Mill Stream," No. 1816, "The Country Lane," No. 1821, and "The Cornfield," No. 1065, one seems to discern the germ of Barbizon landscape. As one so often sees the father in the son—a hint of the elder generation in a passing expression on even the infant's face—so as one looks at these pictures may one catch glimpses of Troyon and Rousseau, Diaz and Millet. The gleaner in the foreground of No. 1065 is sheer Millet. Constable's larger and more painty landscapes, the "Flatford Mill," "The Hay Wain," and so forth, seem to me smaller efforts than some of his more impressionistic and rapid sketches here and elsewhere —at South Kensington and the Diploma Gallery. There is less of inevitable masterly genius about them than in the little "Summer Afternoon after a Shower," No. 1815, which is terrific, and No. 1817, "The Gleaners," and No. 1822, "Dedham Vale". These are to me among the greatest works of English art. Here, too, are various works by David Cox, all left us by Mr. Salting, Bonington from the same hand, a new Henry Walton, and old familiar Wilkies and Morlands.

The next room—XXV—is the last and the greatest of the British School, for here are those portrait painters who ever will be considered its greatest glory, although I personally, for pleasure, prefer Turner, Constable, and Crome: Reynolds, Gainsborough, Romney, and Lawrence, and I am tempted to say, above all (although not perhaps above all here) Raeburn. Gainsborough also has a land-scape, his "Market Cart," and the two great Wilson classical canvases are here too. Among the many Sir Joshuas, all fine, all touched with grandeur and Old-Mastery—I have chosen for reproduction the "Portrait of Two Gentlemen" (No. 754), because it has always fascinated me most. But I would not call it greater per-haps than one or two others—the Johnson, for example, or the Keppel, or the Lord Heathfield, or the very haunting Anne Countess of Albemarle. In the same room are such famous mothers' pictures as the "Age of Innocence" and the "Angels' Heads". London is extraordinarily rich in Reynolds: here, at the Wallace Collection (where they are all beautiful women), at the National Portrait Gallery, and at the Diploma Gallery. Abundance has always marked the greatest English artists, whether with the brush or the pen, the abundance which we find in Reynolds and Turner and Constable, in Shakespeare and Scott, in Fielding and Thackeray and Dickens: the large manner.

The other picture in this room that I reproduce is Romney's "A Lady and Child" (No. 1667), which I have chosen for its charm and for the amazing vitality of the little girl, who is as real, as living, as any figure ever painted, although I do not suggest that the picture is greater technically than his portrait of Lady Craven, or "The Parson's Daughter," close by, or the famous sketch of Lady Hamilton as a Bacchante. Its claims are, how-ever, more urgent—for a mother and child (and such a child) have ultimately—as the great masters knew—a deeper appeal than any woman alone, however beautiful, can have.

But Room XXV to many persons is less noteworthy for the portraits I have named than for No. 683,

Gainsborough's Mrs. Siddons, in the large black hat and
feathers and the blue and white striped dress. This is
the first picture they look at and the last. Brilliant and
masterly as it is, I must confess to a want of interest in
it. I can stand before it quite impassive: it affects me
like a kind of quintessential Burlington House—the Royal
Academy portrait carried out to its highest power. Sir
Thomas Lawrence's Mrs. Siddons, in the same room, seems
to me greater. Before that one has a pulse.

CHAPTER VII

THE NATIONAL GALLERY II: ITALIAN SCHOOLS

IN the first edition of this book I took all the rooms in order; but so many changes are possible—some even now in progress—that it seems to me better, having walked through the six British rooms, merely to enumerate certain of the National Gallery's principal treasures and leave my fellow-wanderers to discover them. Nothing, at any rate, is more delightful than seeking a particular picture in a large and fine collection.

Beginning with the Tuscans, in the first room we are at once among masterpieces—Michael Angelo's "Entombment," with its enormous technical difficulties, the conquest of which must have given the painter such satisfaction; Andrea del Sarto's "Sculptor" (long thought to be his own portrait) and a "Holy Family" from the same serene sad hand; several Botticellis, among them that deeply interesting "Nativity" (No. 1034), in which the painter testifies to his belief in Savonarola; his head of a young man, and his curious pagan "Venus and Mars"; Piero de Cosimo's somewhat smaller but far more whole heartedly and richly pagan "Death of Procris," one of our most beautiful pictures; the same painter's portrait of a warrior; Filippino Lippi's very lovely "Virgin and Child with St. Jerome and St. Dominic," and an "Angel Adoring," a fragment of a fresco from the same hand.

Filippino's Virgins are always adorable : a slip of a girl
he always made Her, with a high innocent forehead, and
Her hair combed back from it, and just a hint of perplexity mixed with the maternal composure which She
has managed to assume, accepting Her great fate very
naturally.   Filippino's scapegrace father's " Annunciation "
(No. 666) should be looked for, and Paolo Uccello's superb
battle scene, perhaps the most decorative thing in all
England, demands much study.   It has a curious grave
harmony which I suppose has never been surpassed.   Its
charm is quite incommunicable : it must be seen, and
seen again and again.   I visit it, whenever I go to the
National Gallery, both on entering and on leaving.   All
these, at the time of writing (and perhaps for some time
to come), are in Room No. I.

Other Tuscan painters in neighbouring rooms include
Fra Angelico with No. 663—" Christ and the Heavenly
Host," so simple and sweet, and filled with such adorable
little people.   Note also the " Virgin and Child Enthroned,"
by his pupil Benozzo Gozzoli.   This picture, though not the
equal of Francesca's " Nativity," has much sweetness and
simplicity ; and the little goldfinches again are not forgotten.   A pupil of Gozzoli is the painter of the very artless
and quaint " Rape of Helen " (No. 591), in which we see
Helen, the World's Desire, for whom Trojan and Greek
blood was to run like water, perched, a cheery little innocent
romp, on the shoulders of her captor.   Other somewhat
kindred pictures are No. 1155, Matteo di Giovanni's spirited
" Assumption," a very heartening if rather artificial work ;
No. 1331, the " Virgin and Child " of Bernardino Fungai,
with its lovely grave colours ; and No. 227, by an unknown
painter of the fifteenth century, " St. Jerome in the Desert "
—once an altar piece at Fiesole—which I always like for
the little kneeling girl with the red cap.

PORTRAIT OF TWO GENTLEMEN
AFTER SIR JOSHUA REYNOLDS' PICTURE IN THE NATIONAL GALLERY

Search also for Pacchiorotto's "Madonna and Child," so sweet and glowing, and his pale tempera "Nativity" next it; Botticini's (or some one else's) "Raphael and Tobias," that distinguished pretty thing, with Raphael light as thistledown; Botticini's very interesting panorama of Florence in the great "Assumption" picture; and Verrocchio's "Virgin Adoring," the perfection of paint and drawing, goldsmithery and sweetness.

Among the best Umbrian paintings are Piero della Francesca's "Nativity" and "Baptism". Of the "Nativity" I have already spoken, but would say here that almost chief among the old masters would it gain by being taken from its gold and framed in black. The gilt frame convention needs breaking down mercilessly again and again in this collection, but most of all, I think, in the case of this picture. The "Baptism of Christ in the Jordan," No. 665, is in its way, though not more ingratiating, more remarkable even than the "Nativity". Surely never did dove so brood before, nor—to take a purely technical point, disregarding the spirit of the work—not even in modern realistic art has any man ever so divested himself of his shirt as the figure in the background. And the sweetness of the whole, and the lovely colouring of it!

Near by are Luca Signorelli's "Triumph of Chastity," Manni's "Annunciation," the unknown "Story of Griselda," worth minute study for its detail and more distant attention for its lovely Umbrian light; Pinturicchio's "Return of Ulysses" and a very fascinating "Madonna and Child". Note the wild flowers in Luca Signorelli's "Nativity" (No. 1133).

Most conspicuous of the Peruginos is the famous Altar Piece, "The Virgin Adoring the Infant Christ". This work is notable not only for its beauty and mastery, but for being the first joyous exultation in colour which we have seen. The picture burns into the mind : to think of it is to feel warmth and content. Incidentally one might say that there are no more charming boys in any Renaissance work of art than this Michael and this Tobias. Other pictures by Perugino (whom the catalogue knows as Vannucci) are his faint and lovely fresco "The Adoration of the Shepherds," which one might say had lent all its own colour to the great triptych, and No. 181, the very sweet little " Virgin and Christ with the infant St. John," who is always a sweet figure but here the solidest little boy in Italian art. The baby Christ plays very prettily with his mother's finger. Raphael's tiny " Vision of a Knight " and his " Procession to Calvary " please me more than his more ambitious works, and I love the " Madonna of the Tower " whoever painted it. Lastly there are Penni's "Holy Family " and the two allegorical subjects by that rare and attractive painter Melozzo da Forli.

Among other Italian pictures (not Venetian) which are still to mention is Correggio's "Venus, Mercury, and Cupid ". I know of no painting of the nude which so grows on one as this : its power, its soft maturity, its charm. It becomes daily more and more beautiful ; the little figure of Cupid becomes more and more roguish.

Hereabouts are Roberti's "Israelites gathering Manna," Bronzino's dashing allegory of Cupid, Venus, Folly, and Time, Ridolfo Ghirlandaio's portrait of Girolamo Benivieni, Sellaio's "Venus and Cupid," Rossi's unknown boy, and Mainardi's unknown girl. Last, but not least, is Leonardo da Vinci's "Virgin of the Rocks," the only Leonardo in the National Gallery. The Louvre is far richer, for it has not only a counterpart of this picture, but

TRAFALGAR SQUARE

several others; but London has the "Holy Family" in the Diploma Gallery, which I reproduce in this volume, and there is nothing anywhere more lovely than that. Of the "Virgin of the Rocks" I have nothing to say. It is—and that is all. And still I have said nothing of Borgognone, Boltraffio, and a number of other painters whose number is at once a delight and a perplexity.

The gallery is very rich in the works of the great Venetians: superb masterful gentlemen who painted for the Doge rather than for Heaven. Occasionally they took a religious subject, but they brought little religion to it. Colour came first. Only in one work here—and that a very little picture—do I find more than a little trace of the simple piety that surrounded us in Fra Angelico's presence: the "Crucifixion" of the rare and wonderful Antonello da Messina, No. 1166.

The greatest names on the Venetian walls are Titian and Tintoretto, Bellini and Moroni, Giorgione and Cima, Moretto and Paolo Veronese, Sebastian del Piombo and Catena. I suppose the glories of the room are Tintoretto's "Origin of the Milky Way" and Titian's "Bacchus and Ariadne," although Charles Lamb would, I feel sure, still remain faithful to No. 1, Piombo's "Raising of Lazarus," in which Michael Angelo was thought to have a hand and which is the picture that began the National Gallery. The Tintoretto seems to me the rarest work of art here—the most amazing, the least copyable; but its appeal is not simple. Titian's Bacchus is simpler and more gorgeous; but I always feel that the Tintoretto transcends it. Comparisons are odious: it is better to delight in both. The National Gallery is strong in Titian: it has his "Holy Family," his "Bacchus and Ariadne," his "Madonna and Child" (the blue of the mountains in the distance!), the new portrait of Aretino. Of Titian, the glorious, the gorgeous, one cannot have too much; but I should hesitate to say the same of Paolo Veronese, who when he is painting his vast panoramic efforts always suggests the contributor to the Salon carried out to his highest power. His "Saint Helena" is to me one of the most beautiful of pictures, but I grudge some of his square yards.

If one had to name the most charming pictures on these Venetian walls, I should pick out Basaiti's "Infant Christ and the Virgin," No. 599 (a reproduction of which will be found in this book), and Giorgione's "Knight in Armour," No. 269, which once hung on the wall of Samuel Rogers, the poet, in St. James's Place. It is one of the pictures one would certainly hasten to save if London fell into the hands of an enemy and looting set in. One could carry it easily. Bellini is always interesting, always the consummate craftsman, always intelligent and distinguished. His finest picture here is, I think, "Christ's Agony in the Garden," No. 726, which is indescribably wonderful in colour.

To two other Venetian painters I would draw attention: both portrait painters, Moroni and Moretto. Moroni is well represented, and I have, I think, chosen his best picture for reproduction: "The Tailor," No. 697. I never tire of this melancholy Italian bending over his cloth, whom one seems to know better than many of one's living acquaintance. Moroni's "Portrait of an Italian Nobleman" —No. 1316—I should put next—so superb and distinguished is it, so interesting a harmony of black and grey. (Surely Velasquez must have seen it.) Comparable with it is the "Italian Nobleman," No. 1025, by Moretto (whom the catalogue calls Bonvicino), another of the great portraits.

Among other pictures to which I return again are No.

636, Palma's "Portrait of a Poet"; No. 1105, Lotto's "Portrait of the Prothonotary," with its curious Surrey common vista; No. 1455, Bellini's "The Circumcision," glorious in colour; No. 234, Catena's "Warrior adoring the Infant Christ," a large rich picture with a lovely evening glow and real simplicity in it; Cima's "Incredulity of St. Thomas," No. 816, with a very charming un-Italian landscape, that Crome might have painted, seen through the left window; No. 173, Jacopo da Ponte's "Portrait of a Gentleman"; No. 1141, a head by Antonello da Messina; No. 1160, a very beautiful little Giorgione; No. 1450, a sombre Piombo; and Romanino's very rich triptych.

Great among other Venetian or Paduan painters is Andrea Mantegna, for whose work in England, however, Hampton Court is the place. He is represented at the National Gallery by a very beautiful "Virgin and Child with St. John the Baptist and the Magdalene," No. 274; by the amazing "Triumph of Scipio," in monochrome, a masterpiece of psychological painting; and by the "Agony in the Garden," curiously like Bellini's, and not inferior though far less glorious in colour. Another Venetian represented here very fully is Carlo Crivelli, in whom I seem to see more ingenuity than greatness, but who certainly drew divinely and made very interesting pictures. All his work bears careful scrutiny, as he had an engaging fancy; but beside Mantegna he is mere confectionery. A painter whom one loves better is Vittore Pisano—for the sheer delight of his "St. Anthony and St. George," so gay and pretty, and the gentle simplicity of his "Vision of St. Eustace". Lastly I must note the Guardis and Canalettos.

Drawings by all or nearly all of these painters may be seen at the British Museum.

CHAPTER VIII

THE NATIONAL GALLERY III: OTHER FOREIGN SCHOOLS

OF early Flemish works we have beautiful examples. Directly one enters the room where Rogier Van der Weyden and Van Eyck are to be seen, one notes that the cheerful piety of Francesca and Fra Angelico, and the sheer love of innocent beauty of Botticelli and Filippino Lippi, are no more. A note of sadness has come in, a northern earnestness, and also the beginning of a realistic interest in humanity. The full materialism of later Netherlandish art is not yet: there is still much left of the rapt religious spirit; but these early Flemish painters have an eye on this world too. It is in their minds that living men and women deserve painting as much as the hierarchy of heaven. We find realism at its most extreme in No. 944, the " Two Usurers " of Marinus van Romerswael, a miracle of minuteness without compensating allurement of any kind. Joachim Patinir introduces us to domestic landscape in Nos. 1084 and 1082, both incidents in the life of the Virgin but more interesting for their backgrounds of fairy tale scenery, busy with romantic Chaucerian happenings. Even more remarkable as innovation is No. 1298, from the same hand, one of the most exquisite pieces of colour in the whole collection—a river scene frankly, and nothing else, painted four hundred years ago. This Patinir, whose work is not often to be seen, was a friend of Dürer, who painted

LADY AND CHILD

AFTER THE PICTURE BY ROMNEY IN THE NATIONAL GALLERY

his portrait and no doubt encouraged him. The three portraits by Mabuse, or Jan Gossaert—Nos. 656 and 946 and 1689—all show his great and rare power, but his masterpiece is, of course, the recent acquisition, "The Adoration of the King," which I reproduce in this book. No. 654, "The Magdalen Reading," possibly by a follower of Rogier Van der Weyden, draws the eye continually by its sweet gravity. For Van der Weyden himself look at No. 664, "The Deposition in the Tomb" (also reproduced in this book), a beautiful work lacking nothing of the true religious feeling, a feeling that is noticeable again with no diminution in the "Virgin and Infant Christ Enthroned in a Garden," No. 686, by Hans Memling, one of the greatest of the Flemings. But the greatest of all, and also one of the earliest, was the painter of No. 186, that amazing achievement of human skill, that portrait of Jean and Jeanne Arnolfini from which sprang half the Dutch school. Earliest and best; for no later painter ever surpassed this forerunner panel, in precision, in colour, or in sincerity. "Johannes de Eyck fuit hic 1434" is its inscription. I give a reproduction in this book, but the picture must be seen if its fascination is really to be felt. Greater minds than Van Eyck's may have arisen in the Netherlands, but never a more interesting one. I look upon Van Eyck's painting of St. Barbe, in the Antwerp Museum, as one of the most beautiful of the works of man; and this picture that we are standing before at this moment, and the Virgin and Child with a saint, at the Louvre, with its wonderful river and town seen beyond the ramparts, and children peeping over, could have been painted only by one who loved his fellow-men and to whom the world was new every morning. Before leaving the Flemings I would draw attention to the " Mystic Marriage

6

of St. Catherine" by Gheerart David, No. 1432, and to certain of the pictures by unknown painters, particularly to No. 653, portraits of a man and his wife, very masterly and living, especially the wife; to No. 943, a portrait of a man; to Nos. 1078 and 1079, which are very interesting; and lastly to the fascinating portrait of a lady, No. 1433.

Among German work we have already seen the fine Holbeins in the earliest of the British rooms, most beautiful of them " Christina, Princess of Denmark " (the Arundel Holbein), one of the sweetest and serenest of all portraits, which England so nearly lost but is now forever ours. The show picture is Holbein's " Ambassadors," which is a great work but hard. Nearer to one's heart comes Durer's portrait of his father, No. 1938, a little like Ridolfo Ghirlandaio's "Girolamo Benevieni," and very satisfying. As with the Flemish School, so with the German, many of the most interesting and beautiful pictures are by unknown hands : such as No. 658 "Death of the Virgin," No. 687 "The Santa Veronica," No. 705 "Three Saints," No. 707 "Two Saints," No. 722 "Portrait of a Lady," No. 1049 "The Crucifixion," and No. 1087 "The Mocking of Christ". These are remarkable either for simplicity or charm or realism, or a blend of all. One should notice too No. 291, "The Portrait of a Young Lady," by Lucas Cranach, a very striking face.

Our Spanish pictures are few but good, and now and then superb. Here are seven and perhaps more Velasquez' —including his "Admiral Pulido-Pareja," his "Boar Hunt," and his "Venus and Cupid". It is no small thing to possess these Velasquez' and those at the Wallace Collection (notably "The Lady with a Fan"). Personally I do not derive so much pleasure from the " Venus and

Cupid " as from those in the master's prevailing manner : it seems too much like his contribution to the Salon : it seems to me to have the least touch of vulgarity, which, before one saw it, one would have said was impossible in anything from that commanding and distinguished brush ; but even feeling like this, one can realise how rare a possession it is and be proud that England owns it. When I think of Velasquez in our two great collections the pictures that alway rise before the inward eye are the " Admiral " here, and " The Lady with a Fan " at Hertford House—both reproduced in this book. The " Admiral " is one of the world's great pictures : a gentleman's picture pre-eminently. Fascinating in another way is the brilliant " Betrothal " (now ascribed to another hand, perhaps Luca Giordano). The " Dead Warrior " is also only attributed to Velasquez ; but whoever painted it was a great man. The " Boar Hunt " is immense and overpowering but it seems to lack air. The other Velasquez' are two Philips, " Christ at the Column," with the exquisite kneeling child, and " Christ in the House of Martha," with the haunting strong sullen face of the servant girl :— altogether a marvellous collection.

Murillo is here too, in both his moods—the sweet pietistic mood in which he painted the " Holy Family " and " St. John and the Lamb," so irresistibly warm and rich, and the worldly and masterful mood which gave us his marvellous " Boy Drinking "—that wonderfully living head. It remains only to mention El Greco, who has a haunting portrait of St. Jerome ; Zurbaran—who might be said to blend Velasquez and Murillo, and who had one of the surest hands among all painters ; Goya's brilliant portrait of " Dona Isabel Corbo de Porcel" ; and the charming little " Virgin and Child " of Morales.

When the first edition of this book was published the French painters were very poorly represented, and there were no modern Dutch at all. The two Claudes and Poussins bulked fairly well, there was a nice Greuze, a Le Brun, and two fair Chardins, but the collection was not what it should be. Since then we have gained enormously in modern French works, chiefly of the Barbizon School, and modern Dutch, through the benefactions of two friends of art, Mr. J. C. J. Drücker and the late George Salting, while other donors have given examples of modern French art and a large Israels. The result is that to-day our Corots and Daubignys alone are worth pilgrimages even from Paris.

Mr. Drücker is indeed a remarkable specimen of the genus man, for with a passion for the best and most sensitive painting, he can find it possible to present from his walls masterpieces which no other person in the world would be able to relinquish. To him we owe examples of the three Marises, Mauve, and Bosboom, and also a fine English Daubigny. The majority of the Daubignys and Corots were from Mr. George Salting. These are very fine, especially the Corots numbered 2628 and 2631. We now have also two Boudins, both admirable, an enchanting sea piece by Courbet, a Michel, a Millet, a superb Diaz, No. 2632, and a very sweet and soothing Rousseau, No 2439.

And now for the wonderful Dutchmen. The Tuscans, Umbrians, Ferrarese, Parmese, Lombardians, Sienese—these found in the Scriptures their principal sources of inspiration; these painted the Holy Child, the Virgin Mary and the blessed company of saints, with a persistence which I for one cannot too much admire and rejoice in. Looking to Rome and Romish patrons for their livelihood, they had little choice, more particularly in the earlier days when simplicity was in their very blood, nor would they have wished a wider field. We may say, at any rate of the Tuscans and Umbrians and Sienese, that their colours were mixed and their panels made smooth for the glory of their Lady. But in the Dutch rooms we are among painters whose art was the servant of the State rather than the Church. Farewell to mild Madonnas and chubby Christs: farewell to holy families and the company of the aureoled. Art has descended to earth: become a citizen, almost a housewife. Heaven is unimportant: what is important is Holland and the Dutch. Let there be Dutch pictures ! A religious subject may creep in now and then, but (but unless Rembrandt holds the brush or the burin) it will not be a religious picture. Worldliness has set in thoroughly. We have travelled very far from Fra Angelico and Francesca's "Nativity".

I hope I shall not be misunderstood about Dutch art, for which I have the greatest admiration. All I mean is that there is no preparation for a loving appreciation of it so unsuitable as the contemplation of the old Italian masters. No emotional student of the Umbrians and the Venetians, no one whose eyes have just been filled with their colour and glory, is in a fit state to understand the dexterity and homeliness of Gerard Dou and Terburg, De Hooch and Jan Steen, the austere distinction of Van Dyck, or even the stupendous power of Rembrandt. Least of all is he able to be fair to Peter Paul Rubens. A different attitude is expected by Italian masters and the northern masters: the Italians ask for wonder, delight ; the Dutch for curiosity, almost inquisitiveness. It is the difference between rapture and interest. Always, however, excepting Rembrandt : he stands alone.

Perhaps one should not combine the north and the south in one visit at all, but confine each visit to a single group. Weak as the National Gallery is, here and there, no one can deny the thoroughness and superlative excellence of its Netherland rooms. The English have always appreciated Dutch art. To have nineteen Rembrandts is alone no small matter; but we have also thirty-two works from Rubens' hand, and five Hals', and four De Hoochs, and nine Jan Steens, and three Terburgs, and fourteen Cuyps, and six Van der Heydens, and two Vermeers, and twenty-one Ruisdaels, and eight Hobbemas, including the best of all. I doubt too if Van Dyck ever surpassed the distinction and power of our "Cornelius van der Geest".

Let us begin with Rembrandt. Here are his fascinating girl's head, No. 237, with the amused expression and ruddy tints of health, and his "Old Lady" in a ruff, No. 775—one of those wonderful heads that come right out of the canvas and seem always to have been our personal acquaintances. Other Rembrandts include the sombre "Jew Merchant," No. 51; the two portraits of himself, as a young man and an old man—Nos. 672 and 221; the "Old Man"; the "Burgomaster"; the other "Old Lady," also in a ruff, No. 1675, a little wizened but immortal; and the "Jewish Rabbi," No. 190. These are the greatest of them, and these alone make our National Gallery priceless. There are also "The Woman Taken in Adultery" and "The Adoration of the Shepherds," two of the pictures with which the collection began: both lighted in that way which added the word Rembrandtesque to the language; the masterly "Woman Bathing," one of his most brilliant oil sketches (look at the way the chemise is painted); and lastly the beautiful grave landscape—beyond Ruisdael or any of the regular Dutch landscape painters: "Tobias and the Angel," No. 72—a picture which always draws me to it. It is stupendous, this man's mastery of his means.

I always wonder if No. 757—" Christ Blessing the Little Children," which is said to be of the School of Rembrandt—was not painted by Nicolas Maes. The child in the foreground seems straight from his brush, and he was Rembrandt's pupil. We come to him with No. 1247, "The Card Players," a very fascinating and powerful work, very near Rembrandt indeed.

Among the great masterpieces are our portraits by Frans Hals, all beggaring one's store of adjectives and all making all other painters of the ruddy human face, even Rembrandt himself, almost fumblers. No one so perpetuated the life of the eye and the cheek as this jovial Haarlemer. Since this book was written the large Family Group by Hals has been added to the collection—a picture not perhaps of this painter's highest quality as a whole, but notable for certain figures. Better perhaps is " The Woman with a Fan," bequeathed by George Salting—a very memorable thing painted like a miracle. The Ruisdaels also have been enriched by the same munificent testator, a perfect little " View near Haarlem " being now our property for ever—unless the suffragettes destroy it in their search for the vote. Among other Dutch pictures added since my first edition are the Salting Jan Steens, chief of which is the perfect " Skittle Players," No. 2560.

Three great landscape painters may be found in the same rooms as the Hals—Ruisdael, Cuyp and Hobbema, but Koninck is next door. Hobbema's wonderful " Avenue at Middelharnis " I reproduce. Chief of the many Cuyps in beauty is No. 822 and next it is No. 53.

Vermeer hangs in a little room. He is represented by pictures of two young ladies which have his peculiar magical skill and charm but are not quite of his finest. Here also hangs Terburg's " Portrait of a Gentleman," in which black cloth is painted with a distinction that I have never seen elsewhere—a picture from which Whistler must have learned much.

Of Rubens I find it always difficult to write. He was so powerful, so vigorous and so abundant. Enough that he may be seen here in every mood, and that personally I like best his landscape and that brilliant sketch for a large picture—No. 57—"The Conversion of St. Bavon". Here you see the great creative hand in its most miraculous form. Of Van Dyck's "Cornelius van der Geest" I have spoken. His portraits of the Marchese and Marchesa Cattaneo, added since the first edition of this book, are superb. The reader must search for the best of the Peter de Hoochs—the "Interior of a Dutch House," No. 834, reproduced in this volume, most marvellously lighted and alive ; and the best National Gallery Metsu, No. 839, "The Music Lesson," in which he is again faithful to the type we observed at the Wallace Collection ; Terburg's "Guitar Lesson" ; Jan Steen's "Music Lesson," No. 856, where the girl is painted—face, dress and hands—as this inspired tippler alone could paint, Gerard Dou's "Poulterer's Shop," the most marvellous example of Dutch minuteness in the collection ; a church interior by Berck-Heyde, and a view in Haarlem by the same efficient brush ; some exquisite street scenes by the adorable Van der Heyden ; and a very beautiful church interior by Saenredam, all cool light. My list is, of course, incomplete, for so far from mentioning all the jewels of this collection, I cannot even name all my own favourites ; but I must not omit the more than lovely "River Scene" (No. 978) by Willem van de Velde. And so we leave the National Gallery (only, I hope, to return to it again and again) with the praises of the late George Salting very genuinely on our lips.

ADMIRAL PULIDO-PAREJA

AFTER THE PICTURE BY VALASQUEZ IN THE NATIONAL GALLERY

CHAPTER IX

THE STRAND AND COVENT GARDEN

I COULD not, I think, explain why, but I have more dis-
taste for the Strand than for any street in London.
I would avoid it as carefully, from pure unreasoning prejudice, as Count D'Orsay or Dick Swiveller avoided certain
other districts on financial grounds. This, I fear, proves
me to be only half a Londoner—if that; for the Strand to
many people *is* London, all else being extraneous. They
endure their daily tasks elsewhere only because such endur-
ance provides them with the means to be in the Strand at
night.

The most Bohemian of London streets, if the Strand
could cross to Paris it would instantly burgeon into a
boulevard. Its prevailing type is of the stage: the blue
chin of Thespis is very apparent there, and the ample

waistcoat of the manager is prominent too. Except at night, on the way to the Gaiety, the fashionable youth avoid the Strand; and indeed the best-dressed men and women are not seen on its pavements, howsoever they may use its carriage way. But with these exceptions, all London may be studied there; and other nations too, for the great hotels and Charing Cross station tend to cosmopolitanise it. Probably at no hour of the day or night are more than half the Strand's population true Londoners.

If the Strand is too much for one, as it may easily be, the escape is very simple. You may be on the banks of the Thames in two minutes from any part of it, or on the beautiful Adelphi Terrace, or among the flowers and greenery of Covent Garden, or amid the peace of the Savoy chapel or the quietude of Essex Street. Standing on the south end of Waterloo Bridge on a sunny afternoon you get one of the best views of London that is to be had and learn something of the possibilities of the city's white stone. Somerset House from this point is superb, St. Paul's as beautiful and fragile as any of Guardi's Venetian domes. Above the green of the trees and the Temple lawns and the dull red of the new Embankment buildings, broken here and there by a stone block, you see Wren's spires pricking the sky, St. Bride's always the most noticeable; and now, far back, gleaming with its new whiteness and the gold of its figure of Justice, is the new Central Criminal Court, to add an extra touch of light. Culminating statues gilded or otherwise are beginning to be quite a feature of London buildings. The New Gaiety Theatre has one; Telephone House in Temple Avenue has a graceful Mercury; over the Savoy portico stands a noble Crusader; over Romano's doorway dance a group of bronze Cupids. Less ambitious but not less pleasing is the gold galleon forming a weather vane on Mr. Astor's embankment office,

THE CITY FROM WATERLOO BRIDGE

which is as fine in its way as the Flying Dragon on Bov
Church in Cheapside.

The Adelphi, which dates from 1768, consists of the
Terrace, standing high overlooking the river, and its neighbouring streets, John Street, Robert Street, James Street,
William Street and Adam Street, together with the arches
beneath. It was the work of the Scotch architects Robert,
John, James and William Adam, who in its generic title
and in these four streets celebrate for ever their relationship
and their names. The Terrace must be seen from the Embankment or the river if its proportions are to be rightly
esteemed ; and one must go within one of the houses to
appreciate the beauty of the Adam ceilings and fireplaces,
which are the perfect setting for the furniture of Heppel-
white and Sheraton. English taste in decoration and design has certainly never since reached the height of delicacy
and restraint it then knew.

No house in the Terrace has been replaced or very seriously tampered with, and all have some interesting association, chief among them being No. 4, where in 1779 the
gaiety of nations was eclipsed by the death of Garrick.
The other Adelphi streets have historic memories too.
Disraeli always believed that he was born at No. 2 James
Street, in a library, although the facts seem to be against
him ; at No. 18 John Street is the Society of Arts, whence
come London's tablets of great men, of which I have
already said something ; and at No. 2 Robert Street lived
Thomas Hood, who sang the "Song of the Shirt".

More ancient is the district between the Adelphi and
the Charing Cross District Railway station. Here we go
back a hundred years before the Adelphi was built, to
associations with the great name of Buckingham—Buckingham Street, Duke Street, and Villiers Street being its chief

quarters. Of these Buckingham Street retains most signs of age. Samuel Pepys lived there for many years, in the south-west corner house overlooking the river, which he probably came to think his own ; Peter the Great lodged at the opposite corner ; Jean Jacques Rousseau and David Hume were together in Buckingham Street in 1765, before they entered upon their great and unphilosophic quarrel ; Etty painted at No. 14 and Clarkson Stanfield's studio was below him.

Pepys' companion diarist John Evelyn resided for a while in Villiers Street, which is now given up to cheap eating-houses and meretricious shops, and on Sunday evenings is packed with rough boys and girls. Steele lived here after the death of his wife. The street is much changed since then, for Charing Cross station robbed it of its western side.

I am inclined to think that Pepys when all is said is the greatest of the Londoners—a fuller, more intensely alive, Londoner than either Johnson or Lamb. Perhaps he wins his pre-eminence rather by his littleness, for to be a Londoner in the highest one must be rather trivial or at least be interested in trivialities. Johnson was too serious, Lamb too imaginative, to compete with this busy Secretary. Neither was such an epicure of life, neither found the world fresh every morning as he did. It is as the epicure of life that he is so alluring. His self-revelations are valuable in some degree, and his picture of the times makes him perhaps the finest understudy a historian ever had ; but Pepys' greatness lies in his appreciation of good things. He lived minute by minute, as wise men do, and he extracted whatever honey was possible. Who else has so fused business and pleasure ? Who else has kept his mind so open, so alert ? Whenever Pepys found an odd quarter of an hour

MADONNA AND THE LAUGHING CHILD

FROM THE CLAY STATUETTE BY DESIDERIO DA SETTIGNANO (?) IN THE VICTORIA
AND ALBERT MUSEUM

he sang or strummed it away with a glad heart; whenever he walked abroad his eyes were vigilant for pretty women. No man was more amusable. He drank "incomparable good claret" as it should be drunk, and loved it; he laughed at Betterton, he ogled Nelly Gwynn, he intrigued with men of affairs, he fondled his books, he ate his dinner, all with gusto and his utmost energy. Trivial he certainly was, but his enjoyment is his justification. Samuel Pepys was a superb artist in living. He was a man of insatiable inquisitiveness: there was always something he considered "pretty to see"; and it was this gift of curiosity that made him the best of Londoners. He had also the true Londoner's faculty of bearing with equanimity the trials of others, for all through the great plague and the great fire he played his lute with cheerfulness.

Turning into the pleasant Embankment Gardens at the foot, one comes at once upon the York Water Gate, which was built by the Duke of Buckingham on the shore of the river to admit boats to his private staithe, those being the days when the Thames was a highway of fashion. To-day it is given up to commerce. But he did not complete his design of rebuilding the old Palace; the gate is all that now remains; and the site of York House is covered by Buckingham Street and its companions—just as the site of Durham House, where Raleigh lived, is beneath the Adelphi, and that of Arundel House beneath Arundel Street and its neighbourhood, and that of old Somerset House beneath the present building of the same name.

Only two relics of the old Strand palaces remain: the York Water Gate and the Savoy chapel, one of London's perfect buildings, dating from 1505 and offering in its quietude the completest contrast to the bustle of the surrounding neighbourhood. The outside walls alone represent the original structure, and they, I fancy, only in parts. Among those who lie beneath its stones are Mrs. Anne Killigrew, whom Dryden mourned, and George Wither the poet, who sang divinely in prison of the consolations of the muse.

Covent Garden being for the most part a wholesale market, it has none of the interest of the Paris Halles, where the old women preside over stalls of fruit and vegetables arranged with exquisite neatness, and make up pennyworths and two pennyworths with so thoughtful an eye to the preservation of economy. We have nothing like that in London. In London if you want two pennyworth of mixed salad you must buy six pennyworth and throw away the balance, economy being one of the virtues of which we are ashamed; nor do we encourage open air stalls except for the poor. Hence where it is retail Covent Garden deals only in cut flowers and rare fruits, although I must not forget the attractive little aviary on the roof at the east end of the central building, where the prettiest of the little cage birds of all countries twitter their appeal to you to take them home and love them.

There is something in the constitution of the London porter, whether he unloads ships or wagons, carries on his head vegetables, fish, or the products of farthest Ind, which arrests progress, keeps him apart and out of the movement. You notice this at the Docks, which are of course remote from the centre, but you notice it also at Covent Garden, within sound of the very modern Strand. Covent Garden remains independent and aloof. New buildings may arise, petrol instead of horses may drag in the wagons from the country, but the work of unloading and distributing vegetables and flowers remains the same, and the porters have an immemorial air and attitude unresponsive to the times; while the old women who sit in rows in the summer shelling peas have sat thus since peas first had pods. Not only does the Covent Garden porter lead his own life insensitive to change, but his looks are ancient too: his face belongs to the past. It is not the ordinary quick London face: it has its scornful expression, of course, because London stamps a weary contempt on all her outdoor sons; but it is heavier, for example, than the Drury Lane face, close by. Perhaps the soil is responsible for this: perhaps Covent Garden depending wholly on the soil, and these men on Covent Garden, they have gained something of the rural stolidity and patience.

One could not have a better view of the Covent Garden porters collectively than fell to my lot one day recently, when I found some scores of them waiting outside the boxing club which used to be Evans's Rooms in Thackeray's day, and before that was Lord's Hotel, looking expectantly at its doors. I waited too, and presently there emerged alone a fumbling stumbling figure, a youth of twenty-four or so, neatly dressed and brushed, but with his cheeks and eyes a mass of pink puff. The daylight smote him almost as painfully as his late adversary must have done, and he stood there a moment on the steps wondering where he was, while Covent Garden, which dearly loves a fight with or without the gloves, murmured recognition and approval. No march of progress, no utilitarian wave, here. Byron's pugilist friend and master, Jackson of Bond Street, could he have walked in, would have detected little change, either in the crowd or the hero, since his own day.

Perhaps the most important event connected with St. Paul's Church, in Covent Garden, which in its original form was built by Inigo Jones to be "the handsomest barn in England," was the marriage in 1773 of William Turner of Maiden Lane to Mary Marshall of the same parish ; for from that union sprang Joseph Mallord William Turner, the painter, who was baptised there in 1775. Among those buried here are Samuel Butler the author of *Hudibras*, and Peter Pindar (Dr. Wolcot) the scarifier of Guelphs and Whitbreads, who wished his coffin to touch that of his great and satirical predecessor ; William Wycherley, who wrote *The Country Wife* ; Sir Peter Lely, who painted Stuart beauties ; Grinling Gibbons, who carved wood like an angel ; Dr. Arne, the musician ; and Charles Macklin, the actor, who lived to be 107.

It was in Maiden Lane, close by, that Turner was born, in 1775, and among famous sojourners there were Andrew Marvell and Voltaire. To-day it is given up to the stage, and it is difficult to pass through it without hearing the chorus of some forthcoming musical piece at practice in an upper room. Rule's oyster shop is here, the modern substitute for the historic Cyder Cellar, where a hundred years ago Porson drank incredible draughts and grew wittier with every potation. And it was in Maiden Lane that poor Terriss, the last of the swaggering romantics of the English stage, was murdered by a madman a few years ago. Close by, in Tavistock Street, at the *Country Life* office, is the best green door in London.

Between Covent Garden and Drury Lane certain eighteenth century traces still remain ; but east of Drury Lane is a wilderness of modernity. Everything has gone between that street and Lincoln's Inn Fields—everything. Men are not made London County Councillors for nothing.

At the time I write the houses in Kingsway and Aldwych have still to be built, a few isolated theatres and offices being all that is yet finished. It remains to be seen whether London, so conservative in its routes, so sentimentally attached to its old rights of way, will make any use of a wide road from the Strand to Holborn, but will not rather adhere to Bow Street and Endell Street or Chancery Lane. It has a way of doing so. Nothing has ever yet persuaded it to walk or drive up or down Shaftesbury Avenue, which for all the use it has been might never have ploughed through the Soho rookeries; while there are many people who would rather be splashed in St. Martin's Lane and among the bird fanciers of St. Andrew's two streets, than use the new and spacious Charing Cross Road. There is yet another reason why one looks with doubt on the usefulness of this new road, and that is that the great currents of London locomotion have set always east and west.

Of Covent Garden's two great theatres I have nothing to say; but the north-east corner house of Russell Street and Bow Street, with its red tiles and ancient façade, has much interest, for it was once, in a previous state, Will's Coffee House, where John Dryden sat night after night and delivered judgments on new books and plays. The associations of Will's are too numerous for me to dare to touch upon them further: they are a book alone. Next door, at No. 20 Russell Street, a hundred and more years later, over what is now a fruiterer's, lodged Charles and Mary Lamb; but the Society of Arts does not recognise the fact, nor even that Lamb was born at 2 Crown Office Row in the Temple, to which we are steadily drawing near. Lamb's rooms I fancy extended to the corner house too, and it was from one of these that, directly they were established there in 1817, Mary Lamb had the felicity to see a thief being conveyed to Bow Street police station.

7

Bow Street has now completely lost its antiquity and is
no longer interesting. Nor would Wellington Street be
interesting were it not for its association with Henry
Irving and the Lyceum. It is true that Henry Irving is
no more, and the Lyceum is transformed and vulgarised;
but the memory of that actor is too vivid for it to be
possible yet to pass through this street without a regret.
The Lyceum, so long the stronghold of all that was
most harmonious and romantic and dignified in the
English drama, is now a home of cheap melodrama, and
never again will that great and courteous gentleman with
whom its old fame is identified be seen on its stage. It
was in a corner of the pit, leaning against the barrier between that part of the house and the stalls, that I saw all
Irving's best performances in recent years, most exquisite
of which to recall being always his Benedick in *Much Ado
About Nothing*—or, as the programme hawkers who
hovered about the queue in the dark passage of the
Lyceum Tavern used to call it, "Much to-do about
Nothing." Of all the myriad plays I have seen—good
plays, middling plays, and plays in which one's wandering
eyes return again and again most longingly to the magic
word "exit"—I remember no incident with more serene
pleasure than the entry of Miss Terry as Beatrice with the
words "Against my will I am sent to bid you come in to
dinner," and the humorous gravity, a little perplexed by
the skill of this new and alluring antagonist, of Benedick's
face as he pondered his counter stroke and found none.
And with it comes the recollection of that other scene
between these two rare and gentle spirits, when, in "Olivia,"
Dr. Primrose, having at last found his weeping daughter,
would take her home again. All reluctance and shame,
she demurs and shrinks until he comes beautifully down to

THE DEATH OF PROCRIS

AFTER THE PICTURE BY PIERO DI COSIMO IN THE NATIONAL GALLERY

level ground with her, by saying, with that indescribably sweet smile of his, "You ran away with one man: won't you run back with me?" and wins the day. Irving may have lacked many qualities of the great actor; but when he died there passed away from the English stage something of charm and distinction and picturesque power that it is not likely in our time to recover; and the world was the poorer by the loss of a commanding gentleman.

It is in the lower part of Wellington Street, between the Strand and Waterloo Bridge, that Sotheby's is situated— that famous sale-room where book-collectors and dealers meet to bid against each other for first editions, and where, in these unpatriotic times, the most valuable of our autograph letters and unique literary treasures are allowed to fall to American dollars.

York Street, which was built early in the seventeenth century, retains much of its old character. It was at No. 4 that De Quincey wrote his *Confessions;* and the superb Elliston, who counted fish at dinner "as nothing," lived at No. 5. I am exploring and naming only the old streets where the actual historic houses still stand, because to walk down a dull street because a great man lived in it before the rebuilder and modern taste had made it dull, is not an attractive occupation. And I am omitting all names but those that seem to me to lend a human note to these pages. Streets such as Arundel Street and Norfolk Street in the Strand, which had many literary and other associations, but have been entirely rebuilt and are now merely business thoroughfares lined with fantastic red brick façades, do not seem to me interesting. But Essex Street, close by, does seem to me interesting, because it retains its old Georgian form, and being a *cul-de-sac* for carriages, is quiet to boot. The Essex Head, it is true, where Sam's Club

met under Doctor Johnson's sway, has been rebuilt; but
the lower part of the street is much as it was when Henry
Erskine learnt oratory at the Robin Hood Club (as some
of the speakers of our day learn it at the Cogers') and when
the Young Pretender lodged at Lady Primrose's.

When I first came to London, Simpson's, the most famous
of the Strand eating-houses, was beyond my purse. Not
for two years did I venture between its doors, and then
was so overawed that I might as well have fasted. I remember that the head waiter, in addition to the charge
for attendance, which was, I think, threepence, although,
such was my obvious unimportance, there had been none,
automatically subtracted a sixpence as my tip to him, thus
saving me the embarrassment of wondering if that were
enough. It was the first thoughtful thing that had occurred
during the meal. But later, when I had learned to call
"Waiter" without a spasm of self-consciousness, I extracted
much entertainment from Simpson's, not only in the
restaurant, but upstairs in the Divan, where one might
watch champions of chess mating in two moves, or read the
current number of *Cornhill*.

But all that is changed. There is no Divan to-day, and no
one there has ever heard of the *Cornhill*, and in place of the
old shabbiness and comfort we have sumptuously-uphol-
stered rooms and all the paraphernalia of modernity. The
chop-house has become a restaurant. The joints are still
wheeled from table to table, but not with the old leisure,
although still not so eagerly that the drivers' licences are
in any danger of endorsement. Simpson's in its new shape
is indeed symptomatic of the times. It even advertises.

The old Chop House is almost extinct, although I know
still of one or two the addresses of which nothing shall induce me to divulge (lest a syndicate corrupt them), where

one still sits in bays, and eats good English food with English names, and waits a long time for it, and does not complain; where there is no cloakroom for hats and coats, and no door porters whose one aim in life is to send you away in a cab; where a twopenny tip goes farther than a shilling elsewhere; and where if one lights a pipe no German-Swiss manager suddenly appears, all suavity and steel, to say that pipes are not allowed. There are still two or three of such places, but probably by the time this book is published they will have gone too and no pipes be left. Londoners, who sing "Rule Britannia" at every smoking concert, turn to water before any foreign *maître d'hotel*.

Although never perhaps so much a slave as when he is in a foreign restaurant, the Londoner loves always to wear shackles. No one accepts slights and insults so much as a matter of course. He may grumble a little, but he never really protests; and the next day he has forgotten. The Londoner has no memory. I say it again and again: he has no memory, and no public spirit or real resentment.

He supports national collections of pictures and books, but is quite happy when he goes to see them on Sunday afternoons, his only opportunity, and finds the door locked in his face.

In the course of a week he wastes hours on 'buses in the cold, during blocks caused by a handful of Italians (London's official road-menders) repairing a hole made by an Electric Light or Gas Company; and though at the time he remarks that it is scandalous, he forgets all about it the instant the block is past.

He pays twice for having his hair cut or his chin shaved, once to the proprietor of the saloon and once to the operator (sometimes to add to the grotesqueness of the proceeding the proprietor and the operator being one). He allows theatrical managers to charge him sixpence for a programme without which he cannot understand the play which he has already paid to see.

He does nothing towards reform when at one minute past eleven on Sunday, one minute past twelve on Saturday, and twenty-nine minutes to one on ordinary nights, he is unable by law to buy anything to drink.

He pays his money day after day for a seat in a train, and cheerfully stands for the whole journey home, hanging perilously to a strap or hat rack, packed closer than the Humane Society (to which perhaps he contributes) would allow any one to pack creatures who lack immortal souls.

Now and then a letter finds its way into the papers pointing out this and other hardships; but that is all. The railway companies and restaurateurs, the theatrical managers and music-hall, know Londoners too well to do more than smile in their sleeves and prepare new forms of aggression. London would be wretched were it not affronted.

In no street out of the city are omnibuses so constant as in the Strand, although to see the London 'bus at its best I think Whitehall is the place. As they come down the hill from Charing Cross into the spaciousness of the road opposite the Horse Guards, at a sharp trot, like ships in full sail, swaying a little under their speed, and shining gaily in all their hues, they are full of the joy of life and transmit some of it to the spectator. What London would be without its coloured omnibuses one dares not think. After the first flush of Spring, almost all her gaiety comes from them. Whitehall is the best at all times, but in April and May, when the trees (always a fortnight earlier than in the country) are vivid on the edge of the Green Park, and the sun has a nearly level ray, there is nothing to equal the smiling loveliness of Piccadilly filled with omnibuses, as seen from the top of the hill, looking east, about Down Street. It is an indescribable scene of streaming colour and gentle vivacity. Words are useless: it needs Monet or Pissarro.

Mention of the slanting sun brings me back to the Strand; for there is nothing more beautiful in its way—certainly a way peculiar to London—than that crowded 'bus-filled street at the same afternoon hour, with the light on the white spire of St. Mary's at the east end, which now, in its isolation, more than ever seems to block the way. It is a graver, less Continental, beauty than Piccadilly's: but it is equally indelible. Almost it makes me forgive the Strand.

St. Mary's church, like St. Martin's-in-the-Fields, is not, as most people would tell you, one of Wren's, but was built by Gibbs. Everything possible was done, some few years ago, to get permission to demolish it, for what were called the "Strand improvements"; but happily in vain. All honour to the resisters. The famous Maypole in the Strand stood on the site of this church. A cedar trunk, one hundred and thirty four feet high, it was erected in 1661 in honour either of the Restoration or (and here comes in the sweet of ignorance) because a Strand farrier's daughter, the wife of General Monk, had become the Duchess of Albemarle.

St. Clement's Inn close by St. Clement Danes, a few years ago was still a backwater of peace, but is now obliterated and new houses bear its name—Clement's Inn, where young Master Shallow of Warwickshire, Little John Doit of Staffordshire, Black George Barnes of Staffordshire, and Francis Pickbone and Will Squele, a Cotswold man, were the devil's own swinge-bucklers. How could we pull it down? But we would pull down anything. And New Inn, close by, of which Sir Thomas More was a member— that has gone too. Men, as I remarked before, are not made County Councillors for nothing.

With St. Clement Danes church, just to the east of St. Mary's Le Strand, and, like that, most gloriously in the very middle of the road, we come at last to the true Wren. It was in this church, one of London's whitest where it is white—of a whiteness, under certain conditions of light, surpassing alabaster—that Dr. Johnson had his pew, from which, we are told, he made his responses with tremulous earnestness. The pew was in the north gallery, where a tablet marks the spot, styling him (and who shall demur?) "the philosopher, the poet, the great lexicographer, the profound moralist and chief writer of his time." Among those buried here are Thomas Otway and Nathaniel Lee, the dramatists; Joe Miller, who made all the jokes, and in addition to being a "facetious companion," as his epitaph says, was a "tender husband" and "sincere friend," as humorists should be; Dr. Kitchiner, the author of *The Cook's Oracle* and himself a "notable fork"; and Acker-mann, the publisher of the *Repository*, which everyone who loves the London of the Regency, its buildings and costumes, in the fairest of all the methods of counterfeiting a city's life, namely copper-plate and aquatint, should know, and if possible possess.

And here at the Griffin, opposite the most fantastically and romantically conceived Law Courts in the world—the most astounding assemblage of spires, and turrets, and gables, and cloisters, that ever sprang from one English-man's brain,—we leave the Strand and pass into Fleet Street, or, in other words, into the City of London.

CHAPTER X

FLEET STREET AND THE LAW

Temple Bar—Charles Lamb—The Retired Cit—The Griffin—Printer's
Ink—An All-night Walk in London—The Temple—Oliver Gold-
smith—Lamb Again—Lincoln's Inn—Ben Jonson—Lincoln's Inn
Fields—Old Mansions—Great First Nights—The Soane Museum—
Dr. Johnson—The Cheshire Cheese—St. Dunstan's and St. Bride's.

WHEN I first knew London—passing through it on
the way to a northern terminus and thence to
school—Temple Bar was still standing. But in 1878 it
was pulled down, and with its disappearance old London's
doom may be said to have sounded. Since that day the
demolishers have taken so much courage into their hands
that now what is old has to be sought out : whereas Temple
Bar thrust antiquity and all that was leisurely and obsolete
right into one's notice with unavoidable emphasis. The
day on which it was decreed that Fleet Street's traffic must
be no longer embarrassed by that beautiful sombre gateway, on that day Dr. Johnson's London gave up the ghost
and a new utilitarian London came into being.

By the way, it is worth while to give an afternoon to a
walk from Enfield to Waltham Cross, through Theobald's
park, in order to stand before Temple Bar in its new
setting. Enfield is in itself interesting enough, if only for
its associations with one who loved London with a love

that was almost a passion, and who never tired of running over her charms and looking with wistful eyes from his rural exile across the fields towards the veil of smoke beneath which she spread her allurements : I mean, of course, Charles Lamb. It was an odd chance, which no one could have foreseen, least of all perhaps himself, to whom it must have stood for all that was most solid and permanent and essentially urban, that carried Temple Bar (beneath whose shadow he was born) to this new home among green fields, very near his own.

The Bar stands now as one of the gateways to Theobald's park. It was bought prior to demolition by Sir Henry Meux, and every brick and stone was numbered, so that the work of setting it up again in 1888 exactly as of old was quite simple. I know of no act of civic piety prettier than this. And there Temple Bar stands, and will stand, beneath great trees, a type of the prosperous cit who after a life of hard work amid the hum of the streets retires to a little place not too far from town and spends the balance of his days in Diocletian repose. What sights and pageants Temple Bar must recall and ruminate upon in its green solitude! The transplantation of the Elgin Marbles from the Parthenon to the British Museum—from dominating the Acropolis and Athens to serving as a source of perplexity to British sightseers in an overheated gallery of Bloomsbury—is hardly more violent than the transplantation of Temple Bar from Fleet Street and the city's feet to Hertfordshire and solitude.

A concrete example of English taste in the eighteen-seventies is offered by the study of the Griffin—the memorial which was selected to mark the site of Wren's gateway. It is curious to remember that the heads of traitors were displayed publicly on the spikes of Temple

Bar as recently as 1772.   Barbarism is always surprising us
by its proximity.

Even less than the Strand's pavements are those of Fleet
Street fitted for loiterers.   In fact we are now in the City,
and urgent haste has begun : not quite as in Cheapside and
Broad Street, for no one here goes without a hat, but
bustle is now in the air, and with every step eastward we
shall be more in the fray.   From Fleet Street, however,
though it may in itself seethe with activity, the escape is
easy into quietude more perfect than any that the Strand
has offered ; for here is the Temple on the south, and on
the north Lincoln's Inn with its gardens ; here also are
Clifford's Inn (now, in 1906, doomed to the speculator) and
Serjeants' Inn ; and here are the oddest alleys, not narrower than those between the Strand and Maiden Lane,
but more tortuous and surprising, the air of all of them (if
you can call it air) heavy with the thick oiliness of printer's
ink.

Printer's ink is indeed the life blood of Fleet Street and
its environs.   The chief newspaper offices of London are
all around us.   *The Times*, it is true, is fixed a little to the
south-east, on the other side of Ludgate Hill station ; but
in Fleet Street, and between it and Holborn on the north
and the river on the south, are nearly all the others.   Here
all day are men writing, and all night men printing it.   If
a tidal wave were to roll up the Thames and submerge
London, the newspapers would go first : a thought for each
of us to take as he will, with or without tears.

On an all-night walk in London, which is an enterprise
quite worth adventuring upon, it is well to be in Fleet
Street between three and five, when it springs into intense
activity as the carts are being loaded with the papers for
the early morning trains.   From here one would go to

Covent Garden and smell the flowers—the best antidote
to printer's ink that has been discovered.

The Temple, which spreads her cool courts and gardens
all unsuspected within a few yards of Fleet Street, is best
gained by the gateway opposite Chancery Lane, by the old
house with a ceiling of Tudor roses that one used to
contemplate as one was being shaved (all barbers' saloons
should have good ceilings). It is now a County Council
preserve. Almost immediately we come to the Temple
church, the most beautiful small church in London and
one of the most beautiful in the world—so grave in character and austere and decisive in all its lines; and yet so
human too and interesting, with its marble Templars lying
there on their circular pavement in a repose that has already endured for five centuries and should last for centuries more. Many of Lamb's old Benchers are buried
beneath this church; and here also lie the learned John
Selden, and James Howell who wrote the *Epistolæ*.

To the north of the church is a plain slab recording that
Oliver Goldsmith, that eminent Londoner and child of
genius, lies beneath it. He died at No. 2 Brick Court, up
two pairs of stairs, in a "closet without any light in it," as
Thackeray, who later had rooms below, described the poet's
bedroom. That was on April 4, 1774, and the next
morning, when the news went out, it was to this door that
there came all kinds of unfortunate creatures to whom he
had been kind—weeping and friendless now.

To name all the illustrious men who have had chambers
in the Temple would not only be an undertaking of great
magnitude but would smell overmuch of the Law. Rather
would I lay stress on the more human names, such as poor
Goldsmith's and Charles Lamb's. It was a little less than
a year after Goldsmith had died at 2 Brick Court that at

the same number in Crown Office Row Charles Lamb was born—on February 10, 1775. The Row is still there, but it has been rebuilt since Lamb's day, or perhaps only refaced. The gateway opposite leading into the garden is the same, as its date testifies. Lamb claimed to be a Londoner of the Londoners; but few Londoners have the opportunity of spending their childhood amid so much air and within sight of so much greenery as he. Perhaps to these early associations we may attribute some of the joy with which in after life, Londoner as he was (having lent his heart in usury to the City's stones and scenes), he would set out on an expedition among green fields.

I ventured just now to mock a little at the Law; and yet it is not fair to do so, for it is the Law that has preserved for London this beautiful Temple where all is peace and eighteenth-century gravity. Yet not everything has it retained, since no longer are the Inns of Court revels held here. It was in the Middle Temple Hall, which is a perfect example of Elizabethan architecture, that *Twelfth Night* was first played.

Lincoln's Inn, the Law's domain on the other side of Fleet Street, has its lawns and seclusion and old world quiet too; but it does not compare with the Temple. The Temple's little enclosed courts, with plane trees in their midst, of the tenderest green imaginable in early spring ; her sun-dials and her emblems ; her large green spaces sloping to the river ; her church and her Master's house; her gateways and alleys and the long serene line of King's Bench Walk — these are possessions which Lincoln's Inn can but envy. And yet New Square is one of the most satisfying of London's many grave parallelo-

grams; and the chapel which Inigo Jones built rises nobly
from the ground; and the old gateway in Chancery Lane
does something to compensate for the loss of Temple Bar.
Its date 1518 disposes of the story that Ben Jonson helped
to build it, with a trowel in one hand and a book in the
other, but I like to believe that he did a little desultory
bricklaying in this way on some extension to it.

Chancery Lane has recently been ennobled by the new
Record Office and made attractive by a little row of the
lions which Alfred Stevens designed for the British Museum
railings but which the British Museum authorities now
keep carefully under cover Some one had the happy
thought to set up copies of these delightful creatures
(which may be bought in plaster of Paris for a few shillings
of Brucciani) on the railings of the west side of the road
opposite the Record Office.

To Lincoln's Inn Fields, which is now lawyers' offices and
a public playing ground, but was once a Berkeley Square,
we come by way of the Inn. On the north and south
sides the rebuilders have already set their mark; but the
west side, although the wave of reform that flung up
Kingsway and Aldwych washes its very roots, is still
standing, much as it was in the great days of the seventeenth century, except that what were then mansions of
the great are now rookeries of the Law. No. 59 and 60,
for example, with its two magnificent brick pillars, was
built by Inigo Jones for the Earl of Lindsay. Inside are
a few traces of its original splendours. The corner house,
now No. 67, with the cloisters, was Newcastle House (previously Powis House) the residence of the great Duke of
Newcastle. Lincoln's Inn Fields Theatre, where Pepys
used to be so vastly amused (going there so often as to
make Mrs. Pepys "as mad as the devil") was on a site

ST. MARY-LE-STRAND

now covered by the Museum of the Royal College of Surgeons, to which the curious are admitted by order. Not for me are physiological whims and treasures of anatomy preserved in spirits of wine; rather would I stay outside and reflect on the first night of Congreve's *Love for Love* on April 30, 1695 with Mrs. Bracegirdle as Angelica, or of the première of *The Beggar's Opera*, thirty and more years later, with Lavinia Fenton so bewitching as Polly Peacham that she carried by storm the heart of the Duke of Bolton and became his Duchess. A little while ago I was reflecting that barbarism, although now, of course, extinct, is yet very recent; but to dip however casually into the history of London is to be continually reminded that for the most part nothing changes. Even as I write the papers are full of the marriages of two noblemen to actresses.

On the north side of Lincoln's Inn Fields is the Soane Museum, a curious medley of odds and ends with a few priceless things among them and a very capricious system of throwing open its doors. One must, however, visit it, for otherwise one would never see Hogarth's delicately coloured election series or "The Rake's Progress" in the original, and since in two or three of the subsidiary figures of "The Humours of an Election Entertainment" he comes nearer Jan Steen than in any of his work this would be a pity; and one would never see Canaletto's fine painting of the Grand Canal—better than any of that master's work at the Wallace Collection, I think; nor Giulio Clovio's illuminations to St. Paul's Epistles; nor a very interesting Watteau; nor several quaint missals, among them one whence the Bastard of Bourbon got his religion; nor a MS. of Lamb's Margaret of Newcastle; nor the MS. of Tasso's *Gerusalemme Liberata*; nor two of

Reynolds' sketch books; nor many exquisite cameos and intaglios; nor Christopher Wren's watch; nor the silver pistol which Peter the Great ravished from a Turkish Bey; nor paintings on silk by Labelle, little delicate trifles as pretty as Baxter prints; nor enough broken pieces of statuary—gargoyles, busts, capitols, and so forth—to build a street of grottoes; nor the famous alabaster sarcophagus of Seti I, King of Egypt about 1370 B.C.

It is the duty of all who now take a walk down Fleet Street to visit the scenes associated with the great name of Johnson. Dr. Johnson's house in Gough Square still stands, throbbing with printing presses: you may still thread Bolt Court: you may worship, as he did, in St. Clement Danes. But whether the wooden seat in the Cheshire Cheese which bears a brass plate sanctifying it to the Doctor was really his is another matter. None the less it has drawn many English sightseers and all Americans. The Cheshire Cheese, together with one or two chop houses in the city where willow pattern plates and two-pronged forks are still used, represents the old guard in English restauration. How long they will be able to hold out I dare not prophesy : but not, I fear, long. There are indeed already signs at the Cheshire Cheese that devotion to old ideas is not what it was. The famous pudding (lark and oyster, steak and kidney) was produced, I seem to recollect, with more ritual, more of an air, fifteen years ago than to-day. I have eaten of it but once, and shall eat of it no more. Not to my charge shall be laid the luring of any sweet-voiced lark into a Fleet Street kitchen, or indeed any kitchen whatsoever; but others have other views, and for them the arrival of the dish has long been one of London's crowded moments. Americans cross the Atlantic to partake of it and write their opinion in the visitors' book, which, not less depressingly facetious than all its kind, is rather more interesting by reason of an occasional name that has some artistic correlation. Old ale, a sanded floor, hot punch, and seats of a discomfort beyond that of the old third class railway compartments or a travelling circus, complete the illusion of Johnsonian revelry.

More than any other street Fleet Street, in spite of all its new buildings, has kept an old London feeling. I think this is due in a great measure to its irregular façades, each one different and some very odd, and its many clocks and signs. To look down Fleet Street on a sunny afternoon is to get a very vivid sense of almost eighteenth century animation. Modern as it all is, it always recalls to my mind the Old London street at one of the early South Kensington exhibitions. Every variety of architecture may be seen here—from the putative palace of Cardinal Wolsey to the *Daily Telegraph* office, from Sell's building, with its sundial, to St. Dunstan's-in-the-West; while to glance down Middle Temple Lane is to have a genuine peep at the eighteenth century.

St. Dunstan's-in-the-West is Fleet Street's jewel, with its very curious, very beautiful, open work tower, as exceptional in its way as St. Dunstan's-in-the-East, although not the artistic equal of that delicate structure. The architect of the western St. Dunstan's was one Shaw, and it is not yet eighty years of age, all the old associations belonging to that which preceded it—the St. Dunstan's under whose shadow Charles Lamb says he was born; in which Donne preached; and which in the seventeenth century was surrounded by booksellers' shops, among them Smethwick's, who published *Romeo and Juliet* and *Hamlet*, and Marriot's, who put forth *The Compleat Angler*. The other Fleet Street church, St. Bride's, which is just off the road on the

8

south, is older and has far more dignity : it is indeed one of Wren's finest efforts. Elsewhere I have said something of the spire under a busy sky. In a house in the churchyard Milton once lived, and beneath the church lies the author of *Pamela* and *Clarissa Harlowe*, under the central aisle.

It is at the Barley Mow, close by, in Salisbury Square, that the ancient society of the Cogers hold their parliament every Saturday night and settle questions of state over pipe and glass. One should certainly visit one of these debates, where so many speakers have first raised their voices and demolished the Government. Students of race will not be surprised to hear that there was never a Cogers' palaver without a brogue in it.

CHAPTER XI

ST. PAUL'S AND THE CHARTERHOUSE

THERE are so many arresting movements in London,
as indeed in all hives of men, that to observe widely
is very difficult. Just as one is said not to be able to see
a wood for trees, so one cannot rightly see a city for its
citizens, London for its Londoners. I believe, to give an
example of defective London observation, that one's tendency is to think that all its greater streets are straight;
whereas hardly any are. Here is a question on that fallacy,
suggested to me one day as I stood at the point which we
have now reached: "From the middle of the road under
the railway Bridge at the foot of Ludgate Hill how much
of St. Paul's do you see?" I would wager that the majority
of Londoners would expect to see the whole façade; but
they would be very wrong.

In one of his delightful books Dr. Jessopp remarks that
whereas country people look up, Londoners look down It

115

is largely this habit that has limited their observing powers ; but London has itself to blame. I assume that one can observe well only by taking large views, and in London this is impossible, even if one would, partly from the circumscribing effect of bricks and mortar, partly from the dim light of a London distance, and partly from the need of avoiding collisions. One's eyes unconsciously acquire a habit of restricted vision : our observation specialises, like that of the little girl in Mrs. Meynell's book, who beguiled the tedium of her walks by collecting shopkeepers named Jones. Perhaps that is the kind of observation for which we in London have become best suited.

I remember how amazed I was, some years ago, when one clear Sunday morning, as I was walking in Fleet Street, I chanced on looking down Bouverie Street to see, framed between its walls, the Crystal Palace gleaming in the far distance. That, however, was an exceptional sight. Far less uncommon yet quite obvious characteristics cause astonishment when they are pointed out. It comes, for example, as a surprise to many people if you refer to the hill in Piccadilly. "What hill?" they ask. Indeed, if there is one thing more remarkable than one's own ignorance of London it is that of other people. Walking one day in Cheapside, from west to east, I was struck by the unfamiliar aspect of the building which blocked the end of that thoroughfare. It turned out to be a new set of offices at the foot of Cornhill, and it caused me to wonder how many people shared my belief that as one walks eastwards down Cheapside one ought to have a full view of the Royal Exchange ; which is not, as a matter of fact, visible until one is almost out of the Poultry. And this error led me to examine other similar fancies, and in many cases to find them equally wrong. I amused myself in consequence by

THE MADONNA AND CHILD, WITH ST. JOHN AND ST. CATHERINE

AFTER THE PICTURE BY TITIAN IN THE NATIONAL GALLERY

drawing up a little paper in London topography, or rather in London observation.   Here are a few of the questions which I jotted down :—

1. If the Nelson column were to fall intact upon its side in a due southerly direction, where would Nelson's head lie ?

2. If circumstances should confine your perambulations to an area comprised in a radius of three hundred yards from the Griffin in Fleet Street, what streets and how much of them would be open to you ? Could you get to the theatre ?

3. Give in detail the route of what is in your opinion the shortest walking-distance from (*a*) St. Pancras to Victoria, (*b*) Paddington to London Bridge, (*c*) the Lyceum to Oxford Circus, (*d*) the Zoological Gardens to the Albert Hall, (*e*) the Bank to the Tower, (*f*) Seat P4 in the British Museum Reading Room to seat C7.

4. Between what points of the compass do the following streets run : the Strand, Northumberland Avenue, Fenchurch Street, Edgware Road, Knightsbridge, Tottenham Court Road, Cockspur Street, Bow Street, Whitehall, Westminster Bridge, Waterloo Bridge and London Bridge ?

5. Give the approximate taxi fare between Charing Cross and (*a*) the Elephant and Castle, (*b*) the Spaniards, (*c*) Liverpool Street, (*d*) the Marble Arch, (*e*) the Brompton Oratory, (*f*) the People's Palace, (*g*) the Agricultural Hall.

6. If you followed that diameter of the four-mile radius which starts from the West Hill, Highgate, where would you collide with the opposite circumference ?

7. Does it surprise you to learn that Westminster Bridge, if continued in a straight line for two or three miles on the Surrey side would run into Tower Bridge, or somewhere very near it ?

8. Where are Hanging Sword Alley and Whetstone Park?

Of St. Paul's Cathedral I find it very difficult to write. Within, it is to me the least genial of cathedrals, the least kindly. It has neither tenderness nor mystery. I would not call it exactly hard and churlish, like some of the white-washed Lutheran temples: it is simply so much noble masonry without sympathy.

Wren, of course, had no religion: one sees that in every church he built. He was a wonderful architect; he heaped stone on stone as no Englishman has ever done, before or since; one feels that he must have known by inspired prevision exactly how the smoke and fog of the future would affect his favourite medium; but he had no religion, no secret places in his soul, no colour. His churches are churches for a business man, and a successful one at that: not for a penitent, not for a perplexed and troubled soul, not for an emotional sufferer. Poor people look out of place in them. Wren's churches are for prosperity.

To make satisfying exteriors—especially to make the right spires—was Wren's happy destiny. He never, or almost never, failed here. Within, his churches are for the most part merely consecrated comfortable rooms: without, they are London's most precious, most magical possession. At first they may not please; but — and especially if one studies the city from a height—one comes to realise their beauty and their extraordinary fittingness. On a bright day of scudding clouds, such as I remember in January of this year, when I was sitting in a room at the highest point of the Temple, the spire of a Wren church can have as many expressions, can reflect as many moods, as a subtle and sympathetic woman. I was watching St. Bride's with absolute fascination as it smiled and frowned, doubted and understood.

St. Paul's of course can hardly be ranked with Wren's churches at all: it is so vast, so isolated. It is too vast in its present Anglican hands for human nature's daily needs. The Roman Catholics, by their incense, their confessionals, their constant stream of worshippers, their little side chapels, their many services, and, perhaps most of all, by their broken-light, bring down even their largest cathedrals to reasonable dimensions, so that one does not feel lost in them. They might humanise St. Paul's. But as it is, St. Paul's is a desert: nothing is done for you, and its lighting is almost commercial. The dominant impression it conveys is of vastness: one emerges with no hush on one's soul.

St. Paul's should, I think, be loved from a distance; an interview should not be courted. The triumph of St. Paul's is that, vast and serene, it broods protectively over the greatest city in the world, and is worthy of its office. The dome is magnificent: there is nothing finer: and that to me is St. Paul's—a mighty mothering dome; not cold aisles and monstrous groups of statuary, not a whispering gallery and worried mosaics, not Americans with red guide books and typists eating their lunch. All that I want to forget.

St. Paul's best appeal, true appeal, is external. It has no religious significance to me: it is the artistic culmination of London city, it is the symbol of London. And as such it is always thrilling. One of the best near views is from the footbridge from Charing Cross to Waterloo; one of the best distant views is from Parliament Hill. By no effort of imagination can one think of London without it.

Yet go to St. Paul's one must, if only to reverse this view and see London from its dome. On a clear day, which in London means a windy day, you cannot have a more interesting sight than this great unwieldy city from the ball of its sentinel cathedral—all spread out on every side, with a streak of river in the midst: all grey and busy right away to the green fields.

To trace the great roads from this height is one of the most interesting things. For it is pleasant to think that all the roads even of the crowded congested business centre take one in time into the country, into the world, right to the sea. In time, for example, Ludgate Hill is going to be Fleet Street, and Fleet Street the Strand, and the Strand King William Street, and so on to Leicester Square and Coventry Street and Piccadilly; and Piccadilly leads to Hounslow and Staines and the west of England. Behind us is Cannon Street, which leads to London Bridge and the Borough High Street and Tabard Street to Watling Street and Gravesend and Rochester and the Kentish coast: or viâ London Bridge and the Borough High Street, to Newington Causeway, to Clapham, Epsom, Leatherhead and Dorking to the Sussex coast; or through Guildford to the Hog's Back and Hampshire. Cheapside leads to Cornhill and Leadenhall Street and Aldgate, and Aldgate to the Whitechapel Road and Romford, Brentwood, Chelmsford and the east; Bishopsgate leads to Edmonton, Hoddesden, Cheshunt, Ware and the north-east; the City Road leads to Islington, Highgate, and the North; and Cheapside to Holborn, Oxford Street, the Edgware Road, St. Albans and the north-west. From the ball of St. Paul's one can follow all these roads for a little way on their great journeys.

A few years ago such eventualities were not considered as they now are, the Londoner associating liberty only with the rail. But now that the motor-car has come, the road has returned to its own again, not only in fact but in our thoughts. No motorist thinks only of the portion of

THE AVENUE, MIDDELHARNIS

AFTER THE PICTURE BY HOBBEMA IN THE NATIONAL GALLERY

road that he happens to be on : he looks ahead and thinks of its course and destination. This is good. This is one of the best things that the motor has done. Compared with such an enlargement of vision, such a quickening of the imagination, its speed is unimportant. The motor's great achievement is its gift of England to the English, the home counties to the Londoner.

It is in St. Paul's that our great soldiers and sailors and painters are commemorated. The painters are modest ; but the monuments to the warriors are large and florid (rather like the Dutch), usually personifying the hero in action. Nothing is so wrong as for sculpture to perpetuate an arrested movement : great art, and particularly marmoreal art, treats of repose ; but the sculptors of St. Paul's, the Bacons, and Bailleys, and Westmacotts, did not think so, and we therefore have Sir Ralph Abercromby for ever falling from his horse, and Sir John Moore for ever being just lowered into his grave, though not at all as the poem describes. Latterly, however, taste has improved, for the completed Wellington monument has dignity and tranquillity, while Lord Leighton's sarcophagus is beautiful.

The old rule which seems to have insisted upon every statue being eight feet high, although doubtless a wise one in so large a building, leads to some rather quaint effects : as when one comes suddenly upon a half-naked Colossus of truculent mien, fit opponent for Hackenschmidt, and finds the name of Samuel Johnson beneath it. Anomalies in marble are so very noticeable. There seems to me to be another of a more serious nature in the bas-relief memorial to the officers and men of the 57th West Middlesex who perished in the Crimea and New Zealand, the subject of which is Christ comforting the mourners : for the logician might so easily point out that had the law of Christ not been broken the cause of mourning would not have existed. One's feeling is that Christ should not be here : it is not so much over dead soldiers as over the living that He must mourn. But every church which, like St. Paul's, glorifies war and warriors, is of course in a very delicate position. England is, however, the last country in which to say so.

For other memorials to distinguished men one must descend, at a cost of sixpence, into the crypt (the soldiers and sailors above are free), where Sir Christopher Wren lies, and where many of the greatest painters are buried—among them Turner and Reynolds, Lawrence and Millais. Here too lie Nelson and Wellington. Latterly the crypt has been set apart as the resting-place or memorial-place of some of our lesser but authentic men of genius, such as W. E. Henley, that burly fighter and sweet poet, and Randolph Caldecott, best of illustrators for the young.

One of the parts of commercial London that I like best is the slope of the hill between St. Paul's and the river. All kinds of old narrow lanes wind down this hill to the water, crossing Upper Thames Street on the way—all strongly stamped by the past and all very busy and noisy. Nowhere in London do the feet of horses make so clattering a disturbance as hereabouts, and the motor vehicle has hardly yet found its way here. These lanes with the odd names—Godliman Street, Benet Lane, Sermon Lane, Trig Lane, Distaff Lane, Little Divinity Lane, Garlick Hill, College Hill, Stew Lane—are all winding and narrow and obsolete, and without exception, contrary to the best interests of business; yet they persist, and one is glad of it. And all make for the wharves and the river, and ultimately the open sea.

The Great Fire made very short work of Thames Street —as indeed a fire always does of riverside buildings—and everything that one now sees dates from the hither side of that disaster. The churches are all Wren's, whose industry amazes more and more :—St. Benet's (where Inigo Jones is buried); St. James's in Garlickhithe (with a figure of the apostle over its fine assertive clock); St. Michael's, on College Hill, with some carving of Wren's confederate Grinling Gibbons, and a window to Dick Whittington, who was buried here as often as he was Lord Mayor of London. By Cannon Street's arch one passes the very thinnest end that any architectural wedge ever had, and so comes into Lower Thames Street, where we quickly find Wren again —at St. Magnus the Martyr, at the foot of Fish Street Hill, on which the Monument, like a tall bully, lifts its head and lies. St. Magnus's is one of London's larger churches, and in its way is very fine. Miles Coverdale, who gave the English their Bible, is buried here. The glass is not good, nor is it good in any Wren church that I have seen, but it rarely reaches a lower point than in St. Dunstan's-in-the-East (which has the beautiful tower). Before we come to this church we pass Pudding Lane, where the Great Fire began (we shall see directly where it stopped), and to Billingsgate fish market. Both the Thames Streets, Upper and Lower, are very genuine, and very interesting, with their warehouses and their wharves; although I should feel there by night that one must meet rats. The whole walk from Blackfriars Station to the Tower is worth taking, with plenty of material to the hand of a Méryon or Muirhead Bone on the way; but at Billingsgate I draw the line—Billingsgate, which is always muddy whatever the weather, and always noisy and slimy and fishy beyond words. One comes away indeed vowing never to eat fish again.

From St. Paul's, when I was last there, I walked to the church of St. Bartholomew the Great in Smithfield, feeling that I needed a little Norman and Early English humanising in the genuine atmosphere of antiquity; for St. Paul's, for all its sacred dust, is too much like the mausoleum of a Lord Mayor. I walked through a

narrow passage into Paternoster Row, and so to Amen
Corner and Warwick Lane. I peeped into Amen Court,
that quiet ecclesiastical backwater where St. Paul's canons
live, but have at the present moment no Sydney Smith
among them; not among the minor canons is there a
Thomas Ingoldsby. I peeped also into Warwick Square,
one of whose old residential houses still stands amid the
offices, with a top hamper of woodwork and a parliament
of pigeons on its coping. And so on into Newgate Street,
where all is changing so rapidly—Christ's Hospital being
no more, and Newgate's dark and sinister prison having
given way to the gleaming new Central Criminal Court
in yellow stone with its gold figure of Justice on top. St.
Sepulchre's Church has not yet been pulled down, it is
true; but I suppose it has merely been overlooked, so
noble is it and worthy of preservation.

St. Sepulchre's, whose four vanes and their inability to
swing exactly together have made a city proverb, has a
long association with crime which, however kindly meant,
lends it a sinister air. Its clock for centuries gave the hours
to the hangman at Newgate across the way: at first to
warn him that it was time to start for Tyburn, and later
that the moment was ripe for the execution in the prison
itself. Life must have been very interesting and full—
to the innocent or undetected—in Holborn and Oxford
Street in those old days when condemned men were hanged
at Tyburn tree: processions so constantly passing, with
every circumstance of publicity and ribaldry. St. Sepulchre's connection with executions did not end at merely
giving the time: it had refinements of torture at its
fingers' ends. By the zeal of a citizen of London named
Robert Dowe, who left a sum of money for the purpose,
the clerk of the church was forced to take his bell in

hand on the eve of a hanging, and proceed twice, once at night and once in the morning, to the prison, where, standing beneath the window of the wretch's cell, he gave out certain tolls and called upon him in a dreary rhyme to make his peace with God if he would avoid eternal flames. And then, on the departure of the cart for Tyburn, the clerk had to appear again and offer prayers; and lest any of these searching attentions were omitted or shirked, the Beadle of the Merchant Taylors' Hall was provided with a stipend to see that the clerk duly carried them out with a becoming Christian rigour. So much for St. Sepulchre's official interest in the condemned; but it played also an amateur part in another and prettier, although not much humaner, ritual, for it was from its steps that a nosegay was presented to every traveller to that Tyburn from which none returned.

Our church has fifteenth century masonry in it, but for the most part is seventeenth, having been destroyed by the Great Fire. St. Sepulchre's was indeed that destroyer's last ecclesiastical victim, for a few yards farther up Giltspur Street, at Pie Corner, it died away and was no more, having raged all the way from Pudding Lane by the Monument. Pie Corner was just by Cock Lane, the scene, in 1762, of the most ridiculous imposture which ever laid London by the heels—the Cock Lane ghost. When last I stood looking down this lane, which now belongs almost entirely to commerce, a catsmeat man went by, pushing a barrow and calling his wares, and it seemed he must have walked straight out of one of Hogarth's pictures.

I have said in an earlier chapter that Shepherd's Market in Mayfair gives one the best impression at this moment of the busy shopkeeping London of the Augustan essayists.

The best idea of a London of an earlier time that still remains, is I think to be found in Cloth Fair and Bartholomew Close, where sixteenth-century houses still stand, and sixteenth-century narrownesses and dirt are everywhere. If there is the true old London anywhere, it is in the passages on the north side of St. Bartholomew the Great.

But before we reach Bartholomew Close we must pass St. Bartholomew's Hospital, or Barts' as it is called, on the south side of Smithfield, one of London's great temples of healing. Its square in summer is quite a little park, with its patients taking the air and the children playing among them, and there is always a bustle of students and nurses and waiting-maids, crossing and re-crossing from one grey building to another.

The way to Bartholomew Close is through the hospital to Little Britain, and so into this ramifying old-world region, once a centre of printers (Benjamin Franklin practised his trade there) and now given up to warehouses and offices and in its narrow parts to small shops; but never for an instant belonging to the twentieth century or even the nineteenth.

The church itself—St. Bartholomew the Great—is one of the architectural jewels of the city. Not that it is so perfect or so beautiful; but that it is so curious, so genuine, so un-Wrenlike, so unexpected, so modest. I think its humility and friendliness are its greatest charm. It hides away behind West Smithfield's houses, with its own little crazy graveyard before it, but keeps its door always open. You enter and are in the middle ages.

I am not attempting to describe the church, which is a very attractive jumble of architectural styles, with a triforium that one longs to walk round, and noble doors,

CHICHESTER CANAL

AFTER THE PICTURE BY TURNER, IN THE NATIONAL GALLERY

and massive Norman pillars, and a devious ambulatory.
Indeed there is no need, for no London church is so often
depicted. On the morning I was last there it was like
students' day at the National Gallery, as many as four
young women being hard at work transferring different
aspects to paper, while two others were engaged on Prior
Bolton's window, which is a kind of private box in the
south side of the choir, built into one of the arches of the
triforium, where this prior, who flourished early in the
sixteenth century, may have sat.

An older relic still is the coloured tomb of the founder—
in the sanctuary—the merry and melodious Rahere, who
founded the Priory of St. Bartholomew in the reign of
Henry I. Seven Henries later it was of course dissolved.
Having loitered sufficiently in the church, one should walk
round its exterior and make a point of seeing the sexton's
house (to which I have already alluded) which clings to
the north wall as a child to its mother—the quaintest old
house in London, with its tiny Tudor bricks and infinitesimal
windows.

Cloth Fair begins here, a congeries of narrow streets and
dreadful old women, where once was the centre of the drapery
trade that now flourishes in St. Paul's Churchyard. From
Cloth Fair I passed into Smithfield's large vacancy, where
Bartholomew Fair—which was in its serious side a fair for
cloth—used to be held every Bartholomew's Day until
1855, when the law stepped in and said No. The pleasure
portion was the most extraordinary chaos of catchpenny
booths, theatricals, *feræ naturæ*, wild beasts, cheap jacks
and charlatans that England has ever seen; and I like
to think that Charles Lamb led William Wordsworth
through it in 1802.

"And were men and women really willing to burn for

their faith?" one asks, as one stands here amid the railway vans. How strange, to-day, it all seems! Unless something very wonderful and miraculous happens there will never be another martyr burnt at Smithfield. Martyrdom is out of fashion; and yet that was only three hundred and fifty years ago.

Through the fleshly horrors of Smithfield Market, where Hebrew middlemen smoke large cigars, I advise no one to wander: it is discipline enough for us to have been created carnivorous; and Charterhouse Square, whither we are now bound, can be reached easily by Long Lane and Hayne Street, well outside the domain of the carcase and the bloodstained porter.

To Charterhouse Square, a region of peace, within sound of Aldersgate's commercial zeal, we are coming, not to see its hotels for city men, or the Merchant Taylors' school, or even the two very charming Georgian houses that are left, but solely to explore the monastery that gives it its name. After a curiously varied career, the Charterhouse is now fixed (I hope for many centuries to come, although the gate porter tells me alarming stories of offers from speculative builders) as an almshouse for old gentlemen. It was built in the fourteenth century as a monastery for Carthusians. Then came the dread Henry VIII with his odd and implacable conscience, hardly less devastating than the speculative builder or the modern County Councillor, who cast out the monks and beheaded the prior, and made the house a private residence for rich courtiers—Sir Thomas Audley, Lord North, the Duke of Northumberland, the Duke of Norfolk, the Duke of Suffolk in turn occupying it and entertaining there. But in 1611 Mr. Thomas Sutton bought it and endowed it with a sum of £200,000 as a hospital and a school. In the school

IN THE TEMPLE GARDENS (FOUNTAIN COURT)

forty boys were to be educated free, with sixty others who paid fees; in the hospital "eighty gentlemen by descent and in poverty" were to be maintained—above the age of fifty, if sound, but of forty, if maimed in war. Both intentions were admirably realised, although changes have come in. In 1872, for example, the school was moved to Godalming, and in 1885 the number of pensioners was reduced by twenty-five owing to loss of revenue. But the fifty-five that remain could not spend their declining days more sweetly and serenely than within these grey walls, with their comfortable rooms and the best fires I saw in London this last winter.

The Charterhouse is very beautiful, very quiet. Its most famous pensioner, although an imaginary one, will always be Colonel Newcome—a proper tribute to the genius of Thackeray, who was educated at the school here. Among its pensioners in real life have been such different dramatists as Elkanah Settle and John Maddison Morton, the author of *Box and Cox*. Among famous schoolboys of the Charterhouse—old Carthusians, as we call them—some of whom are celebrated in the little passage that leads to the chapel, are John Leech and George Grote, Addison and Steele, Crashaw and Blackstone, John Wesley and Sir Henry Havelock.

The last time I went to the Charterhouse was the first day of spring this year, and when I came out the sky was so clear and the air so soft that I gave up all my other plans, and turning into Aldersgate, walked all the way to Highgate: up Aldersgate, which is now wholly commercial but which in Tudor times was fashionable; up the Goswell Road (where Mr. Pickwick lodged with Mrs. Bardell); along Upper Street, that fine old-world highway; past Islington Green, now a municipal enclosure; through Highbury; up

9

the long Holloway Road (where I weakened and took a tram); up Highgate Hill; and so to that healthy northern suburb where time still tarries. All this I did for old sake's sake, because it was at Highgate, on the very top of the hill, that I used to live—just north of the Grove, where Carlyle heard Coleridge discourse endlessly of the sum-jective and the om-jective.

To me Highgate is still London's most fascinating suburb, for it has a quietness and an unpretentiousness that are foreign to Hampstead. On how many sweet May evenings have I walked along Hampstead Lane to the Spaniard's, past Caen's dark recesses, where it is whispered badgers are still to be found, and sitting in one of the tavern's arbours, have heard the nightingale singing in Bishop's Wood. The Spaniard's in those days, ten years ago, was one of the best of the old London inns still surviving—without the German waiter and the coloured wine glasses to bring in the false new note. And I was never tired of leading my friends thither to show them Dick Turpin's knife and fork in a case on the wall. Sometimes we would walk on to Jack Straw's Castle, along that fine high ridgeway across the Heath known as the Spaniard's Road, and watch London twinkling far away beneath us. Or disregarding Jack Straw's Castle (where the Fourth Party were wont to recuperate and plan new audacities), we would plunge down from Constable's Knoll of Scotch firs, over rough sandy bridle paths, to the Bull and Bush in the hollow at North End, and there find refreshment.

I am speaking of the spring and summer; but Hampstead Heath is not less attractive in winter too, and in winter there used to be at the Bull and Bush a brew of barley wine, as it was called, that was very warming. Such brews are no longer common. What one misses from London windows in winter is any alluring invitation to hot cordial drinks. The publicans announce the commencement of the goose club, but there is no longer any tidings of mulled ale. It is sad but true that the Londoner's—indeed I might say the Englishman's—first and last word in alcoholic cheer is whisky. Even in the coldest weather no stand is made for the genial beverages of the past. To the end Dickens brewed punch and saw that it was good; but with Dickens, or very shortly after, passed away all interest in that enkindling Christianising bowl.

And who now asks for a port wine negus? But when I first came to London in 1892, in the good old days when Furnivall's Inn still stood, and Ridler's Hotel beamed hospitably across Holborn, I used to frequent a little inner sitting-room in that hostelry, where long clay pipes were provided, and where a stately waiter, more like the then Speaker of the House of Commons (now Lord Peel) than any waiter has a right to be, used to bring a negus that was worth drinking, with cinnamon floating on the top like drift wood after a wreck.

Will there never come a mixer of hot and kindling beverages who, perhaps taking a Dickensian name, will wean the world from an undiscriminating devotion to whisky? Pineapple rum hot, with three lumps—nowhere now can one drink this fragrant concoction. And the other pleasantly-sounding comforters with which Mr. Pickwick and his friends and the people they met on the top of coaches were wont to make themselves happy and aromatic—where are they? All past, with the stage coaches and the post chaise. This is an age of champagne and whisky, motor-cars and religious novels. Mr. Pickwick and his leisure and his punch are no more.

In Highgate and Hampstead I should love to linger: but they are outside the radius so far as this book is con-

cerned.   Yet of Hampstead I must say a word here, if only
to correct the suggestion that it is pretentious.   Pretentious
only in its modern roads—its Fitzjohn's Avenues, and so
forth : there is no pretentiousness about Church Row,
which, until the flats were built on the north side, was the
most beautiful English street I ever saw, or expect to see,
and is still well worth climbing a hill ten times as steep as
Hampstead's.   With this early simple part of Hampstead,
and the little passages and cottages between Church Row
and the pond on the summit, the memory of Kate Greenaway is in my mind inseparably bound.   To think of one
is to think of the other.   One feels that she must have
lived here ; as indeed she did—just below Church Row, in
Frognal, but not, I grieve to say, in an old house.   Hampstead has had many literary and artistic associations, from
Keats (in Well Walk) to George du Maurier (in the Grove)
but Kate Greenaway is my Hampstead symbol.

I remember what a shock it was to hear that she was
dead.   For one had never thought of death in connection
with this serene and joyous artist.   Her name had called
up for so long only pleasant, sunny associations : memories
of green meadows with grave little girls and boys a-maying ;
quiet, restful rooms (in Church Row !) with tiny fireplaces,
daffodils in blue vases on the high mantelpieces, and grave
little girls and boys a-playing ; and trim streets, where
everything was well-kept and well-swept, and all the roofs
were red and all the garden gates and fences green, and
more grave little girls carried dolls, and more grave little
boys rolled hoops, and very young mothers with high waists
gossiped over their grave little babies' infinitesimal heads.
Some such scenes as these had for twenty years been rising
before one whenever Kate Greenaway's name was heard,
bringing with them a gentle breath of ancient repose and

CORNELIUS VAN DER GEEST

AFTER THE PICTURE BY VAN DYCK IN THE NATIONAL GALLERY

simplicity and a faint scent of pot pourri. And to think the hand that devised this innocent communism of quaintness and felicity, this juvenile Arcadia, was still for ever!

That was in 1901, when for some years Miss Greenaway had not been the power that once she was. Her greatest triumphs were in the early eighties, when she illustrated Ann and Jane Taylor's *Original Poems*, and wrote and illustrated verses of her own writing, and put forth every Christmas a little almanack, with scenes fitting to every month and delicate and dainty borders of the old-world flowers she loved best. It might almost be said that she invented the daffodil. That was the time when flowers were being newly discovered, and while the æsthetes were worshipping the sunflower and the lily Miss Greenaway was bidding the cheeriest little daisies spring from the grass and the chubbiest little roses burst from the bushes, and teaching thousands of uninitiated eyes how beautiful the daffodil is. Wordsworth had done so before, it is true; but between Wordsworth and Kate Greenaway how wide a gulf of stuffy taste was fixed—the forties, the fifties, the sixties, and the seventies! Kate Greenaway came like a fresh southern breeze after a fog. The æsthetes were useful, but they were artificial: they never attained to her open-air radiances. In the words of a critic whom I was reading somewhere the other evening, Kate Greenaway newly dressed the children of England; and the effects of her influence will probably never be lost. And to a great extent she refurnished England too. There is not an intelligent upholsterer or furniture dealer in the country at this moment whose warehouses do not bare witness to Miss Greenaway's unobtrusive, yet effectual, teaching. She was the arch-priestess of happy simplicity.

As an illustrator of dramatic stories, such as the domestic tragedies set forth by the sisters Taylor, or Bret Harte's

Queen of Pirate Isle, or *The Pied Piper of Hamelin*, Miss Greenaway was not quite successful. Her genius bent rather to repose than action; or, at least, to any action more complex than skipping or dancing, picking flowers, crying, or taking tea. (No one in the whole history of art has drawn more attractive tea tables—old Hampstead tea tables, I am sure.) Drama was beyond her capacity, and her want of sympathy with anything unhappy or forceful also unfitted her. Her pictures prove her the soul of gentleness. Had she set out to make a tiger it would have purred like the friendliest tabby; nothing could induce her pencil to abandon its natural bent for soft contours and grave kindlinesses. Hence her crones were merely good-natured young women doing their best—and doing it very badly—to look old; her witches were benevolent grandmothers. To illustrate was not her *métier*. But to create—that she did to perfection. She literally made a new world where sorrow never entered—nothing but the momentary sadness of a little child—where the sun always shone, where ugliness had no place and life was always young. No poet can do much more than this. It seems to me that among the sweet influences of the nineteenth century Kate Greenaway stands very high. The debt we owe to her is beyond payment; but I hope that some memorial will be considered. Randolph Caldecott has a memorial in the crypt of St. Paul's; Lewis Carroll in the Great Ormond Street Children's Hospital; Kate Greenaway ought to have a group of statuary (in the manner of the Hans Christian Andersen monument) in Church Row, Hampstead.

And now we must get back to the city again, but before we do so let us, since it is Friday, turn our steps to a very curious place on that day. I wonder how Mr. Wilfred Whitten, that inveterate and glowing Metropolitan, would reply to the question, Where, if anywhere,

in London is to be seen in this year of 1913 the best
approximation to a Hogarthian scene ? But let me share
with all propounders of riddles (except a few unhappy ones
baffled by the cleverness or tactlessness of the company) the
triumph of supplying also the answer. The answer is the
Caledonia market on a Friday. I was last there on a bitter
afternoon, and the thought of Hogarth was continuous in
that vast concourse of dealers and bargain-hunters.

It was a killing day : an east wind swept the eminence :
Caledonia was at its sternest and wildest. The dealers
were blue with cold ; their wives huddled over braziers ;
every hot-chestnut man was hemmed in by a little warmth-
seeking crowd as closely as though he was in a fit ; on
the floor of this vast open space were spread the wares
of the day, all of which had been brought thither that
morning, and arranged to best advantage, and most of
which would have to be packed up and taken away
that evening. Horses and carts were anchored here and
there for the removal of the more prosperous merchants'
goods, the horses shivering in the blast ; for the rest there
were hand barrows by the hundred. The goods covered,
I suppose, several acres ; and a hundred pounds would
have cleared the market. For the most part it was
rubbish—old iron, old clothes, old household utensils,
such curiosities as a pawnbroker lends nothing on, "dud"
Sheffield plate, tools, oleographs, and so forth, all huddled
together. But there were specialists too. One dealer, for
example, had nothing but old corsets, and if there is a less
engaging sight than a huddle of old corsets I hope never
to see it. Another had fire-irons and nothing else ;
another, painters' brushes which had seen their best days ;
another, odd pieces of wainscotting ; another, old umbrellas ;
and so forth. But these specialists were few ; the majority
of the stocks were miscellaneous.

As to the dealers themselves, their general air was of a willing receptivity rather than aggressive disburdenment. Here and there one proclaimed the merits of his wares; the majority shivered and watched. Perhaps it was the grey chill of the day; perhaps in warmer weather all are vocal. Few of them were properly dressed for such bleakness; all had the cynical expression of the Londoner under Heaven's ban; a Hogarthian plainness, if not ugliness, heightened by the exposure, marked every face.

The bargain-hunters were more prosperous looking, and happier because less cold, for they at any rate had the the power of locomotion denied to one who wished either to sell or preserve his wares. Rumour has it that many of the articles which are offered for sale at this market have been acquired by the most primitive means known to acquisitive man; and there is no doubt that among the frequenters of the market are many who hold that hands were made before title-deeds. The merchant therefore, even if he has given up hope of selling, must still be rooted to his pitch.

Many of the crowd were as purely sight-seeing as myself; but there were the intent ones too, with their string bags or other bags, hoping always for a find, whether for their own domestic use or to sell again: keen-eyed men and women with long eager fingers.

For the real bargains, I am told, one must go early; and it is a reasonable precaution. But to what extent the real bargain is obtainable I have no notion. Most persons, I find, have a remarkable story of Caledonian luck; but it has happened always to others, not to themselves. No doubt there have been *coups*, especially when the dealer had the best reason for wishing that his own

THE VIRGIN AND CHILD, WITH ST. JEROME AND ST. DOMINIC

AFTER THE PICTURE BY FILIPPINO LIPPI IN THE NATIONAL GALLERY

temporary ownership of the article should cease at the earliest possible moment and the purchaser hurry away with it; but I not only saw with those eyes on that Friday nothing that a collector of any taste would buy, but nothing that any but a confirmed and undiscriminating kleptomaniac would steal.

More fun was that partially covered portion of the market where the stalls have new articles. This was a downright fair, and the spirit of the fair prevailed. Every household requisite was offered at I suppose a far cheaper rate than a shopkeeper with his rent to pay could possibly manage, and when you had bought your fill you could eat winkles and cockles and mussels and shrimps or drink hot coffee. Nothing lacking but roundabouts and cocoanuts, and everywhere signs that buying and selling and chaffering are still among the deepest of human joys, and that London in the twentieth century, when put to it, can reproduce the eighteenth with amazing fidelity.

CHAPTER XII

CHEAPSIDE AND THE CITY CHURCHES

Crowded pavements—Sunday in the City—A receded tide of worshippers —Temples of Cheery Ease—Two Weekday Congregations—St. Stephen's, Walbrook—Bishopsgate Churches—The Westminster Abbey of the City—Houndsditch toy shops—Postmen's Park—Bunhill Fields—The City Road—Colebrooke Row and Charles Lamb— London Pigeons—The Guildhall—The Lord Mayor in State—The City and Literature—In the wake of John Gilpin—To Tottenham and Edmonton—A Discovery and a Disillusionment.

WE are now in a part of London that really is too busy to wander in. London neither likes you to walk faster than itself nor slower; it likes you to adopt its own pace. In the heart of the city you cannot do this and see anything. To study Cheapside and its narrow tributaries, the very narrowness of which is eloquent of the past and at the same time so much a part of the present that it is used in a thoroughly British manner to imprison carts and carters for five or six hours a day, you must choose a Sunday; but if you can loiter in these parts on a Sunday without becoming so depressed as to want to scream aloud, you are made of sterner stuff than I. For my part, I would rather be actually bruised by the jostlings of Cheapside on Monday than have solitary elbow room there on the day of rest, when the cheerful shops are shut and the dreary bells ring out. For the city on Sunday is to me a wilderness of

138

ST. PAUL'S FROM THE RIVER

melancholy. Church bells are tolerable only when one hears a single peal: to hear many in rivalry is to suffer.

The city churches are many and are well cared for; but their day is over. During the week we are too busy making money, or not making it, to spare time for religion; while on Sunday we are elsewhere. What do these churches here? one asks. Other gods reign here. I do not wish to suggest that there are not city men who value the opportunity which the open doors of the churches give them for a little escape from Mammon during the day; but for the most part the city church strikes one as a monument to the obsolete. It belongs so completely to the period when merchants not only made their money in the city but lived there too; before Sydenham Hill and Brighton, Chislehurst and Weybridge were discovered. No one lives in the city any longer, save the Lord Mayor and a few caretakers; and all the gentlemen who would once have convoyed their wives and families up the aisles into the lethargic pews are now either doing the same thing in the suburbs or evading that duty on the golf links.

Times change: the city church remains, calm and self-possessed, offering sanctuary to any one who needs it; but one cannot believe that were they all pulled down to-morrow any one would really resent it except a few simple-hearted old fashioned city gentlemen and an æsthetic minority writing to the papers from Kensington, while the competition for the sites on which to erect commodious and convenient business premises would be instant and terrific. Personally I rarely go into the city without spending a few minutes in one or other of these abodes of peace; but that is a circumstance of no value, because I go to the city only out of curiosity. I am not of it; indeed I am lost in it and I can find myself again only by resting a while in one of these very formal havens. Silent they are not: the roar of the city cannot be quite shut out; but one hears it only as one hears in a shell the murmur of the sea.

Comfort—ecclesiastical comfort—is the note of the city church. It reflects the mind of the comfortable citizen for whom it was built, who liked things plain but good, and though he did not want so far to misbehave as to think of religion as a cheerful topic, was still averse from Calvinistic gloom. (In St. Michael's on College Hill, for instance, is a notice over the door bearing the congenial promise to the congregation: " Plenteousness within His palaces ".) The city church, although unmistakably a temple for the worship of the God of the Old Testament, has yet a hint of the kindliness that would belong to the New if Christians would only permit it. Take for example St. Mary Woolnoth's, just by the Mansion House. It is light, almost gay, but, I hasten to add, without a suggestion of the gaudiness of Rome. The black woodwork and the coloured walls have a pleasant effect. The pulpit is an interesting example of the cabinetmaker's art. There is seating accommodation for very few persons, and that guards against overcrowding. The heating arrangements are good. St. Botolph's, in Aldgate, at the corner of Houndsditch, is another bright and cheery little church. This has a gallery and some elaborate plaster work on the ceiling. Comfort and well-being are strongly in evidence—not to the point of decimating a golf links, of course, but comfort and well-being none the less.

On Sundays these churches may be filled, for aught I know; but my experience of their week-day services is not happy.

One of the most unexpected of London churches is St. Stephen's, Walbrook (behind the Mansion House), into the

MERCURY INSTRUCTING CUPID
AFTER THE PICTURE BY CORREGGIO IN THE NATIONAL GALLERY

side of which a bookshop has been built. Without, it is nothing uncommon and its spire is ordinary Wren; but within it is very imposing and rather fine, having a lofty dome and a number of stately pillars. There is of course no religious feeling in it, but as a piece of grandiose architecture it has merit. I do not, however, agree with a London friend whose advice to me was to disregard all the city churches so long as I saw this one. At the opposite pole is St. Ethelburga's in Bishopsgate Street Within, a very modest shrinking little fane. Like All Hallows, Barking, St. Ethelburga's escaped the Fire, and it stands, a relic of Early English architecture, in the midst of the busiest part of the city. But beyond its isolation, age and simplicity, it has little to recommend it. The famous city church of St. Helen's is in Great St. Helen's Place, a little to the south, and it is worth visiting for the tombs alone—for here lie London's greatest merchants, from Sir Thomas Gresham downwards: it is the Westminster Abbey of the city, the Valhalla of commerce. It has, however, one poet too; for the possibility that a William Shakespeare who lived in the parish in 1598 was the Swan of Avon has led an American gentleman to erect a window to the dramatist.

Elsewhere I have said something of Norton Folgate and Shoreditch, the northern continuation of Bishopsgate Street. I might here remark that Houndsditch, which really was once a ditch, just outside the wall, is now the centre of the toy and cheap jewellery trade. It was in a shop there, after much hunting, that I ran down one of the old weather-cottages, with a little man and a little woman to swing in and out and foretell rain and shine—wrongly, for the most part, but picturesquely.

In Leadenhall Street one may see where Lamb's India

House stood; and Leadenhall Market, which fills several estuaries here, is interesting for its live-stock shops, where one may buy puppies and bantams, Persian cats and bull-finches, and even, I believe, foxes for the chase—if one sinks so low. Cornhill has two churches almost touching each other—St. Peter's and St. Michael's—but neither is interesting, although St. Michael's tower can catch the sun very pleasantly.

For the most part the city church no longer has its graveyard; or if it has, the graves have been levelled and a little green space for luncheon-hour recreation has been made instead. One of the pleasantest of these is that of St. Botolph Without, Aldersgate, which is known as Postmen's Park. It is here that the late G. F. Watts, the great painter, erected memorials to certain lowly heroes and heroines not in either of the heroic services, who saved Londoners' lives and perished in the effort. If any one has a strong taste for graveyards he should certainly visit Bunhill Fields at Finsbury—if only to lose it. A crazy dirty place is this, with its myriad stones saturated with London soot and all awry, and the hum of factories on the northern side. Defoe's tomb is here, with an obelisk over it, and here also lie Bunyan and Isaac Watts, and William Blake and Thomas Stothard, two gentle old men who were rivals only in their painting of Chaucer's Pilgrims; but one comes out in the depths of depression and had better perhaps not have entered. Opposite is a little museum of relics of John Wesley, whose statue is there too. Another great spiritual man, George Fox, lies close by, in the Friends' burial ground; but the Friends' museum is not here but in Devonshire House, in Bishopsgate Street Without, where many very interesting prints and books and pamphlets of the quiet folk may be seen.

From Bunhill Fields one may climb the City Road on a tram—the City Road, once important, once having its place in the most popular comic song of the day, but now a kind of wilderness. The Eagle is now an ordinary public house, the Grecian's Corinthian period is over; and when I was here last, that most dismal sight, the demolition of a church, was to be seen. But the City Road is worth traversing if only for Colebrooke Row, at the end of which, in the last house on the north side, adjoining Duncan Terrace and next a ginger-beer factory, Charles Lamb once lived, in the days before the New River was covered over; and it was down Lamb's front garden that George Dyer walked when he fell into that stream.

Colebrooke Row is still old-fashioned; hardly anything has been done beyond covering the waterway. I descended to the banks of the canal, which, in its turn, runs at right angles beneath the New River, and talked with the captain of the tug which pulls the barges through the long low tunnel. And then I climbed to Colebrooke Row again and roamed about Upper Street and all that is left of Islington Green, where a statue of Sir Hugh Myddleton stands, and wondered at the success with which Islington has kept itself a self-contained town entirely surrounded by houses, and walked a while in Islington churchyard, and then descended the squalid heights of Pentonville to King's Cross. I cannot call either Pentonville or Clerkenwell interesting, except for preserving so much of the London of a hundred years ago.

But meanwhile we are due in Cheapside again.

The British Museum has the first name for pigeons in London—the pigeon being our sacred bird, our ibis—and truly there are none bigger: they have breasts like cannon balls; but the Guildhall's birds are even tamer. In crossing the courtyard in front of the Guildhall one really has to step carefully to avoid treading on them, so casual are they and so confident that you will behave.

The Guildhall has in its basement a collection of articles relating to the history of the city, which are sufficiently interesting to be well worth a visit. Relics of Roman occupation; old inn signs, including the Boar's Head in Eastcheap which Falstaff frequented; instruments of punishment from Newgate; old utensils and garments; prints and broadsheets; and so forth. But the chief collection of such articles is now to be seen at the London Museum proper, which we have not yet reached.

The Lord Mayor's departure for or from the Guildhall is a piece of civic pomp that never fails to please the tolerant observer. He drives in a golden chariot, with four horses to draw it and two footmen to stand behind; while an officer in a cocked hat, carrying a sword, rides on in front, and mounted policemen serve as an escort. The Lord Mayor climbs in first, a figure of medieval splendour, in robes and furs and golden chain, more like a Rabbi in a Rembrandt picture than a London magistrate about to send a costermonger to prison; then another elderly and august masquerader is pushed in; and then the mace bearer is added, holding that bauble so that its head is well out of the window. The golden carriage, which is on cee springs and was built to carry Cinderella and none other, swings like a cradle as these medievalist sink into their seats. The powdered footmen leap to their station at the back; the coachman (who has recently figured on the London hoardings with a recommendation for metal polish, and is more than conscious of his identity) cracks his whip; and the pageant is complete. Then the crowd of cynical Londoners—porters, clerks, errand boys, business men, who have, as Londoners always will, found time to observe the spectacle (and it is all one to them whether it is a Lord Mayor or a horse down)—melts, and the twentieth century once more resumes its sway.

I am quite aware that I am treating the city too lightly; but it cannot be helped. One chapter is useless: it wants many books. No sooner does one begin to burrow beneath the surface of it into the past than one realises how fascinating but also how gigantic is the task before one. Reasons of space, apart from other causes, have held my pen. The literary associations of the city alone are endless. It is in Threadneedle Street that Lamb's old South Sea House stood; in Leadenhall Street we have just seen the modern representative of his East India House. It was in a house in Birchin Lane that the infant Macaulay opening the door to his father's friend Hannah More, asked her to step in and wait while he fetched her a glass of old spirits, such as they drank in *Robinson Crusoe*. It was at the corner of Wood Street that Wordsworth's poor Susan imagined herself in the country; and here still stands a famous city tree, but its limbs are sadly lopped.

It was in Cheapside that John Gilpin lived. I once made an interesting little journey from his house, which properly was at the corner of Paternoster Row, opposite the statue of Sir Robert Peel, in order to follow his great ride. It was some years ago, before the present building superseded the old: the shop part was then a bookseller's, and above were various tenants, among them an aged instructor in the language of chivalry and Spain. It seemed to me that it would be an amusing thing to proceed on foot from John Gilpin's to the Bell of Edmonton, in the wake, so to speak, of this centaur *manqué*; and indeed it was, and more so, for it led to a grievous discovery.

10

With the exception of the old parish churches that rise here and there from the waste of newer masonry, there now remains little between Cheapside and Tottenham that the Gilpins would recognise. The course of the highway is the same, but since their jaunt to Edmonton most of the houses have been built, and rebuilt, and built again; railways have burrowed under or leapt across the road; tram metals have been laid down; fire-stations have arisen; and lamp-posts, like soldiers, have stepped out to line the pavements. These changes would hold the Gilpins spellbound were they suddenly re-incarnated to drive to Edmonton again to-day. Most, perhaps, would they marvel at the bicycles darting like dragon-flies between the vehicles, and the onset of the occasional motor-car. Probably had motor-cars come in in John Gilpin's day he would never have essayed that ride at all. If the braying of an ass were too much for his horsemanship, what of the horn and the exhaust pipe and the frantic machinery of the new vehicles? The press of people would amaze them too, and the loss of green meadows sadden them. On the other hand, the absence of turnpike gates and charges would go far to restore gladness to Mrs. Gilpin's frugal mind.

By the time Tottenham was reached, however, they all would be more at home again. The edge of their wonder would have been taken off, and familiar landmarks coming into view would cheer them. The broad road of the comfortable Tottenham of to-day was not broader in 1750, which was, I estimate, approximately the date of the great expedition. On the common I found two goats feeding, and there were surely goats in 1750. The Cross stood then where it now stands, albeit in the interim the renovator may have touched it; and there were of yore the roadside trees, though not, perhaps, so severely pollarded as now.

THE CHARTERHOUSE

Where there is absolutely no change at all, save faint traces of age, is in the two rows of alms-houses—those of Nicholas Reynards, built in 1736, and those of Balthazar Sanchez, for eight poor men and women, built in 1600. Many of the square red-brick houses on each side of the road date from far earlier than 1750. Here, for instance, is one with a sundial bearing the year 1691. The inns, too, are in many cases merely re-faced (how much to their disadvantage!) but there are a few butchers' shops that seem to have undergone no modification. Butchers are under no compulsion to march with the times: civilization or no civilization, meat is meat and you must have it.

North of Tottenham the air of prosperity disappears, and a suggestion of squalor is perceptible. Deserted houses are common, the inns are poverty-stricken, the impression that one is in a decaying neighbourhood is unavoidable. The Bell at Edmonton has now a stucco front, and if it were not for the fresco depicting John Gilpin at full gallop, one would deny that it could be the same house from whose balcony Mistress Gilpin watched her husband. Edmonton itself is a mile farther on the road. More decay is here. A strip of the Wash is still left, and a butcher's cart splashes through it, but the low level railway passes over the larger portion. The Cross Keys looks hospitable, but the largest house in the village, once a substantial mansion graced with a sundial, is now surmounted by three brass balls. The glory of Edmonton has departed. Indeed there is no more emphatic example of a decayed neighbourhood than this. Beautiful Georgian houses in their own grounds, with spreading cedars on the lawn and high fruit walls, can be rented at a ridiculously low rate. Once they were the homes of retired citizens and men of leisure and wealth; now they have fallen to market

gardeners. London is like that: she has no pity, no
sentiment, no care for the past. She will abandon and
forget old associations instantly, at the mere sound of the
words "convenience" and "utility" or "good form"; she
will create a new residential neighbourhood almost in a
single night, and never give the old another thought.
It having been decreed that Liverpool Street is not a
gentleman's line—at least, that no gentleman travelling
from it can buy a ticket for any station nearer London
than (say) Bishop's Stortford—the decay of Edmonton
and Enfield, Waltham Cross and neighbourhood must
follow.

So much for the route. Now for my grievous discovery.
Briefly, my grievous discovery was this—that the Wash
is a mile farther from London than the Bell. To understand its significance we must turn to the ballad of the
Gilpins. At present it sounds a little enough matter, and
yet, as will be seen, the reputation of a poet is thereby
jeopardised and another illusion threatened with extinc-
tion.

The chaise and pair to contain Mrs. Gilpin and her three
children and Mrs. Gilpin's sister and her child, drew up
just three doors from John's shop, and the party took their
seats there. It was a bright morning in the summer of 1750
or thereabouts. Mr. Gilpin would have accompanied them,
but he was delayed by three customers whom he valued too
much to entrust to his apprentice. Then—after an inter-
val, say, of half an hour,—he started too. His horse began
by pacing slowly over the stones, but immediately the road
became smoother he trotted, and then, thinking very little
of his rider, broke into a gallop. Neither curb nor rein
being of any service, Mr. Gilpin took to the mane. This
gallop, as I understand the ballad, the horse kept up all

the way to Edmonton and Ware and back again. But if John proceeded at this breakneck pace, how is it that the six persons in the chaise and pair reached Edmonton before him, and were able to watch his mad career from the balcony?

How was it that Mrs. Gilpin reached the Bell first? The natural answer to this problem is that John Gilpin took a roundabout course. Indeed, we know that he passed through Islington, whence, presumably, the traveller to Edmonton would proceed by way of the Seven Sisters Road, or even the Essex Road, and so into Tottenham, which from Cheapside is less direct a course than by way of Threadneedle Street, Bishopsgate, Shoreditch, Kingsland Road, and Stamford Hill. But Gilpin must have made a wider *détour* even than this, because, according to the ballad, he came to the Wash before he came to the Bell. This means he was approaching Edmonton from the north, because as the exploration of Edmonton revealed, the Wash is a mile farther from London than the Bell. Very well, then; Mrs. Gilpin in a loaded chaise reached the Bell sooner than her husband on a galloping horse, for the reason that he chose a devious course; and the poet's reputation is saved.

"Let me see, how was it," now whispers the devil's advocate, "that John did not stop at Edmonton to dine?" Because, I reply, quoting the ballad,

> "his owner had a house
> Full ten miles off at Ware."

The horse, then, was making for his stable at Ware. But Ware is thirteen miles farther north than Edmonton, on the same road out of London. So, although horses that run away to their own stables usually run straight, Mr. Gilpin, when he passed the Bell, was riding south, full speed in the direction of London again. Topography is conclusive; there is no argument against it. But, it may be urged, perhaps it was another Ware. That is unlikely, for is not the Johnny Gilpin an inn just outside the town to this day, and do not the people of Ware show the house where the Calendar dwelt, now a draper's? These un-willing eyes have seen both. One word more. Edmonton is seven miles from London, and Ware is thirteen from Edmonton, twenty in all, and it is twenty miles back again. John Gilpin's horse, a Calendar's hack, covered the distance at a gallop with but one halt.

You see how much may proceed from a little. I had merely intended to take a walk from Cheapside to Edmon-ton and think of the merry ballad of John Gilpin on the way. But by so doing I hit upon a great fraud, and Cowper, most amiable of men that ever wore a nightcap, stands convicted of having for upwards of a century hood-winked his fellows by inducing them by poetical cunning to believe in a ride that could never have been accomplished, in a route that could never be followed. Sad is it when faith in our household poets fails. One would begin to wonder if the *Royal George* really sank, were it not for the relics of it in Whitehall. William Tell was discredited long ago, Robin Hood is no more than a myth, Shakespeare is Bacon; alas, that John Gilpin should go too!

CHAPTER XIII

THE TOWER AND THE AMPHIBIANS

ON the way to the Tower from Mark Lane station one
crosses Tower Hill—perhaps, if the traffic permits,
walking over the very spot on which stood the old scaffold.
When I was last there a flock of pigeons was feeding
exactly where I judged it to have been—that scaffold on
which so many noble heads were struck from their shoulders,
from Sir Thomas More and Surrey the poet to Strafford
and Algernon Sidney, and a few ignoble ones, not the least
of which was Simon Fraser, Lord Lovat's, the last man to
be beheaded in England, the block on which he laid his
wicked old neck being still to be seen, full of dents, in the
Tower itself. Standing here it is extraordinary to think
that (in 1913) only 166 years have passed since it was
possible to behead a man publicly in broad day in the
middle of a London street. Only five generations : the
late Baroness Burdett-Coutts could have seen it.

Opposite Mark Lane Station, and at the corner of Great

Tower Street, which leads into Little Tower Street, and that in its turn into Eastcheap and the city proper, is All Hallows Church, whither many of the victims of the Tower Hill scaffold were carried for burial, among them the Earl of Surrey, Bishop Fisher and Archbishop Laud. All three were, however, afterwards removed elsewhere, Laud, for example, to St. John's College, Oxford. William Penn, who lived to speak contemptuously of churches as steeple-houses, was baptised here in 1644, and the bloody Judge Jeffreys, who harried Penn's sect so mercilessly, was married here to his first wife in the year following the Great Fire, which spared All Hallows by a kind of miracle—just thrusting out a tongue or two to lick up the porch and then drawing them back. The church, though it has a new spire, is, within, a fine example of medieval architecture, and its brasses are among the best that London contains. Among them is one of William Thynne and his wife, Thynne being worthy of all commendation as the man responsible for the first printed collection of Chaucer's works in 1532.

Another interesting Great Tower Street building, or rather re-building, is the Czar's Head, an inn on the same side as the church, which stands on the site of an older inn of that name to which Peter the Great, when learning at Deptford to build ships, resorted with his friends. Muscovy Court, out of Trinity Square, close by, derives its style from the same monarch. Little Tower Street has in a different way an equally unexpected association, for it was in a house there that James Thomson, the poet of *The Seasons*, wrote "Summer".

Harrison Ainsworth's romance *The Tower of London*, which I fear I should find a very tawdry work to-day, twenty and more years ago stirred me as few novels now

VIRGIN AND CHILD

AFTER THE PICTURE BY BOTTICELLI IN THE NATIONAL GALLERY

are able to, and fixed the Tower for all time as a home of dark mystery. Not even the present smugness of its officialdom, the notice boards, the soldiers in its barracks, the dryness of its moat or the formal sixpenny tickets of admission, can utterly obliterate the impression of Ainsworth's pages and Cruikshank's engravings. I still expect to see Gog and Magog eating a mammoth pasty; I still look for Xit the dwarf; and in a dark recess fancy I hear the shuddering sound of the headsman sharpening his axe. No need however for Ainsworth's fictions:—after reading the barest outline of English history, the Tower's stones run red enough. Anne Boleyn, Katherine Howard, Lady Jane Grey, Sir Thomas More, the Earl of Essex—these are a few who were beheaded in state within its walls; but what of the others who died secretly by force, like the little Princes and Sir Thomas Overbury, and those other thousands of prisoners unknown who ate their hearts out in the cells within these nine-feet walls?

The ordinary tickets admit only to the jewels and the armour, but a written application to the Governor procures an authorisation to see also the dungeons, in the company of a warder. The room in the Bloody Tower in which the little Princes were smothered is no longer shown, as it has become part of a private dwelling; but the window is pointed out, and with that husk you must be satisfied. Among the sights to which a special order entitles you is the cell in which Raleigh wrote the *History of the World*, and that narrow hollow in the wall of the White Tower, known as Little Ease, in which Guy Fawkes was immured while waiting for justice and death.

St. John's Chapel, in the White Tower, has a naked simplicity beyond anything I know, and a massiveness out of all proportion to its size, which inspires both confidence and reverence. In its long life it has seen many strange and moving spectacles—from the all-night vigils of the Knights of the Bath, to Brackenbury's refusal at the altar side to murder the little Princes and the renunciation by Richard II of his crown in favour of Bolingbroke. I had the history of this chapel from a gentle old Irish beef-eater who sits in a chair and talks like a book. The names of monarchs and accompanying dates fell from his tongue in a gentle torrent until I stopped it with the question "Do *all* the warders in the Tower take snuff?" He had never been asked this before, and it knocked all the literature and history out of him and re-established his humanity. He became instantly an Irishman and a brother, confessed to his affection for a pinch (as I had detected), and we discussed the merits of the habit as freely as if the royal body of Elizabeth of York had never lain in state within a few yards of us, and no printed notice had warned me that the place being holy I must remove my hat.

In the Tower armouries every kind of decorative use has been made of old muskets, ramrods and pistols, resulting in ingenious mural patterns which must strike the schoolboy visitor as a most awful waste of desirable material. The armouries contain also some very real weapons indeed: to students of the machinery of death they are invaluable. The evolution of the sword and gun of all nations may be traced here, in glass cases which are so catholic as to contain not only the corkscrew dagger of Java but the harpoon gun of Nantucket. I think nothing impressed me more than a long and sinister catchpole—surely the most unpleasant weapon that ever assailed a man's comfort and dignity. The models of knights in armour cannot but add to the vividness of *Ivanhoe*. Among the more recent relics is the uniform which the Duke of Wellington wore as the

Constable of the Tower, and the cloak, rolled up far too tightly and squeezed under glass, in which Wolfe died on the Heights of Abraham. It should be spread out. The drums from Blenheim touch the imagination too.

But the best things about the Tower are the Tower itself—its spaces and gateways, and old houses, and odd corners, and grave, hopping ravens—and St. John's Chapel. Interesting as the armour no doubt is, I could easily dispense with it, for there is something very irritating in being filed past policemen in the pursuit of the interesting; and one sees better crown jewels in any pantomime. Of medieval gravity one never tires; but medieval ostentation and gaudiness soon become unendurable. Yet I suppose more people go to the Tower to see the jewels than to see anything else. The odd fact that the infamous but courageous Colonel Blood, by his historic raid on the regalia in 1671, rose instantly from a furtive skulking subterraneous existence to a place at Court and £500 a year might have had the effect of multiplying such attempts; but it does not seem to have done so. No one tries to steal the crown today. And yet precedent is rarely so much in the thief's favour.

But the Tower as a whole—that is fine. There is a jumble of wooden walls and windows on one of the ramparts overlooking the river, where I would gladly live, no matter what the duties. What are the qualifications of the Governor of the Tower I know not, but I am an applicant for the post.

London's wild beasts, which now lend excitement to Regent's Park, used to be kept at the Tower, and the old guide books to it, a hundred and more years ago, are inclined to pay more attention to them than to history. A living lion was more to the authors of these volumes (as to

the sightseers also) than many dead kings.   One such book
which lies before me now, dated 1778, begins with this
blameless proposition: "The Desire of seeing the Antiquities
and Rareties of our Country is allowed by all to be a laud-
able Curiosity : to point them out therefore to the Inquisitive, and to direct their Attention to those Things that
best deserve Notice, cannot be denied its degree of Merit."
The guide then plunges bravely into history, but quickly
emerges to describe, with a degree of spirit rare in the
remainder of his work, the inhabitants of the menagerie.
The chief animals at that time were the lions Dunco,
Pompey, Dido, Cæsar, Miss Fanny, Hector, Nero, Cleony
and Helen, and the tigers Sir Richard, Jenny, Nancy, and
Miss Groggery, who, "though a tigress, discovers no marks
of ferocity."   The old custom of calling the lions after the
living monarchs of the day seems just then to have been
in abeyance.   In 1834 the menagerie was transferred to
Regent's Park ; but I think they might have left a cage or
two for old sake's sake.

From the Tower, when I was there last, I walked to
Jamrach's, down what used to be the Ratcliffe Highway,
where De Quincey's favourite murderer Williams (who
must, said George Dyer, have been rather an eccentric
character) indulged in his famous holocaust a hundred years
ago.   It is now St. George's Street, and one reaches it by
the wall of St. Katherine's Dock, through the scent of
pepper and spice, and past the gloomy opening of Nightingale Lane, which has no reference to the beautiful singing
bird of May, but takes its name from the Knighten Guild
founded by King Edgar in the days when London was
Danish.

Jamrach's is not what it was, for the wild beast trade,
he tells me, no longer pays any one but the Germans,

And so the tigers and leopards and panthers and lions and other beautiful dangers are no more to be seen crouching in the recesses of his cages; and instead I had to be satisfied with the company of parrots and macaws, the bul-bul of Persia and the mynah of India, lemurs and porcupines, cockatoos and blue Siberian kittens. These were in the shop, and in the stables were Japanese deer, and some white greyhounds from Afghanistan with eyes of milky blue, and a cage of wild turkeys. And, more interesting still, in the square at the back were six Iceland ponies, shaggy as a sheep dog and ingratiating as an Aberdeen terrier, and so small that they might be stabled under one's writing desk.

On this occasion I returned to Mark Lane station from Jamrach's by way of Wellclose Square, which saw the birth of Thomas Day, the author of *Sandford and Merton*, and was the site of the Magdalen Chapel of the famous Dr. Dodd, who found Beauties in Shakespeare and was the indefatigable friend of London's unfortunates until he took to luxury and excesses, became a forger, and died, as we saw in an earlier chapter, at Tyburn Tree. The square was once the centre of Denmark in London and is still associated with the sea, a school for seamen's children standing where the old Danish church stood, and seamen's institutes abounding hereabouts. Much of the square's ancient character has been preserved, and on one house are still to be seen some very attractive bas-reliefs of children pursuing the arts. The rebuilder is, however, rapidly drawing near, and already has cleared away a large tract of old houses by the Mint.

Another reminder of the sea is the Trinity House in Trinity Square, looking beyond the Tower to the river. From these offices the Brothers of the Trinity House control our lighthouses and lightships.

Into the Mint I have never penetrated; but the Tower Bridge I have climbed often, on clear days and misty. The noblest bridge I know (although its stone work is but veneer, and iron its heart), it is imposing however one sees it, broadside, or obliquely, or looking down from the Bridge Approach: with the roadway intact, or the bascules up to let a vessel through. It is the only gateway that London retains.

A few years ago the district over which the Tower Bridge stands as a kind of sentinel, and of which the docks are the mainstay, had no special significance. It was merely largely populated by those that follow the sea or the seaman. But since then has come Mr. Jacobs to make it real, and now no one who knows his engaging stories can ever walk about Wapping and Shadwell, Limehouse and Rotherhithe, without recalling the humour of this writer. It is a high compliment to a novelist and an indication of his triumph when we can say that he has created a new world, although from the circumstance that we say it only of the comic novelists, it has, I suppose, also a suggestion of limitation. A novelist whose characters for the most part behave like real people escapes the compliment: their world is also ours. We do not talk of Thackeray's world, of George Eliot's world. But we talk often of Dickens' world, which means that Dickens' love of eccentricity so impregnated his characters as to give them all a suspicion of family resemblance, branding them of his world rather more perhaps than of ours. Mr. Jacobs also thus stamps his seafaring men, so that we are coming to talk of the Jacobs' world too. Not that he —or not that Dickens—is false to life, but that both, liking people to be as they like them, tone up life a little to please their own sense of fun. It is one of the differences between the realist and the romancist that the romancist wants to give himself pleasure as well as his reader. The realist is more concerned to do only his duty.

I wish that one might enter the Jacobs' world now and then instead of going to Switzerland or Scotland or the other dull countries where one makes formal holiday. But I fear it is not to be: I fear that the difference between fact and Mr. Jacobs' presentation of it will never be bridged. I have wandered much and listened much in Wapping and Rotherhithe, but have heard no admirable sarcasms, have met no skippers obviously disguised as women. I have listened to night-watchmen, but they have told me no tales like "The Money Box" or "Bill's Lapse". A lighterman at Rotherhithe (on the green balcony of the Angel) once told me a good story, but it is quite unfit for print and belongs peculiarly and painfully to our own world. I have heard the captains of barges and wherries exchanging repartees, but they were for the most part merely beastly. It is sad but true: the Jacobs' world is not accessible. Even if one followed Mr. Jacobs about, I doubt whether one would come to it: none the less may one live in hope as one wanders among the wharves and streets of this amphibious district.

If one would explore it with any thoroughness one must walk from the Tower to the East India Docks: it is all there. But the quickest way to the East India Docks is to take the train from Fenchurch Street—that almost secret city terminus—to Blackwall.

If one were to ask a hundred people to name London's most interesting railway terminus, some would choose Charing Cross, some Waterloo, some Euston, some Paddington, and so forth. Not one would say Blackwall; and yet in its way Blackwall is more interesting than any of these others. It is at the end of one of the short grimy lines from

Fenchurch Street, through Stepney and Poplar : one of the lines which carry you on a raised rail level with the chimneys of small houses, all alike apparently for ever and ever, broken only by a factory chimney, or a three-master, or the glimmering spire of a white stone church. It is these miles of chimneys which keep me out of East London and South London, so oppressive are they, so desolating, so fatal to any idealistic view of humanity. Doomed to live in such squalor, such deserts of undersized similar houses, so that the identification of one's home becomes more wonderful than a bird's identification of its nest, how can we, one asks oneself, be anything but larger ants ? What future is there for such groundlings ? Is it not monstrous that our chances of eternity should be determined by conduct in an infinitesimal span of years under conditions such as these—with poverty and dirt and fog thrust on us from our birth —not our own poverty and dirt, but so powerful as to resist all efforts ?

One has the same gloomy atheistic oppression as one comes into London on the South Eastern, and in fact on every line where the carriage window is above these squalid London roofs and chimneys. One gets it again on the top of the Monument or St. Paul's or the tower of the new Roman Catholic cathedral at Westminster, looking down at the ceaseless activities of what surely must be insects—so busy about trifles or nothing at all, so near the ground, so near annihilation.

In a lighter mood I have sometimes as I looked out of the window of a railway carriage in the country allowed myself to dwell on the thought that there is not a square inch of this green England through which we are passing but possesses title-deeds reposing in some lawyer's safe. The same thought if indulged in one of these London trains, cannot but land one in a feeling for the law which, beginning with something like respect, must culminate in reverence. Everything belongs to someone—that is the truism which finally emerges. In the country, where there are unfenced heaths and hills and commons, one can forget it; but never in a city, where for every open space a code of regulations must be drawn up and displayed, and where every house in a small terrace may have a different owner. A further reflection is that although the lawyers may not inherit the earth (indeed they are expressly excluded by the beatitude), they will at any rate be indispensable at the negotiations.

To come into London between the roofs of Bermondsey on the South Eastern, as I do very often, has, however, its compensations: for in the distance the shipping is always to be seen to carry one's thoughts afar. It was on one occasion, when this scene was new to me, that I found myself composing these stanzas:—

Between New Cross and London Bridge,
    I peered from a third-class "smoker,"
Over the grimy chimney pots
    Into the yellow ochre.

When lo! in a sudden lift of the fog
    Up rose a brave three-master
With brand new canvas on every spar
    As fair as alabaster.

And, gazing on that gallant sight,
    In a moment's space, or sooner,
The smoke gave place to a southern breeze,
    The train to a bounding schooner.

11

Again the vessel stood to sea,
　　Majestic, snowy-breasted;
Again great ships rode nobly by,
　　On purple waves foam-crested.

Again we passed mysterious coasts,
　　Again soft nights enwound us;
Again the rising sun revealed
　　Strange fishermen around us.

The spray was salt, the air was glad—
　　When—bump—! we reached the station:
But what did I care though fog was there,
　　With *this* for compensation?

The interest of Blackwall station is its unique and romantic situation hard by the north bank of the Thames.
You get into the train at Fenchurch Street, and in the
company of shipping agents and mates, ships-chandlers and
stewards, emigrants and engineers, you travel through the
chimney pots and grime of London at its grimiest to this
ugly station. And suddenly, having given up your ticket,
you pass through a door and are in the open world and a
fresh breeze, with the river at your very feet—a wherry or
two beating up against the wind, a tug dragging out a
schooner, and a great steamer from Hong Kong looking
for her berth! It is the completest change, and on a fine
day the most exhilarating.

And of all London termini Blackwall is most emphati-
cally a terminus, for another yard and your train would be
at the bottom of the East India Docks.

Docks are docks all the world over, and there is little
to say of the East India Docks that could not be said of
the docks at Barry in Wales, at Antwerp or Hamburg.

One is everywhere confronted by the same miracles of berthing and extrication. Perhaps at the East India Docks the miracles are more miraculous, for the leviathans of Donald Currie which lie here are so huge, the waterways and gates so narrow.

The last time I was there I returned on foot—down the East India Docks Road, through Poplar and Limehouse and Stepney : past hospitals and sailors' homes and Radical Clubs, and here and there a grave white church, and here and there, just off the main thoroughfare, a Board School with the side street full of children ; and public houses uncountable, and foreign men on the pavement.

Just by Jack's Palace, which is the newest of the sailors' homes, at the corner of the West India Docks Road, I met a little band of five Chinese sailors in dirty blue linen. They were making, I suppose, for Limehouse Court,—an odd little street which is given up to lodging houses and grocers' shops kept by silent discreet Chinese who have married English women and settled down in London. They stand at their doors, these stolid Celestials, beneath their Chinese signs, for any one to see, and are, I am told, among the best citizens of the East End and the kindest husbands.

A little west of Jack's Palace one ought to turn off to the south just to see the barges in Limehouse Basin, because it is here that they enter the river from Regent's Canal, that sluggish muddy waterway upon which one is always coming unexpectedly in the north-west district of London, and by which, if one were so minded, one could get right away into the heart of green England. Very stealthily it finds its slow and silent way about London, sometimes underground for quite long distances, as at

Islington, where the barges are pulled through by a steel hawser—almost scraping the sides and the roof as they go. By Regent's Park and at Paddington you may see boys angling from the tow path; but no one ever saw them land a fish. I have long intended one day to strike a bargain with a bargee and become his shipmate for a while and see a little of England in this way; but somehow the opportunity never comes. Yet it should, for outside the city—at Hemel Hempsted or Berkhampsted for example —these craft are gay and smiling as any in Holland, and the banks are never dull.

At the hospital just opposite the entrance to the East India Docks and the Blackwall Tunnel—that curious subterranean and subaqueous roadway beneath the Thames, through which one may ride on the top of an omnibus, as one rides beneath Kingsway in a tram—notice boards are set up asking the drivers, for the sake of those that are ill within, to walk their horses past the building. That is a common enough request, but what gives it a peculiar interest here is that the carter having complied (or not) with the modest demand, is confronted at the end of the façade by another board saying "Thank you, driver."

In this and other of the poorer quarters of London, where every one else is engaged in the struggle for life, one feels a little that it is an impertinence to be inquisitively wandering at all: that one has no right here unless one is part of the same machine. A little bold Jewess, aged nine or thereabouts, on her way home from school, seemed to share this view, for she looked at me with impudently scrutinising eyes (not ceasing the while to scratch her leg), and then shouted something which I failed to understand but which her companions enjoyed to the full. It was an epithet of scorn, I am sure, and it seemed to challenge my right to be there, doing nothing but examining the fauna of the district for superior literary purposes. And I quite agreed with her. I left her still scratching her leg, the triumphant heroine of her circle, the satisfied author of the *mot juste*.

CHAPTER XIV

WHITECHAPEL AND THE BORO'

East of Bishopsgate—A new London and a New People—Love and Death
—A Little Tragedy—The Female Lightning Extractor—A broad and
vivid Road—The Trinity Almshouses—Epping Forest—Victoria
Park—The Sandbank and the People's Palace—The Ghetto—Norton
Folgate—The Book Stalls of London—The Paris Quais—Over
London Bridge—St. Saviour's—Two Epitaphs—Debtors' Prisons—
Dickens and Chaucer—Guy's Hospital.

LONDON east of Bishopsgate Street is another city
altogether. It leads its own life, quite independent
of the west, has its own social grades, its own pleasures, its
own customs and code of morality, its own ambitions, its
own theatres and music halls, its own smart set. The
West End is in the habit of pitying the East: but the
young bloods of the Mile End Road, which is at once the
Bond Street, Strand and Piccadilly of this city, have as
much reason to pity the West End. Life goes quite as
merrily here: indeed, more so. There is a Continental
bustle in this fine road—a finer, freer road than the rest of
London can boast—and an infinitely truer feeling of
friendliness. People know each other here. Friends on
'buses whistle to friends on the pavements. Talkative
foreigners lend cheerfulness and picturesqueness. In the
summer the fruit stalls are almost continuous—in early
autumn purple with grapes. Nowhere else in London, in
England, is fruit so eaten. Sunday here is no day of

166

gloom: to a large part of the population it is shopping day, to a large part it is the only holiday.

There is no call to pity the Mile End Road or Whitechapel High Street. It is they rather than Bloomsbury and Bayswater that have solved the problem of how to live in London. If the art of life is, as I believe, largely the suppression of self-consciousness, these people are artists. They are as frank and unconcerned in their courtships as the West Enders are in their shopping. They will embrace on the top of a 'bus: anywhere. The last summer evening I was in the Mile End Road Cupid was terrifically busy.

But the last winter day I was there, I remember, it was the other end of life that was more noticeable; for funeral after funeral went by, all very ostentatious and all at the trot. Most of them were babies' funerals: one carriage only, with the poor little coffin under the box seat, and the driver and bearer in white hat bands; but one was imposing indeed, with a glass hearse under bushes of plumes—an ostrich-feather shrubbery, a splendid coffin snowed under flowers, half a dozen mourning coaches filled with men and women in the blackest of black, three four-wheelers, a hansom or so, two crowded wagonettes of the kind that licensed victuallers own and drive on Sundays, and a market cart packed with what seemed to be porters from Spitalfields market. I guessed the deceased to have been a fruit salesman. He was going home well, as those that die in the East End always do. No expense is spared then.

These many babies' funerals reminded me vividly of my first visit to the East End twelve or thirteen years ago. A girl of sixteen, a hand in an umbrella shop, unmarried, had become a mother, and her baby had died under suspicious circumstances. The case was in the papers, and a humanitarian friend of mine who was not well enough to go herself asked me to try and see the girl or her people and find out if she needed any help. So I went. The address was a house in one of the squalid streets off the Commercial Road, and when I called the landlady said that the girl was at work again and would not be in for two hours. These hours I spent roaming the neighbourhood, for some time fascinated by the despatch, the cleverness, and the want of principle of a woman who sold patent medicines from a wagonette, and pulled out teeth for nothing by way of advertisement. Tooth after tooth she snatched from the bleeding jaws of the Commercial Road, beneath a naphtha lamp, talking the while with that high-pitched assurance which belongs to women who have a genius for business, and selling pain-killers and pills by the score between the extractions.

After a while I went back to the house and found the little wan mother, a wistful but wholly independent child, who was already perplexed enough by offers of help from kindly aliens in that other London (to say nothing of local missionaries), but had determined to resume her own life as if nothing had happened. And so I came away, but not before her landlord had pitched a tale of his own embarrassments that far transcended, to his mind, any difficulty that the girl might be in. And then I rode back to London on a 'bus, behind a second engineer who was taking a Limehouse barmaid to the Tivoli.

I believe that an observant loiterer in the Mile End Road would bring away a richer harvest than from any street in London. There seems to me always to be light there, and it is so wide and open that one's eyes are not worried and perplexed. Here also, and in its continuations, the Whitechapel High Street and Aldgate, one can reconstruct the past almost more easily than anywhere in London. There

ST. DUNSTAN'S-IN-THE-EAST

are fewer changes; the width of the road has not been tampered with; some of the inns still retain their sign posts with a swinging sign; and many old houses remain— such as those in Butchers' Row in Aldgate, one of the most attractive collections of seventeenth century façades that have been left. There is something very primitive and old-English in the shops too, not only of the butchers, but the ancient wine merchant's in the midst of them, whose old whisky is very warming to the dealers who assemble for the hay market in the middle of the road, just above here, three mornings a week.

But the architectural jewel of the Mile End Road is the Trinity Almshouses—a quiet square of snug little residences dating from the seventeenth century, for old men who have been mariners, and old women who are mariners' widows or daughters—sixty and more of them. In the midst is a grass plot, and at the end a chapel, and the Governor's house is by one gate and the Reading Room by the other. Home is the sailor, home from the sea, in this still backwater; and here he smokes and gossips till the end, within sound of the roar not of his ancient element but of humanity.

On a fine Sunday afternoon in summer the Mile End is crowded with vehicles—dog-carts, wagonettes, donkey-carts, every kind of democratic carriage, on its way to Wanstead and Epping and the River Lea, which is east London's Jordan. Epping Forest is out of the scheme of this book, or I could write of it with some fervour: of its fine seclusion and its open air, its thickets of hornbeam and groves of beech, its gorse and rivulets, its protected birds and deer, its determined roads and shy footpaths, and its occasional straggling Georgian towns with Victorian trimmings and far too many inns. The Forest, although motor-cars rush through it, is properly the last stronghold of the gig; the bicycle also, which is fast disappearing from patrician roads, may still be counted in its thousands here. Epping Forest knows nothing of progress : with perfect content and self-satisfaction it hugs the past and will hug it. It is still almost of the days of *Pickwick*, certainly not more recent than Leech.

The Sunday gigs and wagonettes, the donkey-carts and bicycles are, as I say, on their way to Epping and the open country : the trams and omnibuses are packed with people bound for one of the cemeteries or Victoria Park. This park, which lies between Hackney and Bethnal Green, is a park indeed : an open space that is really used and wanted, in a way that Hyde Park and Regent's Park and St. James's Park are not wanted. London in its western districts would still have air without them; but Hackney and Bethnal Green would have nothing were it not for Victoria Park. Battersea Park is made to do its work with some thoroughness; but it is a mere desolate unpeopled waste compared with Victoria Park. Whether the sand bank which a few years ago was placed there for children to dig in, still remains, I know not; but when I was there last in warm weather, a few summers since, it was more populous than an ant hill and the most successful practical amelioration of a hard lot that had been known —in a district which had just seen the total failure of the People's Palace, that huge building in the Mile End Road that was to civilize and refine this wonderful East End nation, but which all too soon declined into a college and a desert. I sometimes doubt indeed if it is not the Mile End Road's destiny to civilize the rest of London. As I have said, these people lead far more genuine and sensible lives—and to do that, though it may not be all civilization, is a long way towards it.

THE ADORATION OF THE KINGS

FROM THE PAINTING BY JAN DE MABUSE IN THE NATIONAL GALLERY

There is no difficulty in naming the prevailing type in Aldgate and Whitechapel High Street—olive skin, dark hair, hook nose. Here the Jews predominate. But if you would see them in their masses, unleavened by Christian, go to Middlesex Street (which used to be called Petticoat Lane) on Sunday, or Wentworth Street any day except Saturday. Wentworth Street is almost impassable for its stalls and chafferers. Save for its grime, it is impossible to believe it in England and within a few minutes of the Bank. The faces are foreign; the clothes are foreign, nearly all the women being wrapped in dark red shawls; the language is largely foreign, Yiddish being generally known here; and many of the articles on the stalls are foreign—from pickled fish and gherkins to scarfs of brilliant hue. Most of the Jews one sees hereabouts have some connection with the old clothes trade, the central exchange of which is just off Houndsditch—in Phil's Buildings—for the right to enter which you pay a penny, and once inside would gladly pay five shillings to be let out. Yet I suppose there are people who take season tickets.

Norton Folgate and Shoreditch are very different from Whitechapel High Street and the Mile End Road. They are quieter and much narrower. But they too have their old houses, and a chemist at a corner, I notice, still retains his old sign of a Golden Key. The London streets in the days of the hanging signs and gables must have been very picturesque. One does not see that we have gained anything to compensate for their loss—electric light and roll shutters do not count at all in the balance. Spital Square, off Norton Folgate, has been little impaired by the rebuilder, and some of its Georgian doors might open at any moment, one feels, to allow a silk merchant in knee breeches to step forth.

Shoreditch, like Aldgate High Street, has its stalls: many for whelks and oysters, which are steadily patronised, quite as a matter of course, all day long, and a few for old books. I bought for threepence when I was there last a very unprincipled satire in verse on poor Caroline of Brunswick, entitled *Messalina;* a work on Female Accomplishment (as much unlike the other as a book could be); and *Little Henry and His Bearer.* The Aldgate stalls are famous for the bargains one may find there; but one must look long under unfavourable conditions, and I have had no luck. The Farringdon Street stalls have served me better. London having no quays, as Paris has, it is here and to the Charing Cross Road that one must go for old books—to Aldgate and Farringdon Street in particular. I wonder that the West End has no street of stalls where one might turn over books and prints.

The Embankment, since it leads nowhere, is utterly neglected. The Londoner hates to be out of the swim, and therefore he would rather be jostled in Parliament Street and Whitehall, the Strand and Fleet Street, on his way to Blackfriars from Westminster, than walk direct but unaccompanied beside the river. Hence a mile of good broad coping on the Embankment wall is unused, where in Paris it would be bright with trays of books and prints and curiosities.

It is at Aldgate that on the east the city proper ends; but although the pump still stands, the gate is no more. Chaucer was once the tenant of the dwelling-house over the gate and, being a wine-merchant, of the cellars beneath it. Mention of the poet reminds me that we have not yet been to the Borough to see the Tabard; and this is a good opportunity—by 'bus—it will need two 'buses—to London Bridge. Not the London Bridge of the old prints, with its houses and shops massed higher and thicker than any on Firenze's Ponte Vecchio, but the very utilitarian structure that ousted it eighty years ago.

London Bridge is the highest point to which great vessels can come: beyond are only tugs and such minor craft as can lower their funnels or masts and so creep beneath the arches. It has always typified London's business to me, because when I used as a child to come to town on my way to school, we came to London Bridge station, and the first great excitement was to cross the river here: the second, to lunch at Crosby Hall amid Tudor trappings. I still always loiter on London Bridge—looking over at the bustling stevedores and listening to the donkey engines and the cranes. From this point the Tower Bridge is the gate of London indeed, and the Tower indescribably solemn and medieval. St. Dunstan's-in-the-East hangs in the sky, a fairy spire, the only white and radiant thing amid the dun and grey.

St. Saviour's, which is now grandly known as Southwark Cathedral, is architecture of a different type, but it is beautiful too and sits as comfortably as any brooding hen. It is interesting both in its old parts and its new—very new indeed, but harmonious, and carefully reproducing what has been lost. In the vestry you may still see a Norman arch or two from the twelfth century. After a fire in the thirteenth century it was built again; and again and again since has it been enlarged and repaired. But it should now rest a while, secure from masons. Be sure to ask the verger for the story of St. Mary Overy, who founded the priory of which this is the church: he tells it better than I could, and believes it too. He will also give you some interesting views on American glass as you stand before the window presented by Harvard University, and will recite epitaphs to you, with much taste and feeling, in cluding the lines on the World's Nonsuch, a beautiful and holy virgin of fourteen. Among these epitaphs is one upon Lockyer, the Cockle and Holloway, Beecham and Carter of his time—the middle of the seventeenth century:—

> His Virtues and his Pills are so well known
> That Envy can't confine them under Stone.
> But they'll survive his dust and not expire
> Till all things else at th' Universal Fire.

Yet where are the pills of Lockyer? Where are the galleons of Spain? Of another worthy parishioner, Garrard a grocer, it was written:—

> Weep not for him, since he is gone before
> To Heaven, where Grocers there are many more.

The church has old tombs and new windows, those in the new nave being very happily chosen and designed: one to Shakespeare, for his connection with Bankside and its Theatres; one to Massinger, who is buried here; one to John Fletcher, who is buried here too; one to Alleyn the actor; one to Gower, the Father of English Poetry, who is buried here and founded a chantry; one to Chaucer, who sent forth his pilgrims from the Tabard hard by; and one to Bunyan, erected with pennies subscribed by Southwark children. Although the church is so lenient to literature and the stage, no hero from the neighbouring bear pit and bull baiting arena is celebrated here.

The Tabard to-day is just a new inn on the site of the old and is not interesting; but there is an inn close to it, a few yards north, on the east side of the High Street, which preserves more of old coaching London than any that is now left, and is, I think, the only one remaining that keeps its galleries. I mean the George. When I came to

London the White Hart, a little to the north of this, still retained its yard and galleries—just as in the days when Samuel Weller was the boots here and first met Mr. Pickwick on his way to catch Jingle and Miss Wardle. So did the Bull and the Bell in Holborn. But these have all been renewed or removed, and the George is now alone. It stands in its yard, painted a cheerful colour, and the coffee room has a hot fire and high backed bays to sit in, and the bar is a paradise of bottles. Surely the spirit of Dickens, who so loved the Borough, broods here. Surely the ghosts of Bob Sawyer and Ben Allen drop in now and then from Lant Street, and it is not too far for Mr. Micawber's genial spook to send for a bottle of something encouraging, from the King's Bench prison.

A few other old houses remain in the High Street—the Half Moon, with its flying bridge and old world stables, and No. 152, with a window standing out as in the old London prints; and one generally has the feeling that one is in a London of a many years earlier date than that across London Bridge. Perhaps it is beer that keeps progress in check, for the hop merchants congregate here.

The church of St. George the Martyr—brick and stone (you see the spire in Hogarth's "Southwark Fair")—brings other memories of Dickens, for it was in the vestry here that little Dorrit slept, while the prisoners who died in the Marshalsea and King's Bench prison lie in its burial ground, now partly built over. The King's Bench prison, which existed so largely for debtors, had many illustrious visitors besides Mr. Micawber, sent thither not only by the eternal want of pence but also for some of the more positive offences. Among them was John Wilkes (for libel), Haydon, who painted his "Mock Election" here, William Combe, who wrote Syntax's tours here, and William Hone, who edited his *Table Book* while in captivity. Hone was not in the prison but in its "rules"—which included several streets round about, but no public house and no theatre. Alleviations were however found. The Dorrit family were in the Marshalsea, which adjoined the King's Bench and had, like all the debtors' prisons, a skittle alley in which the gentlemen might, in Dickens's phrase, "bowl down their troubles". If you walk into Leyton's Buildings, which is very old and picturesque and has a noble timber yard at the end of it, you will be within this prison area. The Marshalsea not only harboured gentlemen who could not meet their bills, but had a compound for smugglers also. Nearly three hundred years ago some of the sweetest notes that ever struck a bliss upon the air of a prison cell rose from the Marshalsea, for here George Wither wrote his "Shepherd's Hunting".

One should certainly walk up St. Thomas's Street, if only to see the doorway of the house to the east of the Chapter House, and also to peep into Guy's, so venerable and staid and useful, and so populous with students and nurses, all wearing that air of resolute and assertive good health—more, of immortality—that always seems to belong to the officers of a hospital. And yet—and yet—John Keats was once a student at this very institution!

THE MONUMENT

CHAPTER XV

HOLBORN AND BLOOMSBURY

The changing seasons—London at her best—Signs of Winter—True
Londoners—Staple Inn—Ely Place—Gray's Inn—Lord Bacon—
Dr. Johnson and the Bookseller—Bedford Row—The Foundling
Hospital—Sunday Services—Culture and Advanced Theology—The
Fifth Commandment—Queen Square—Edward Irving—Lord Thur-
low—Red Lion Square and the Painters—St. George's and the
Brewer—St. Giles's—Bloomsbury—Gower Street and the Wall Fruit
—Egypt and Greece in London.

I HAVE so often by a curious chance been in Holborn
on those days in February and October when the
certainty of spring and winter suddenly makes itself felt
that I have come to associate the changing seasons inseparably with that road. One can be very conscious
there of the approach of spring, very sure that the reign
of winter is at hand. Why, I do not know, unless it is
that being wide and on high ground Holborn gives the
Londoner more than his share of sky, and where else
should we look for portents?

I must confess to becoming very restless in London in
the early spring. As one hurries over the asphalt the
thought of primroses is intolerable. And London has a
way of driving home one's losses by its many flower-sellers
and by the crocuses and daffodils in the parks. But later
—after the first rapture is over and the primroses no
longer have to be sought but thrust themselves upon one

12   177

—I can remain in London with more composure and wait
for the hot weather.   London to my mind has four periods
when she is more than tolerable, when she is the most
desirable abode of all.   These are May, when the freshness
of the leaves and the clarity of the atmosphere unite to
lend her an almost Continental brightness and charm;
August at night; November at dusk when the presages
of winter are in the air; and the few days before Christmas,
when a good-natured bustle and an electric excitement
and anticipation fill the streets.   Were I my own master
(or what is called one's own master) I would leave London
immediately after Christmas and never set foot in her
precincts again till the first match at Lord's; and soon
after that I would be off again.

But November would see me back; for although London
beneath a May sun is London at her loveliest, it is when
the signs of winter begin to accumulate that to me she
is most friendly, most homely.   I admire her in May, but
I am quite ready to leave her: in November I am glad
that I shall not be going away for a long time.   She
assumes the winter garb so cheerfully and naturally.   With
the first fog of November she begins to be happy.   "Now,"
one seems to hear her say, "now I am myself again.
Summer was all very well, but clear air and warmth are
not really in my line.   I am a grey city and a dingy:
smoke is the breath of my life: stir your fires and let us
be comfortable and gloomy again."   In the old days one
of the surest signs of winter in London was straw in the
'buses; but there is not much of it now.   The chestnut
roasters, however, remain: still as certain harbingers of the
winter as the swallows are of the summer.   At the street
corners you see their merry little furnaces glowing through
the peep-holes, and if you will, and are not ashamed, you

may fill your pockets with two-pennyworth, and thus, at a ridiculously small expenditure, provide yourself with food and hand-warmers in one. A foreign chestnut-vendor whom I saw the other day in the Strand kept supplies both of roast chestnuts and ice-cream on the same barrow, so that his patrons by purchasing of each could, alternately eating and licking, transport themselves to July or December, Spitzbergen or Sierra Leone. The hot potato men are perennials, although perhaps they ply their business with less assiduity in summer than winter. I like best those over whose furnace is an arch of spikes, each one impaling a Magnum Bonum—like the heads that used to ornament Temple Bar. ("Behold the head of a tater," as a witty lady once remarked.) The sparrows now are a thought tamer than in summer, and the pigeons would be so if that were possible. The chairs have all gone from the parks.

From the fact that I have already confessed to a desire to leave London for quite long periods, and from the confession which I now make that few pleasures in life seem to me to surpass the feeling of repose and anticipation and liberty that comes to one as one leans back in the carriage of an express train steaming steadily and noiselessly out of one of the great London stations, the deduction is easy that I am but an indifferent Londoner. With the best intentions in the world I cannot have deceived any reader into thinking me a good one. I am too critical: the true Londoner loves his city not only passionately but indiscriminately. She is all in all to him. He loves every aspect of her, every particular, because all go to the completion of his ideal, his mistress. None the less (although I suggest that my travels would assist in disqualifying me), his love does not prevent him from leaving her: you meet true Londoners all over the world; indeed it is abroad that you find them most articulate, for the London tendency to ridicule emotion and abbreviate displays of sentiment (except on the melodramatic stage) prevents them at home from showing their love as freely as they can do abroad. At home they are sardonic, suspicious, chary of praise; but in the lonely places of the earth and in times of depression all the Londoner comes out.

Every one knows how Private Ortheris, in Mr. Kipling's story, went mad in the heat of India and babbled not of green fields but of the Strand and the Adelphi arches, orange peel, wet pavements and flaring gas jets; and on the day on which I am writing these words I find in a paper a quotation from an article in a medical magazine, by the lady superintendent of a country sanatorium for consumptives, who says that once having a patient who was unmistakably dying, and having written to his friends to receive him again, they replied that his home off the Euston Road was so wretched that they hoped she could keep him; which she would have done but for the man himself, who implored her to send him back "where he could hear once more the 'buses in the Euston Road". There, in these two men, one in India and one dying in East Anglia, speaks the true Londoner. No transitory visitor to the city can ever acquire this love; I doubt if any one can who did not spend his childhood in it.

The Londoner speaking here is the real thing: the home sickness which he feels is not to be counterfeited. It is not the least sad part of Charles Lamb's latter days that he was doomed to Enfield and Edmonton, and that when he did get to London now and then it was peopled by ghosts and knew him not. No wonder he shed tears to find that St. Dunstan's iron figures—the wonders of his infancy, as those in Cheapside have been the wonders of ours—had vanished. This is the real love of London, which I for one cannot pretend to, much as I should value it. London is neither my mother nor my step-mother; but I love her always a little, and now and then well on the other side of idolatry.

There is that other type of Londoner, too, that is in love not with its sights and savours but with its intellectual variety—a type fixed for me in an elderly man of letters of considerable renown, the friend of some of the rarest spirits in modern life, whom when, almost a boy, I was for the first time in his company, I heard say that he "dared not leave London for fear some new and interesting figure should arrive during his absence and be missed by him." That speaker was a true Londoner too.

Meanwhile what of Holborn and Bloomsbury?

Holborn is chiefly remarkable for that row of old houses opposite Gray's Inn Road which gives so false an impression of this city to visitors who enter it at Euston or St. Pancras or King's Cross, and speeding down the Gray's Inn Road in their hansoms, see this wonderful piece of medievalism before them. "Is London like that?" they say; and prepare for pleasures that will not be fulfilled. The houses, which are piously preserved by the Prudential directors, form the north side of Staple Inn, one of the quietest and most charming of the small Inns of Court, with trees full of sparrows, whose clamour towards evening is incredibly assertive, and a beautiful little hall. It is all very old and rather crazy, and it would be well for us now to see it as often as we can, lest its knell suddenly sound and we have not the chance again. Something of the same effect of quietude is to be obtained in the precincts of the Mercers' School, a little to the east, especially in the outer court;

but this is a very minute backwater. For quietude with space you must seek Gray's Inn.

But before exploring Gray's Inn one might look into Ely Place on the other side of the road, at the beginning of Charterhouse Street, for it is old and historic, marking the site of the palace where John of Gaunt died. Sir Christopher Hatton, who danced before Elizabeth, secured a part of the building and made himself a spacious home there, a tenancy still commemorated by Hatton Garden, close by, where the diamond merchants have their mart. Ely Place, as it now stands, was built at the end of the eighteenth century, but the chapel of the ancient palace still remains, and has passed to the Roman Catholics, who have made it beautiful. The crypt is one of the quietest sanctuaries in London.

Gray's Inn has let the rebuilder in here and there, but he has been well watched, and in a very little time, under London's grimy influence, his work will fall into line with the Inn's prevailing style. The large Square is still the serene abode of antiquity—not too remote, but sufficiently so for peace. The most illustrious of Gray's Inn's members is Francis Bacon, Lord Verulam, who acted as its treasurer and kept his rooms here to the end. He identified himself with all the activities of the Inn, grave and gay, and helped in laying out its gardens. To meditate upon the great Chancellor most fittingly one must saunter at evening in Gray's Inn Walk, beneath the trees, the descendants of those which he planted with his own hand. It was here perhaps that his own sage and melodious thoughts on gardens came to him.

Among Gray's Inn's other illustrious residents for long or short periods were Ritson the antiquary and vegetarian, Oliver Goldsmith, Southey and Macaulay. It was behind

Gray's Inn that Mr. Justice Shallow fought with Sampson Stockfish, a fruiterer. Tonson, the publisher and bookseller, had his shop by Gray's Inn Gate in Holborn before he moved to the Shakespeare's Head in the Strand. Osborne, the bookseller of "impassive dulness," and "entirely destitute of shame," whom Dr. Johnson knocked down, had his shop here too. The story goes that the Great Lexicographer there floored him with a folio and set his learned foot upon his neck; but this, it is sad to relate, was not so. "Sir, he was impertinent to me and I beat him. But it was not in his shop: it was in my own chambers"—that is the true version. Booksellers (perhaps from fear) have rather abandoned this neighbourhood now, although there are a few in the little alleys about—in Red Lion Passage for example, and in both Turnstile Streets; but curiosity shops abound.

Through Gray's Inn one may gain Bedford Row, which might almost be a part of the inn itself, so quiet and Georgian is it—the best-preserved and widest Georgian street in London, occupied in its earliest days by aristocrats and plutocrats, but now wholly in the hands of the Law. I like to think it was at No. 14 that Abernethy fired prescriptions and advice at his outraged patients. Bedford Row is utterly un-modern.

I noted as I passed through it one day recently a carriage and pair of old-fashioned build drawn up before one of the houses. It had the amplitude of the last century's youth. There was no rumble, but had there been one it would have seemed no excrescence. A coronet was on the panel, and the coachman was aged and comfortable and serene. The footman by the door had also the air of security that comes of service in a quiet and ancient family. Suddenly from the sombre Georgian house emerged a swift young clerk with a sign to the waiting servants. The coachman's back lost its curve, the venerable horses lifted their ears, the footman stood erect and vigilant, as a little, lively, be-ribboned lady and her portly and dignified man of law appeared in the passage and slowly descended the steps. The little lady's hand was on his arm; she was feeble and very old, and his handsome white head was bent towards her to catch her final instructions. They crossed the pavement with tiny steps, and with old-world gravity and courtesy he relinquished her to the footman and bowed his farewells. She nodded to him as the carriage rolled steadily away, and I had a full glimpse of her face, hitherto hidden by her bonnet. It wore an expression kindly and relieved, and I felt assured that her mission had been rather to add an unexpected and benevolent codicil than to disinherit any one. It all seemed so rightly a part of the life of Bedford Row.

By Great James Street, which is a northern continuation of Bedford Row on the other side of Theobald's (pronounced Tibbald's) Road, and, like it, Georgian and wainscotted with oak and out-moded, one comes to Mecklenburgh Square and the Foundling Hospital (known locally as the "Fondling"): the heart of old Bloomsbury. Visitors are shown over the Hospital on certain days in the week; and I think I advise the visit to be made. It is a pleasant institution to see, and on the walls of the long low rooms are some interesting pictures—its founder, the good Captain Coram, painted by Hogarth, who was closely associated with the charity; scriptural texts illustrating our duties to the fatherless translated into paint by the same master and by such contemporaries as Highmore, Wills and Hayman; portraits of governors by the score; and a portion of a cartoon by Raphael. Here also may be seen medals belong-

JEAN ARNOLFINI AND JEANNE, HIS WIFE
AFTER THE PICTURE BY JAN VAN EYCK IN THE NATIONAL GALLERY

ing to foundlings who have become warriors; cases of odd trinkets attached to foundlings in the old days when these poor little forlorn love-children were deposited in the permanent cradle at the gates; signatures of kings; old MSS.; and the keyboard and tuning fork that were used by the great George Frederick Handel when he was organist here. All these and other curiosities will be shown you by a sturdy boy, who will then open the door suddenly upon foundlings in class, and foundlings at play, the infant school being packed with stolid and solid children all exactly alike in their brown clothes and white pinafores and all profoundly grateful for a visitor to stare at.

The boys for the most part become soldiers and sailors: the girls go into service. In the early days the boys were named after heroes of the battle field and the ocean, and the girls after whom I know not, but St. Xita is their patroness, one and all. To-day there may be a new system of nomenclature; but if not, one may expect to find Drakes and Rodneys, Nelsons and Collingwoods, Beresfords and Fishers, Wellingtons and Havelocks, Gordons and Burnabys, Roberts and Kitcheners. The first boy baby admitted was very prettily named Thomas Coram, and the first girl baby Eunice Coram, after their kindly stepfather and stepmother.

London, as I have hinted, does little enough for its guests on Sundays; but morning service at the Foundling Hospital must certainly be grouped among its entertainments. We are not as a people given to mingle much taste or charm with our charity: we never quite forgive the pauper or the unfortunate; but there is charm here. Anyone that wishes may attend, provided that he adds a silver coin to the offertory (here emerging the shining usefulness of the threepenny bit!). It has for some years been the custom to

appoint as chaplain a preacher of some eloquence or intellectual bravery, or both. I remember that the first sermon
I listened to in this square and formal Georgian temple
touched upon the difference that must always exist in the
experience of eye-witnesses, an illustration being drawn by
the divine from "the two bulky volumes on Persia by Mr.
George Curzon which doubtless many of you have read". I
certainly had not read them ; and although the gods stand
up for bastards I doubt if any of his congregation proper
had ; but there they sat, row upon row, in their gallery,
all spick and span with their white caps and collars and
pink cheeks, and gave as little indication as might be that
they were intensely uninterested, if not positively chilled.
Perhaps they have their own human sermons too, when
the silver-edged stranger is not admitted. I hope so.

If the sermon is ever too advanced for the visitor (and I
seem to remember that now and again it was so in the
days of the gifted Momerie) he will always find the children
worth study.   "Boy," said the terrible James Boyer of
Christ's Hospital to the youthful Samuel Taylor Coleridge
"boy, the school is your father: boy, the school is your
mother . . . let's have no more crying." It was not quite
true of Coleridge, who had a real enough mother in Devonshire ; but it is literally true of the children here.   Yet
when the communion comes round their response to the
fifth commandment is as hearty as to any other, and as
free from apparent irony.

Before the Foundling Hospital was built, in 1739, there
were fields here, and in 1719 a very early cricket match
was played in them between the Men of Kent and the Men
of London for £60. I know not which won. At No. 77
Guilford Street, in 1803, lived Sydney Smith. Although
in the centre of Queen Square, which leads out of Guilford

Street to the west, stands a statue of Queen Charlotte, the enclosure was named after Queen Anne, in whose reign it was built. Many traces of its early state remain. Hospitals now throng here, where once were gentlemen and scholars: among them Antony Askew, physician and Grecian and the friend of all learning ; and Dr. Campbell of the *Biographia Britannica*, whose house Dr. Johnson frequented until the shivering fear came upon him that the Scotsmen who flocked there might accuse him of borrowing his good things from their countrymen. Another friend of Johnson, Dr. Charles Burney, also lived in Queen Square. In a house on the west side, an architect once told me, is still to be seen a perfect example of an ancient English well. Having no opening into Guilford Street except for foot passengers, Queen Square remains one of the quietest spots in London, and scholars might well live there now. Perhaps they do. Such houses would naturally harbour book-worms and scholiasts.

Few streets have changed less, except in residents, than Gloucester Street, running between Queen Square and Theobald's Road, which dates from Anne or George I and has all its original architecture, with two centuries of dirt added. It is long and narrow and gives in perfection the old Bloomsbury vista. At No. 19 lodged Edward Irving, the preacher, when he first came to London, little dreaming perhaps that his followers some forty years later were to build the cathedral of the Catholic and Apostolic, or Irvingite, body in Gordon Square. Great Ormond Street, reading out of Queen Square on the east, has much history too, especially at No. 45, lately the working Men's College, for it was here that Lord Chancellor Thurlow was living when in 1784 the great Seal was stolen. Here also Thurlow entertained the poet Crabbe and thought him " as like

Parson Adams as twelve to a dozen". Macaulay lived at No. 50 from 1823 to 1831, but the house is now no more: part of the Children's Hospital stands on its site. No. 44 Great Ormond Street is one of the most attractive of the old Georgian houses, with some fine iron work to increase its charm.

From Great Ormond Street we gain Lamb's Conduit Street, which, crossing Theobald's Road, becomes Red Lion Street, an old and narrow street between Bedford Row and Red Lion Square. No. 9 Red Lion Street is famous as being the house in which the firm of William Morris first began its existence and entered upon its career of revolutionising taste in furniture and driving Victorian stuffiness from our houses. At No. 17 Red Lion Square lodged Burne-Jones and Rossetti. Haydon, another painter of individuality, lived on the west side of the square ; and Henry Meyer, at his studio at No. 3, in the spring of 1826, gave sittings to a little dark gentleman in knee-breeches with a fine Titian head "full of dumb eloquence," who had just left the India House on a pension—Charles Lamb by name. The picture may be seen at the India Office in Whitehall to-day, commemorating if not the most assiduous of its clerks the one who covered its official writing paper with the best and tenderest literature.

Between Red Lion Square and the British Museum, whither we are now bound, one object of interest alone is to be seen—St. George's Church in Hart Street, famous for its pyramidal spire, culminating in a statue not of George the Saint but of George the First; placed there, to London's intense amusement, by Hucks the brewer. Hogarth, who liked to set a London spire in the background of his satirical scenes, has this in his terrible "Gin Lane," just as St. Giles, close by, is in his "Beer Street".

STAPLE INN

Munden the actor, whose grimaces and drolleries Lamb has made immortal, was buried in the churchyard of St. George's, now transformed into a recreation ground. Above the old player with the bouquet of faces Bloomsbury children now frolic.

St. Giles's-in-the-Fields is so near that we ought perhaps to glance at it before exploring the Museum and the rest of Bloomsbury. It is still in the midst of not too savoury a neighbourhood, although no longer the obvious antipodes to St. James's that it used to be in literature and speech. When we want contrasts now we speak of the West End and the East End. St Giles's is a dead letter. The present church is not so old as one might think : much later than Wren : and it is interesting rather for its forerunner's name than for itself, and also for being the last resting place of such men as George Chapman, who translated Homer into swinging Elizabethan English, and the sweetest of garden poets, Andrew Marvell.

Bloomsbury, which is the adopted home of the economical American visitor and the Hindoo student; Bloomsbury, whose myriad boarding-houses give the lie to the poet's statement that East and West can never meet; is bounded on the south by Oxford Street and High Holborn; on the north by the Euston Road; on the east by Southampton Row; and on the west by Tottenham Court Road. It has few shops and many residents, and is a stronghold of middle class respectability and learning. The British Museum is its heart : its lungs are Bedford Square and Russell Square, Gordon Square and Woburn Square : and its aorta is Gower Street, which goes on for ever. Lawyers and law students live here, to be near the Inns of Court; bookish men live here, to be near the Museum; and Jews live here, to be near the University

College School, which is non-sectarian. Bloomsbury is discreet and handy: it is near everything, and although not fashionable, any one, I understand, may live there without losing caste. It belongs to the Ducal House of Bedford, which has given its names very freely to its streets and squares.

To my mind Gower Street is not quite old enough to be interesting, but it has had some very human inhabitants of eminence, and has one or two still. Millais lived with his father at No. 87; the great Peter de Wint, who painted English cornfields as no one ever did before or since, died at No. 40. In its early days Gower Street was famous for—what? Its rural character and its fruit. Mrs. Siddons lived in a house there, the back of which was "most effectually in the country and delightfully pleasant"; while Lord Eldon's peaches (at the back of No. 42), Col. Sutherland's grapes (at No. 33), and William Bentham's nectarines were the talk of all who ate them.

Every one who cares for the beautiful sensitive art of John Flaxman, the friend of Blake, should penetrate to the dome of University College, where is a fine collection of his drawings and reliefs. The College also possesses the embalmed body of Jeremy Bentham. Other objects of interest in this neighbourhood are the allegorical frescoes at University Hall in Gordon Square, filled with portraits of great Englishmen; the memorial to Christina Rossetti in Christ Church, Woburn Square; and two unexpected and imposing pieces of architecture—St. Pancras Church in the Euston Road, and Euston station. Euston station, seen at night or through a mist, is one of the most impressive sights in London. As Aubrey Beardsley, the marvellous youth who perished in his decadence, used to say, Euston station made it unnecessary to visit Egypt. I would not add that St. Pancras Church makes it unnecessary to visit Greece; but it is a very interesting summary of Greek traditions, its main building being an adaptation of the Ionic temple of the Erectheion on the Acropolis at Athens, its tower deriving from the Horologium or Temple of the Winds, and its dependencies, with their noble caryatides, being adaptations of the south portico of the Pandroseion, also at Athens.

Bloomsbury, as I have said, gives harbourage to all colours, and the Baboo law student is one of the commonest incidents of its streets. But the oddest alien I ever saw there was in the area of the house of a medical friend in Woburn Square. While waiting on the steps for the bell to be answered I heard the sound of brushing, and looking down, I saw a small negro boy busily polishing a boot. He glanced up with a friendly smile, his eyes and teeth gleaming, and I noticed that on his right wrist was a broad ivory ring. "So you're no longer an Abolitionist!" I said to the doctor when I at last gained his room. "No," he answered: "at least, my sister isn't. That's a boy my brother-in-law has just brought from West Africa. He didn't exactly want him, but the boy was wild to see England, and at the last minute jumped on board." "And what does the ring on his arm mean?" I asked. "O, he's a king's son out there. That's a symbol of authority. At home he has the power of life and death over fifty slaves."

When I came away the boy was still busily at work, but he had changed the boots for knife-cleaning. He cast another merry smile up to me as I descended the steps— the king's son with the power of life and death over fifty slaves.

CHAPTER XVI

THE BRITISH MUSEUM AND SOHO

The Bloomsbury History of the World—Great statuary—Julius Cæsar
and Demeter—The Elgin Marbles—Terra-cotta and bronze—MSS.—
London's foreign quarter—Soho Square and Golden Square—Soho—
Cheap restaurants—The old artists' quarter—Wardour Street and
Berners Street—The great Hoax—Madame Tussaud's—Clothes
without Illusion—The Chamber of Horrors—Thoughts on the Killing
of Men—The Vivifying of *Little Arthur*—Waxworks at Night—An
Experience in the Edgware Road.

THE British Museum is the history of the world: in
its Bloomsbury galleries the history of civilization,
in its Cromwell Road galleries the history of nature. The
lesson of the Museum is the transitoriness of man and the
littleness of his greatest deeds. That is the burden of its
every Bloomsbury room. The ghosts of dead peoples, once
dominant, inhabit it; the dust of empires fills its air.
One may turn in from Oxford Street and in half an hour
pass all the nations of the earth, commanding and servile,
cultured and uncouth, under review. The finest achiev
ments of Greek Sculpture are here, and here are the painted
canoes of the South Sea islander; the Egyptian Book of
the Dead is here, and here, in the Reading Room, is a copy
of the work you are now judiciously skipping; the obelisk
of Shalmaneser is here, and here are cinematoscope records
of London street scenes.

It is too much for one mind to grasp. Nor do I try. The Roman Emperors, the Graeco-Roman sculptures, the bronzes, the terra-cottas, the Etruscan vases, the gems, the ceramics and glass, the prints, the manuscripts, the Egyptian rooms—these, with the Reading Room, are my British Museum. Among the other things I am too conscious of the typical museum depression: it is all so bleak and instructive.

In vain for me have the archipelagos of the Pacific been ransacked for weapons and canoes; in vain for me have spades been busy in Assyria and Babylonia. Primitive man does not interest me, and Nineveh was not human enough. Not till the Egyptians baked pottery divinely blue and invented most of civilization's endearing ways did the world begin for me; but I could spare everything that Egypt has yielded us rather than the Demeter of Cnidos, the serenest thing in England, or the head of Julius Cæsar. For although at the Museum the interesting predominates over the beautiful, the beautiful is here too; more than the beautiful, the sublime. For here are the Elgin Marbles: the Three Fates from the Parthenon, and its bas-reliefs, which are among the greatest works of art that man has achieved. We may not have the Winged Victory of Samothrace, or the Venus of Milo, the Laocöon or the Dying Gladiator; but we have these, and we have the Demeter and the Julius Cæsar and the bronze head of Hypnos.

One reaches the sculpture galleries by way of the Roman Gallery, where the Emperors are, culminating in the Julius Cæsar, surely the most fascinating male head ever chiselled from marble. I pause always before the brutal pugilistic features of Trajanus, and the Caracalla, so rustic and determined, and the mischievous charm of Julia Paula. In

13

the Second Graeco-Roman room is a superb Discobolos, and here also is a little beautiful torso of Aphrodite loosening her sandal—that action in which the great masters so often placed her, that the exquisite contour of the curved back might be theirs.   My favourites in the Third Graeco-Roman room are the head of Aphrodite from the Townley collection—No. 1596; the boy extracting a thorn from his foot, No. 1755; the head of Apollo Musagetes, No. 1548, the beauty of which triumphs over the lack of a nose in the amazing way that the perfect beauty of a statue will—so much so indeed that one very soon comes not to miss the broken portions at all.   It is almost as if one acquires a second vision that subconsciously supplies the missing parts and enables one to see it whole; or rather prevents one from noticing that it is incomplete.   I love also the head in Asiatic attire—No. 1769—on the same side, and the terminal figure opposite—No. 1742—on which the winds and the rains have laid their softening hand.

But all these give way to the Ceres, or Demeter, in the Greek ante-room.   This is to me the most beautiful piece of sculpture in the British Museum.   It came from the sanctuary of Demeter at Cnidos—a temple to worship in indeed!   I know of no Madonna in the painting of any old master more maternal and serene and wise and holy than this marble goddess from the fourth century B.C., a photograph of which will be found on the opposite page.

In a case on the right of the Ephesus Room, as you enter from this ante-room, are two gems—another little Aphrodite, No. 1417, with a back of liquid softness; and a draped figure of the same goddess, from her temple at Cyrene—the lower half only—the folds of the dress being exquisite beyond words.

And so we enter the room which brings more people to

THE DEMETER OF CNIDOS

AFTER THE STATUE IN THE BRITISH MUSEUM

Bloomsbury than any other treasure here—the room of the Elgin Marbles, which certain sentimentalists would restore to Greece but which I for one think better here. The group of Fates is the most wonderful; and it is difficult to imagine how much more impressive they would be if they were unmutilated. As it is, they have more dignity and more beauty than the ordinary observer can witness unmoved. Broken fragments as they are, they are the last word in plastic art; and one wonders how the Athenians dared look at their temple in its perfection. On a lower plane, but great and satisfying and beautiful beyond description, are some of the reliefs from the frieze—the perfection of the treatment of the horse in decorative art. Such horses, such horsemen: life and loveliness in every line.

From marble it is interesting to pass to terra-cotta: from the sublime to the charming: from the tremendous to the pretty. It is, however, charm and prettiness of a very high order, some of the little figures from Tanagra and Eretria being exquisite. Note in particular these numbers for their grace and their quaintness: C. 299, an aged nurse and child; C. 278, mother and child; C. 245, a girl with a fan; C. 214, the writing lesson; C. 250, a woman draped and hooded (this is reproduced in the admirable official catalogue); C. 308 a little girl, and C. 196r a Cupid. The domesticity of so many of these figures— the women with fans, the girls playing astragali, and so forth—always brings to my mind that idyll of Theocritus in which the two frivolous women chat together.

After the terra-cottas we come to the bronzes, chief among which is the wonderful Hypnos from Perugia. Of the treasures of these rooms I can say nothing: they are endless. And so we pass on to the four Vase rooms, and then come to ancient Egypt, where everything that we do now and deem novel and exciting (short of electricity and motors) seems to have been old game.

Parallel with the Egyptian rooms are a series of smaller rooms illustrating the history of religion, leading to the Ethnographical Gallery, which leads in its turn to netsukés (the variety and perfection of which are alike bewildering), ceramics and prints.

The collection of English and foreign pottery and porcelain and glass is fascinatingly displayed, and one may lose oneself completely here, whether it is before Lowestoft and Chelsea or old Greek prismatic glass, Delft or Nankin, Sèvres or Wedgwood, Persian tiles or Rhodian plates.

One reaches the ground floor again by way of the Medieval Room, which contains many odd treasures but is perhaps rather too much like an old curiosity shop, such as Balzac describes in the *Peau de Chagrin* or Stevenson in *Markheim*. In the room at the end of the porcelain gallery an exhibition of drawings and engravings from the print department is usually on view. At the moment at which I write it is given up to mezzotints.

But before descending again, one ought to see the ornaments and gems—marvellous intaglios and cameos beyond price from Egypt and Greece and Rome; precious stones of every variety, and wonderful imitations of precious stones of every variety, which, false as they may be, are still quite precious enough for me; gold work of all periods; the famous Portland Vase of blue glass; and frescoes from Pompeii.

One of the most interesting things in the Hall of Inscriptions on the way to the Reading Room is the slab of marble which used to be hung outside a Roman circus, with the words on it, in Latin: "Circus Full. Great Shouting.

Doors Closed." Few things bring the modernity of Romans, or the ancientry of ourselves, so vividly before one.

A continuous exhibition of illuminated books, famous MSS., letters and early printed books is held in the cases in the library galleries to the right of the Entrance Hall. Here one may see Books of Hours, Bibles and missals, with quaint and patient drawings by Flemish and Italian artists; the handwriting of kings and scholars, Boer generals and divines; manuscripts of poems by Keats and Pope, illustrating the laborious stages by which perfection is reached; an early story by Charlotte Brontë in a hand too small to be legible to the naked eye; a commonplace book of Milton's; and books from the presses of Caxton and Gutenberg. Here also are manuscript pages of the *Iliad* and the *Odyssey* from old Greek libraries, with comments by old Greek scholars.

It is not until one has wandered in the British Museum for some weeks that one begins to realise how inexhaustible it is. To know it is impossible; but the task of extracting its secrets is made less difficult by acquiring and studying its excellent catalogues, which are on sale in the Entrance Hall. Apart from their immediate use they are very good reading.

The quickest way to Soho from the Museum is down Shaftesbury Avenue; or one may fight one's way through the blended odours of beer, pickles and jam, all in the making, to Soho Square, and recover one's self-respect in the Roman Catholic church of St. Patrick, which is there. So Italian is its interior that you cannot believe you are in London at all.

Soho proper lies between Oxford Street, Charing Cross Road, Leicester Square and Warwick Street; but the corresponding parallelogram north of Oxford Street, bounded by the Tottenham Court Road, the Euston Road and Great Portland Street, is now almost equally foreign, the pavements of Great Portland Street in particular being very cosmopolitan. I have been told that in the Percy Street and Cleveland Street neighbourhood many of the great anarchist plots have been hatched; certain it is that London has offered as many advantages to the political desperado as any city, except perhaps Geneva.

The foreign residents of Soho proper are almost exclusively French; north of Oxford Street we find Italians too and Germans. Poorer Italians still, organ grinders from Chiaveri, monkey boys from further south and ice cream men from Naples live on Saffron Hill, by Leather Lane; Swiss mechanics live in Clerkenwell; poor Jews live in Whitechapel, as we have seen; middle class Jews in Maida Vale; rich Jews in Bayswater. American settlers are fond of Hampstead; American visitors like the Embankment hotels or Bloomsbury. Although there are many exceptions, one can generalise quite safely on London's settlements, not only of foreigners, but of professional and artistic groups. Thus the artists live in Chelsea, Kensington, St. John's Wood and Hampstead; the chief doctors are in and about Harley Street; Music Hall performers like to cross the river on their way home; musicians congregate about Baker Street; Kensington has many literary people.

In addition to Leicester Square, which is however far less French than it used to be, Soho has two squares—Soho Square and Golden Square. It is Soho Square which gives the name to the district—"So ho!" an old cry of the harriers, but why thus applied no one knows. The story that it was previously called Monmouth Square and King's Square, and changed to Soho Square after Sedgemoor, where "So

KENSINGTON PALACE FROM THE GARDENS

ho!" was Monmouth's battle-call, is, I believe, disproved; the reverse being the fact—the battle-cry coming from the neighbourhood. The Duke of Monmouth was the first resident here—in 1681—his house being on the south side, between Frith Street and Greek Street. Other residents in the Square were Sir Cloudesley Shovel, the admiral, "Vathek" Beckford and Sir Joseph Banks, the botanist. A statue of Charles the Second used to stand in the centre, facing the house of his unlucky natural son. George the Second still stands in Golden Square, half a mile to the west, which a few years ago it would have been imperative to visit, for it had, on the south side, one of the comeliest of London's Georgian houses; but that too has now gone and the square is uninteresting. Miss Kilmansegg ought to have lived here, but did not. Golden Square was, however, the abode of Ralph Nickleby, and in real life, among others, of Angelica Kaufmann, the artist (Mrs. Ritchie's charming "Miss Angel"), and Cardinal Wiseman, who may or may not have been Bishop Blougram who apologised.

Soho has never been the same since Shaftesbury Avenue and the Charing Cross Road ploughed through her midst, and to eat in her restaurants became a fashion. Before those days she was a city apart, a Continental city within a London city, living her own life; but now she is open to all. In fact you now see more English than French in her Lisle Street and Gerrard Street and Old Compton Street restaurants. It is the English who eat there, the French and Italian proprietors who retire with fortunes. In the old days Wardour Street may be said to have been the main artery of Soho, but now her most characteristically French street is Old Compton Street. Here are comestible shops, exactly as in the Rue St. Honoré, and the greatest profusion of cheap restaurants, most of which soon have their day and disappear. Since the habit of eating away from home has seized London, it has become quite a pursuit to discover new eighteen-penny *tables d'hôte* in this neighbourhood. We now swap catalogues of their merits as we used to swap stories.

Many of Soho's streets retain their old character. Gerrard Street, for example, although the headquarters of telephoning, is yet full of the past. One of the cheap restaurants here is in Edmund Burke's old house; a little farther east, on the same side, at No. 43, is the house where Dryden died: it is now a publisher's office. Both have tablets. At the corner of Gerrard Street and Greek Street, at the Turk's Head, the "Literary Club" which Reynolds founded used to meet. Here also the Artists' Club met; for a hundred and fifty years ago this was the centre of the artists' quarter. Hogarth and Reynolds lived in Leicester Square; Hogarth's painting Academy was in St. Martin's Lane. Reynolds, Wilson, Hayman and Gainsborough, met at the Turk's Head with regularity and limited themselves to half a pint of wine apiece. Sir Thomas Lawrence lived in Greek Street, and there Wedgewood had show rooms.

Frith Street was the early home of Edmund Kean, and Macready had lodgings there in 1816. At No. 6 (a tablet marks the house) William Hazlitt died, in 1830. Charles Lamb stood by his bed. "Well, I've had a happy life," Hazlitt said; but he was bragging. He was buried at St. Anne's, between Dean Street and Wardour Street.

The artists' quarter extended due north beyond Oxford Street to Newman Street and Berners Street. Dean Street was full of artists—Thornhill, Hayman, Hamilton, Bailey, James Ward, all lived there, and Christie's auction rooms were there too. It was Fanny Kelly, Lamb's friend, who built the Royalty Theatre. In Newman Street lived and died Benjamin West—at No. 14; Stothard at 28. Fanny Kemble was born in this street.

Berners Street is still one of the most sensible streets in London, of a width that modern vestries have not had the wit to imitate. With the Middlesex Hospital at the end it has a very attractive vista. This also was given up to the painters: Fuseli was at No. 13, Opie at No. 8, Henry Bone, whose miniatures we saw at the Wallace Collection, at 15. At No. 7 lived the wretched Fauntleroy, the banker and forger, whom Bernard Barton, the Quaker poet, was urged by a mischievous friend never to emulate. It was upon the lady at No. 54, a Mrs. Tottingham, that Theodore Hook played his dreary " Berners Street hoax," which consisted in sending hundreds of tradesmen to her door at the same hour with articles she had not ordered and did not want, including a hearse. David Roberts, who painted cathedrals like an angel, did not live here, but it was while walking along Berners Street that he received the apoplectic stroke from which he died.

If I do not dally longer in this part of London it is because I do not care much for it. It is a little seamy, and after Berners Street no longer quite the real thing—not old enough on the one hand, or clean enough on the other. Let us look at the old curiosity shops of Great Portland Street and so pass through the discreet medical district of Harley Street and Welbeck Street to a British institution which it would never do to miss—Madame Tussaud's.

The imposing red façade of Madame Tussaud's in Marylebone Road must give the foreigner a totally false impression of English taste in amusement; for the exhibition does not really bear the intimate relation to the city that its size might lead one to expect. Who goes to

Madame Tussaud's I cannot say. All I know is that whenever I have asked friends and acquaintances of my own (as I have been doing lately) if they have been, they reply in the negative, or date their only visit many years ago. I wonder if men of eminence steal in now and then to see what their effigies are like and what notice they are drawing, as painters are said to lurk in the vicinity of their canvases at the Royal Academy to pick up crumbs of comfort. I wonder if Mr. Kipling has ever seen the demure figure that smirks beneath his name; I wonder if the late Dr. Barnardo really wore, "in the form," as the spiritualists say, a collar such as he wears in his waxen representation? Has Lord Kitchener ever examined the chest which his modeller has given him? Were he to do so he would probably feel as I always do in the presence of the waxen—that they ought to be better. There is hardly a figure in this exhibition that conveys any illusion of life. Their complexions are not right; their hair is not right. Their clothes are obviously the clothes of the inanimate; they have no notion what to do with their hands.

Thinking it over, I have come to the conclusion that not only the unreality, but also the eeriness, almost fearsomeness, of a waxwork, reside principally in its clothes. A naked waxwork, though unpleasant, would not be so bad: it is the clothes wanting life to vivify and justify it that make it so terrible, just as clothes on a corpse add to the horror of death. One wonders where the clothes come from. Do they also, like the features and hair of these figures, approximate to life, or are they chosen at random? Mr. Burns, it is well known, relinquished one of his blue serge suits in exchange for a new one; but the others? Mr. Balfour, for example? Are there underclothes too? Does the Tussaud establishment include a tailor and a modiste? To these questions I could no doubt obtain a satisfactory reply by merely writing to the exhibition; but there are occasions when it is more amusing to remain in the domain of conjecture. This is one.

I wandered into Madame Tussaud's a little while ago entirely for the purpose of saying something about it in this book. As it was a foggy day, I had some difficulty in disentangling the visitors from the effigies; but when I did so I saw that they wore a provincial air. I felt a little provincial myself as I passed from figure to figure and turned to the catalogue to see if I were looking at the late Daniel Leno or Mr. Asquith.

The Chamber of Horrors at Madame Tussaud's is London's Cabaret des Néants, London's Wiertz Museum. Horrors are not encouraged in England, and London has no other official collection of them, if we except the assemblage of articles of crime that Scotland Yard cherishes. But jemmies and pistols and knives are not in themselves horrors, whereas wax decapitated heads dropping blood, coloured pictures of diseases, models of criminals being tortured, a hangman and a condemned man on the scaffold —these exist by virtue of their horrifying power, and you are asked for an extra sixpence frankly as a payment for shudders.

It is all ugly and coarse, and in part very silly, as when you are confronted by a dock crammed with effigies of the more notorious murderers (the only really interesting murderers, of course, being those who have escaped detection or even suspicion : but how should Madame Tussaud's patrons know this?) all blooming with the ruddy tints of health. Seeing them packed together like this for execration, one may reflect, not perhaps wholly without

admiration and certainly with pity, that they are here
less because they were wicked than because they dared to
anticipate the laggard steps of Fate. One may be a little
perplexed too, if one knows anything of history, by the
disrepute into which this business of killing a man has
fallen. That these poor, shabby, impulsive, ill-balanced
creatures should be the only unlicensed shedders of blood
that are left! And had Madame Tussaud lived in Iceland
in the twelfth century would she have modelled Gunnar
of Lithend and Scarphedinn to the same vulgar purposes?

But one must not wholly deprecate. The exhibition as
a whole may be supplying a demand that is essentially
vulgar: many of its models may be too remote from life
to be of any real value: the Chamber of Horrors may be
beyond question a sordid and hideous accessory: yet in
the other scale must be put some of the work of Madame
Tussaud herself—her Voltaire, which is to me one of the most
interesting things in London, as his life mask at the Carnavalet is one of the most interesting things in Paris; a few
of her other heads belonging to the reign of Terror,
notably the Robespierre; the very guillotine that shed so
much of France's best and bravest blood; and the relics of
Napoleon. We must remember too that it is very easy
and very tempting to be more considerate for the feelings
of children than is necessary. Children have a beautiful
gift of extracting pure gold from baser material without
a stain of the alloy remaining upon them; and we are apt
to forget this in our adult fulminations against vulgarity
and ugliness. For children Madame Tussaud's will always
be one of the ante-rooms to the earthly paradise, whether
they go or not. The name has a magic that nothing can
destroy. And though they should not, if I were taking
them, ever set foot in the subterranean Temple of Tur-

pitude, they would, I have very good reason to know, come away from the study of kings and queens of England, and the historical tableaux—the finding of Harold's body, and the burning of the cakes by Alfred the Great, the execution of Mary Queen of Scots and the death of Becket, the signing of Magna Charta and other scenes in *Little Arthur*—with a far more vivid idea of English history and interest in it than any schoolmaster or governess could give them. And that is a great thing.

None the less, not willingly do these footsteps wander that way again; and I would sooner be the chairman of the Society for Psychical Research's committee for the investigation of haunted houses than spend the night among these silent, stony-eyed mockeries of humanity. Surely they move a little at night. Very slowly, I am sure, very cautiously. . . . You would hear the low grinding sound of two glass eyes being painfully brought into focus. . . .

I could go mad in a waxwork exhibition. Once I nearly did. It was in the Edgware Road, and the admission fee was a penny. A small shop and house had been taken and filled with figures, mostly murderers. The place was badly lit, and by the time I had reached the top floor and had run into a poisoner, Mrs. Hogg and Percy Lefroy Mapleton, I was totally unhinged.

CHAPTER XVII

THE PARKS AND THE ZOO

FOR those who have to get there, London's finest open
space—or "lung," as the leader-writers say—is
Hampstead Heath. But Hampstead Heath is a journey
for special occasions: the Parks are at our doors—Hyde
Park and Kensington Gardens, St. James's Park and Green
Park, Regent's Park and Battersea Park. What London
would be like without these tracts of greenery and such
minor oases as the gardens of her squares one cannot think,
In hot weather she is only just bearable as it is. (Once
again I apply the word London to a very limited central
area: for as a matter of fact there are scores of square
miles of houses and streets in the East End that have no
open space near them, Victoria Park having to suffice for
an immense and over-crowded district, whereas the West-
ender may if he likes walk all the way from Kensington to
Westminster under trees.)

Each of these parks has its own character; but one sight
is common to all, and that is the supine slumberer. Even

immediately after rain, even on a sunny day in February (as I have just witnessed), you will see the London working-man (as we call him) stretched on his back or on his front asleep in every park. I have seen them in the Green Park on a hot day in summer so numerous and still that the place looked like a battle-field after action. Do these men die of rheumatic fever, one wonders, or are the precautions which most of us take against damp superfluous and rather pitifully self-protective?

To come to characteristics, Battersea Park is for games; St. James's Park for water fowl; the Green Park for repose; Hyde Park for fashion and horsemanship; Kensington Gardens for children and toy boats; and Regent's Park for botany and wild beasts. You could put them all into the Bois de Boulogne and lose them, but they are none the worse for that; and in the early spring their bulbs are wonderful. One has to be in London to see how beautifully crocuses can grow among the grass.

I have said that Hyde Park is for fashion and horsemanship; but it is for other things too—for meets of the Four-in-Hand club (which still exists in spite of petrol): for flag-signalling: for oratory. Just within the park by the Marble Arch is the battle-ground of the creeds. Here on most afternoons, and certainly on Sundays, you may find husky noisy men trimming God to their own dimensions or denying Him altogether: each surrounded by a little knot of listless inquisitive idlers, who pass from one to another quite impartially. To be articulate being the beginning and end of all Marble Arch orators, the presence of an audience matters little or nothing. Now and then an atheist tackles a neo-Christian speaker, or a Christian tackles an atheist; but nothing comes of it. Such good or amusing things as we have been led to suppose are then said are (like the retorts of 'bus drivers) mostly the invention of the descriptive humourist in his study.

Unless you want very obvious space, an open sky and straight paths enclosed by iron railings, or unless you want to see fashionable people in carriages or in the saddle, my advice to the visitor to Hyde Park is to walk along the north side until he reaches the Serpentine, follow the east bank of it (among the peacocks) to the bridge, and then cross the bridge and loiter in Kensington Gardens. In this way he will see the Serpentine at its best, remote from the oarsmen and the old gentlemen who sail toy boats; he will see all the interesting water fowl; and he will have been among trees and away from crowds all the time

Personally I would view with composure a veto prohibiting me from all the parks, so long as I might have the freedom of Kensington Gardens. Here one sees the spring come in as surely and sweetly as in any Devonshire lane; here the sheep on a hot day have as unmistakable a violet aura as on a Sussex down; here the thrush sings (how he sings!) and the robin; here the daffodils fling back the rays of the sun with all the assurance of Kew; here the hawthorns burst into flower as cheerily as in Kent; here is much shade, and chairs beneath it, and cool grass to walk on. Here also is a pleasant little tea-house where I have had breakfast in June in the open air as if it were France; while in winter the naked branches of the trees have a perfectly unique gift of holding the indigo mist: holding it, and enfolding it, and cherishing it.

Here also are dogs. In all the residential parts of London dogs are very numerous, but Kensington Gardens is the place if you would study them. Ordinary families have one dog only; but the families which use the Gardens have many. There is one old gentleman with eight dachshunds. And the children. . . . But here I refer you to *The Little White Bird*, where you will find not only the law of the Gardens by day, but are let into the secret of Kensington Gardens by night, when the gates are locked, and all is still, and Peter Pan creeps into his cockle shell boat. . . . Peter himself, in bronze, triumphant on a rock with fairies all about him, and little woodland animals such as squirrels and rabbits to play with too, now and for ever dominates the Serpentine, Sir George Frampton's charming creation having been secretly unveiled one spring night in 1911.

Regent's Park has the Botanical Gardens and the Zoological Gardens to add to its attractions. The Park itself is green and spacious, yet with too few trees to shade it, and too many wealthy private residents like unto moths fretting its garment. The stockbroker who stealthily encloses strips of a Surrey common must have learned his business in Regent's Park. But to any one who cares for horticulture or wild beasts this is the neighbourhood to live in—in one of the cool white terraces on the park's edge, or thereabouts. When I first came to London I had rooms near by, and every Monday morning I visited the otter and the wombats and the wallabys—Monday being a sixpenny day.

All that the Zoo needs to perfect it is the throwing open of its doors on Sunday, the one day on which so many Londoners have a chance of visiting it. Open on Sundays it now is, it is true, but only for members and their friends, who, being well-to-do, could go on any other day equally well. London Sabbatarianism breaks down in the summer so completely on the Thames, and in the winter in Queen's Hall, the Sunday League concert rooms, the cinema theatres, and the chief restaurants, that a few steps more might surely be taken.

14

Every frequenter of the Zoo has his favourite animals. Personally I am most interested in the apes in the basement of the ape-house, those almost too human creatures, the King Penguin and the seals and sea-lions. The elephant in England is soon learned ; the giraffes, so frail and exotic, I always fear will die before I can get out ; monkeys make me uneasy, and lions and tigers, pacing behind their bars, are, however splendid, pathetic figures. But the sea-lions and the seals do not suggest captivity : they frolic while 'tis May, and May is continual with them. But I suppose the best time to see them is half-past three, when they are fed. In their fine home, which is a veritable mermaid's pool, with rocks and caverns and real depth of water, they have room for evolutions of delight : and as their keeper is a particularly sympathetic man with a fine dramatic sense, this makes feeding-time a very entertaining quarter of an hour. It is worth making a special effort to be there then, if only to see how one of these nimble creatures can hurl itself out of the water to a rock all in one movement. It is worth being there then to note the astounding and rapturous celerity with which the sea-lions can move in the water—beyond all trains and motor-cars—and the grace of them in their properer element.

Seals and sea-lions, it is getting to be well known, are the real aristocrats of the brute creation. One had always heard this ; but it is only lately, since troupes of them have been seen on the variety stage, that one has realised it. When an ordinary wet seal from some chilly northern sea—a thing that we kill to keep warm the shoulders of rich men's wives—can balance a billiard cue on its nose with as much intelligence as the superb Cinquevalli, it is time to wonder if there is not some worthy mental destiny for it more useful in its way than any comforting property of its fur. That most animals can be

CHRIST WASHING PETER'S FEET

AFTER THE PICTURE BY FORD MADOX BROWN IN THE TATE GALLERY

taught routine, I know; that they can be coached into mechanical feats is a commonplace; but to get one to understand the laws of gravity is a miracle. Not only in a stationary position can this amphibian balance the cue, but move flappingly along the stage with its precarious burden and mount a pedestal. This is very wonderful. And at the Music Hall where I saw this feat other things happened too—displays of humour, well-reasoned games of ball between two sea-lions while their trainer was off the stage, and so forth—which show that it is time for us to revise our notions of these gentle creatures. Here is a potential new force. It is undoubtedly time to clothe our wives in other material, and think of the seal less as a skin than a mind. We might try experiments. Suppose the Lord Chancellor really were a Great Seal. . . .

Perhaps the seal is the superman of the future. In any case it should be the subject of a scientific memoir. When seals and sea-lions come nearer our own vaunted abilities than any other member of the brute creation we are entitled to be told why. "Go to the ant" was never a piece of counsel that aroused me; but "Go to the seal" has logic in it.

When the summer comes it is not, however, Hyde Park with its breadth of sky and its peacocks, not Kensington Gardens with its trees and the Round Pond's argosies, not Regent's Park even at sheep-shearing time, not St. James's Park with its water fowl; it is none of these that call me. My open space then is Lord's cricket ground in St. John's Wood (where acacias and lilac flourish). For the Oval, the great south London ground, where Surrey used to beat all comers and may do so again, I have never much cared: it is not comfortable unless one is a member of the Club; it is too big nicely to study the game; there are too many pot-houses around it; and I dislike gasometers. But Lord's I love, although I wish that one could see the game while strolling as once one could. It is now too much of a circus with raised seats. Still, sitting there at ease one may watch minutely the best cricket in the world. It was there that, scarlet with shame, I saw the Australian team of 1896 dismissed on a good wicket for 18, one after another falling to Pougher of Leicestershire, who had rarely terrified batsman before, and terrified none after; it was there that I saw Mr. Webbe bowled by Mordecai Sherwin, who took off the gloves for the purpose, leading to the batsman's famous *mot* that he "felt as if he had been run over by a donkey cart"; it was there that I saw Mr. Stoddart straight drive a ball from the nursery end along the ground so hard that it rebounded forty measured yards from the Pavilion railings; it was there that I saw three distinct hundreds scored in the University match of 1893; it was there that I saw Sir T. C. O'Brien and Mr. F. G. J. Ford heroically pull the Surrey and Middlesex match out of the fire in, I think, the same year. It was there in 1912 that I saw the great little McCartney miss his 100 by one run. But when Albert Trott at last realised his ambition of hitting the ball clean over the Pavilion I was not there. Perhaps some one will do it again: cricket is full of thrills, and what man has done man can do.

I like to approach Lord's through Dorset Square, which was the site of the original ground, because then I feel I may be passing over the exact spot where Alexander, Duke of Hamilton, was standing when he made his great drive —a hit which sent the ball one hundred and thirty-two yards before it touched earth. A stone was erected to commemorate this feat. Where is it now?

CHAPTER XVIII

KENSINGTON AND THE MUSEUMS

Two Burial Grounds—Kensington's Charm—Kensington's Babies—
Victorian Influence—Kensington Palace—The London Museum—
Holland House—Two Painters—The Model Buildings—The Albert
Memorial—Indian Treasures—Machinery for Miles—Heartrending
Bargains—A Palace of Applied Art—Raphael's Cartoons—Water
Colours—John Constable—The Early British Masters—The Jones
Bequest—The Stage and some MSS.—A Perfect One-man Collection
—The Natural History Museum.

KENSINGTON in itself, no less than in its beautiful
name, is the most attractive of the older and con-
tiguous suburbs. The roads to it are the pleasantest in
London, whether one goes thither through the greenery of
the park and Kensington Gardens, deviously by the Serpentine and among the trees, or by Kensington Gore, south of
the Park, or by the Bayswater Road, north of it.

The Bayswater route is the least interesting of the three,
save for its two burial grounds—one spreading behind the
beautiful little Chapel of the Ascension, which is opened
all day for rest and meditation and guards the old cemetery
of St. George's, Hanover Square, now no longer used, where
may be seen the grave of Laurence Sterne: and the other
the garden of the keeper's lodge at Victoria Gate, which is,
so far as I know, the only authorised burial ground for
dogs, and is crowded with little headstones marking the last
resting place of Tiny and Fido, Max and Prince and Teufel.

Kensington is of course no longer what it was; but the old Palace still stands on its eastern side, and Holland House still stands on its western side, and Kensington Square is not much injured on the south, and Aubrey House is as beautiful as ever, on the very summit of the hill, and Cam House and Holly Lodge (where Macaulay died) are untouched, below it. It is true that Church Street, which still has many signs of the past, is to be widened, and that great blocks of flats have risen and are rising—one of them to the obliteration of old Campden House, and that Earl's Terrace and Edwardes Square are to be pulled down and built over in the next few years, and that no doubt all Phillimore Terrace will soon be shops. Yet active as the builder and rebuilder are they have not been allowed to smirch this reserved and truly aristocratic neighbourhood. Notwithstanding all its flats and new houses it still has its composure and is intellectually contented. Kensington knows: you can teach it nothing.

With Edwardes Square, by the way, will vanish perhaps the best specimen of the small genteel square of a hundred years ago that still exists: every house minute, and all cheerful and acquainted with art. It is impossible to avoid the impression as one walks through it that Leigh Hunt once lived here—and as a matter of fact he did!

I said something in an earlier chapter about St. James's Street and Pall Mall and Savile Row being men's streets. Almost equally is the south pavement of Kensington High Street a preserve of women. In fact Kensington is almost wholly populated by women. Not until this year, I am told, was a boy baby ever born there—and he, to emphasise the exception and temper his loneliness, brought a twin brother with him. Why girl babies should so curiously outnumber the boy babies of Kensington is a problem which I cannot attempt to solve. The borough has plenty of scientific men in it—from Dr. Francis Galton and Professor Ray Lankester downwards—to make any hazardous conjectures of mine unnecessary; but I would suggest with all deference that the supply of girl babies may be influenced (1) by the necessity of maintaining the feminine character of the High Street, and (2) by fashion, the most illustrious and powerful woman of the last hundred years having been born at Kensington Palace. I rather lean to the second theory, for Kensington being so much under the dominion of the Victorian idea—with the Palace on the edge of it, the amazing souvenir of the queen (a kind of granite candle) in the High Street, her statue in the gardens, and a sight of the Albert Hall and Memorial inevitably on one's way into London or out of it—it is only natural that some deep impression should be conveyed.

Although Kensington Palace began its royal career with William and Mary, and it was Anne who directed Wren to add the beautiful Orangery, the triumph of the building is its association with Victoria. It was there that on May 24, 1819, she was born; and there that she was sleeping when in the small hours of June 20, 1837, the Archbishop of Canterbury and the Lord Chamberlain awakened her to hail her queen—and "I will be good," she said, very prettily, and kept her word. Both these historic rooms—the room where she was born and the room where she slept—are now incorporated in the London Museum here; and her toys you may see, her dolls' house and her dolls, dear objects to the maternal sightseer, and also her series of amazingly minute official uniforms, together with pictures of herself, her ancestors and children, in great numbers.

The Palace is principally Wren's work and is staid and comely save for a top hamper of stone on the south façade which always troubles my eye. But the little old houses north of the main building on the west are quite charming and may be used as a collyrium. Of the charm of these and many of Kensington's older houses and some of its new I have spoken in the first chapter : although I said nothing there in praise of the Princess Beatrice's stables, which are exquisitely proportioned and always give me a new pleasure.

When the first edition of this work was ready there was no London Museum. I do not pretend that anything that I then said about the want of one had any influence ; but the fact remains that there is one to-day, and its model was (as I suggested it should be) the Carnavalet in Paris. The London Museum is only in its infancy and will soon be changing its quarters.[1] The collection, as it now stands, which owes much to generous lenders, is exceedingly catholic, the word London acquiring in these rooms an elasticity sometimes beyond belief, as when the cradle of Henry V at Chepstow Castle is encountered, while a chair in which Charles Dickens once sat to be photographed, although it is true that the camera trained upon him was in a London studio, is, one feels, lucky to be here. Some more personal relic of that greatest of Londoners might, one would think, be obtained. No matter; even if the Directors' net is full of things that not every one would call strictly metropolitan fish, they all make for entertainment, and there is no real call for cavil. The personal relics are naturally the most interesting—such as the Victorian souvenirs I have already mentioned, augmented by many

[1] Stafford House is to be its new home ; but at the present moment (June, 1913) it is still at Kensington.

articles of clothing, King Edward VII's first shoes and first gloves and a tiny pair of buckskin breeches; a pair of gloves that old Sarah Jennings, Duchess of Marlborough, wore; the Duke of Kent's medicine chest, from which, no doubt, the great Queen-Empress was more than once uncomfortably dosed; Dr. Johnson's chair from Thrale's (now Barclay & Perkins's) brewery; gambling counters from the Field Club; bone passes to the theatres; a gold and crystal ring which belonged to Queen Mary II, who once resided here, so that it has returned to its old home; a little oil painting of the barges and boats returning from Nelson's funeral in St. Paul's; models of men-of-war which James II once owned; too many royal robes and dresses; three of Victoria's bonnets dated respectively 1851, 1887 and 1897; wedding-cake boxes belonging to the Royal Family; one of Edward VII's cigar cases, and I suppose he had hundreds; the Marquis of Hertford (" Lord Steyne ")'s dressing case; Phelps' costume as Wolsey in *Henry VIII*, and Sir Herbert Beerbohm Tree's in the same part; twenty-one plates from Nell Gwynne's kitchen, and Sir Thomas Gresham's steel yard. These come to memory as I write. In addition, countless pictures and prints, including an interesting series of suggested reconstructions of London and Londoners in early and prehistoric times, in which we see the palæolithic Londoners and the neolithic Londoners pursuing their daily avocations amid mammoths and savagery. That they are truly the ancestors of the present race is easily proved by a visit to a bargain-sale counter in Oxford Street.

Before descending to the Orangery and the Annexe, look again from the windows over the pleasant grounds of Kensington Palace, which now include a formal sunken garden, and away to the Round Pond with its busy naval life. One has but to narrow the vision a little, and it is the Solent in Cowes Week. And away beyond is the City of London smoking above the grimness. Truly Kensington Gardens forms a very delectable oasis. "How thick the tremulous sheep-cries come!" wrote Matthew Arnold, there, half a century ago, and it is still true; one may indeed even see the sheep sheared beneath the elms; and quite one of the most unexpected and charming things to do in London on a June morning is to have breakfast outside the pavilion near the Princes Gate entrance.

The Orangery now preserves specimens of the obsolete—or nearly obsolete—passenger vehicles of London: a four-wheeler, a hansom, and so forth. The Annexe is more interesting, for here is the great iron door from Newgate prison, with the shackles again hanging over it; and here is the famous Roman galley from the bed of the Thames, reconstructed with the tenderest care. Here also are two or three cells from Wellclose prison set up again with exactitude, and wax prisoners to show how it was done; and a very miserable sight for the young these prisoners are. On the wooden walls are carved many names still decipherable, among which I noticed those of Edward Burk, William Thompson, E. Lovemann and Francis Britain Peto. Little did any of them think, hacking away out of sheer boredom two or more centuries ago, that their names would get into a book in the year 1913.

Another rare possession of Kensington is Holland House, which stands half-way up the hill, half a mile to the west of the Palace, and may be seen dimly through the trees from the main road and, hiding behind its cedar, more or less intimately through the iron gates in Holland Walk. Holland House is the nearest country mansion to London; while in the country itself are none superior in the picturesque massing of red brick and green copper, and none stored more richly with great memories. It was built in 1607: James the First stayed there in 1612; in 1647 Cromwell and Fairfax walked up and down in the meadow before the house discussing questions of state; William Penn lived there; Addison died there, exhibiting his fortitude *in extremis* to the dissolute Earl of Warwick. At last the house came to Henry Fox, Lord Holland, father of Charles James Fox and grandfather of the famous Lord Holland, the third, who made it a centre of political and literary activity and who now sits in his chair, in bronze, under the trees close to the high road, for all the world to see. A statue of Charles James Fox stands nearer the house.

Of the great days of Holland House less than a hundred years ago let the occupant of the neighbouring Holly Lodge tell—in one of his fine flowing urbane periods :—"The time is coming when perhaps a few old men, the last survivors of our generation, will in vain seek amidst new streets and squares and railway stations for the site of that dwelling which was in their youth the favourite resort of wits and beauties, of painters and poets, of scholars, philosophers and statesmen. They will then remember with strange tenderness many objects once familiar to them, the avenue and the terrace, the busts and the paintings, the carving, the grotesque gilding, and the enigmatical mottoes. With peculiar fondness they will recall that venerable chamber in which all the antique gravity of a college library was so singularly blended with all that female grace and wit could devise to embellish a drawing-room. They will recollect, not unmoved, those shelves loaded with the varied learning of many lands and many ages, and those portraits in which were preserved the features of the best and wisest Englishmen of two generations. They will recollect how many men who have guided the politics of Europe, who have moved great assemblies by reason and eloquence, who have put life into bronze and canvas, or who have left to posterity things so written as it shall not willingly let them die, were then mixed with all that was loveliest and gayest in the society of the most splendid of capitals. They will remember the peculiar character which belonged to that circle, in which every talent and accomplishment, every art and science, had its place. They will remember how the last debate was discussed in one corner, and the last comedy of Scribe in another: while Wilkie gazed with modest admiration on Sir Joshua's Baretti, while Mackintosh turned over Thomas Aquinas to verify a quotation: while Talleyrand related his conversations with Barras at the Luxembourg, or his ride with Lannes over the field of Austerlitz. They will remember, above all, the grace, and the kindness far more admirable than grace, with which the princely hospitality of that ancient mansion was dispensed."

Within Holland House I have never set foot, but I know its gardens—English and Dutch and Japanese—and I know how beautiful they are, and when one is in them how incredible it seems that London is only just across the way, so to speak.

A little west of Holland Park, in Holland Park Road, is Leighton House, the stately home of the late Lord Leighton, which has been made over to the people as a permanent memorial of the artist. Here one may see his Moorish hall and certain personal relics, and some of his very beautiful drawings and water colour sketches of Greece and the southern seas. Exhibitions of pictures are from time to time held here. In Melbury Road, until recently, might be seen on Sunday afternoons a little collection of the

CANNON STREET STATION FROM THE RIVER

paintings of G. F. Watts, but these are now dispersed.   In
Lisgar Terrace, however, a few minutes farther west, is the
Garden Studio of the late Sir Edward Burne-Jones, the
friend and contemporary of these artists, where a number
of his drawings and paintings are permanently preserved,
to be seen on certain days by any one who presents a visit-
ing-card.   Here are the studies for many famous pictures,
here are pencil sketches, and a few unfinished works.   No
modern had a more sensitive pencil than this master, and
the Garden Studio should be sought for its drawings
alone, apart from its other treasures.

To pass from the true Kensington to South Kensington
is to leave gold for silver.   South Kensington is all wealth
and masonry.   Here are houses at a thousand a year and
buildings that assault the heavens.   The Albert Memorial
is the first of a long chain of ambitious edifices so closely
packed together as to suggest that they are models in a
show yard and if you have the courage you may order
others like them.   Albert Memorial, Albert Hall, the
Imperial Institute, the Royal College of Music, the Natural
History Museum, the School of Science and Art, the Victoria and Albert Museum, Brompton Oratory—these, together with enormous blocks of flats, almost touch each
other : a model memorial, a model concert hall, model
museums, model flats, model institutes, and so forth.

By the way, the groups of statuary at the four corners
of the base of the Albert Memorial, symbolising Europe,
Asia, Africa and America, always seem to me very felicitous
and attractive.   The bison and the cow, the elephant and
the camel, are among the kindliest animals that stone ever
shaped.   I have an artist friend who wishes to treat the
Round Pond in a similar spirit, and set up groups to celebrate Grimm and Andersen and Kate Greenaway and Lewis

Carroll—since the Round Pond is the children's Mediter-ranean. A very pretty project it seems to me ; too pretty ever to be carried out.

One thinks of the Victoria and Albert Museum as the Museum at the corner of Exhibition Road and the Crom-well Road only: but that is only part of it. The Museum extends into the Imperial Institute, where one may walk for miles, as it seems, among the wonders of the East. I cannot describe these riches: all I can say is that India, China, Japan, Persia, Egypt and Turkey have given of their best—in pottery and carving, glass and porcelain, embroidery and tapestry, bronze and jade. But nothing is to my imagination more interesting and quickening than the first thing that one sees on entering the east door in Imperial Institute Road—the façade of two houses in teak from Ahmadabad in Gujarat. This is old domestic India at a blow. They are wonderful: nothing else in the ex-hibition is so unexpected.

Crossing Exhibition Road to the Art Museum we may prepare for real pleasure once more : for this is one of the most fascinating museums in the world—filled with beauty and humanity. Not a mummy in it, not a South Sea trophy, not a fossil. All is friendly and all interesting. It is South Kensington's mission to instruct England in domestic beauty. Everything that is most beautiful and wonderful in architecture and furniture, sculpture and metal work, jewellery and embroidery, pottery and glass, may here be studied either in the original or in facsimile. The best goldsmith's work in the world is here in electro-type, the best sculpture in casts. The Venus of Milo is here, and the Laocöon, the Elgin Fates, the Marble Faun, Michael Angelo's giant David : everything famous except the Winged Victory of Samothrace, Donatello's great equestrian statue at Padua and Verrocchio's great equestrian statue at Venice; I have not found those.

It is of course impossible to write of any museum adequately, even in a whole volume, and I have but a few pages. But this I can say, that there are at South Kensington original works of decorative art — carvings, enamels, lace, pottery, metal vessels, sculpture, glass—before which one can only stand entranced, so beautiful are they. The lace and embroidery alone are worth a long journey. The Della Robbias are worth a longer. The Museum furthermore is made the despair of every collector by the custom—a very interesting one and a very valuable one—but often devastating in its triumph—of appending to many of its treasures the price that was paid for it. Some are high; but the bargains! The bargains are heart-breaking.

The Victoria and Albert Museum has been largely rebuilt since this book was written, and its new imposing façade has quite changed the neighbourhood, while from any distance its dome is nobly visible. The complete rearrangement of the treasures of this most wonderful museum will take long, but certain rooms are now fixed, among them the galleries on the right of the main entrance given to Renaissance sculpture, to which I always go first and where I remain longest. For here are certain great works the possession of which will always make us envied, even by Berlin, where Herr Bode has brought together so magnificent an assemblage of kindred masterpieces. At South Kensington Donatello may be studied in all his periods and in all his media : light relief, deep relief, marble, terra-cotta and bronze. Here is the Madonna and laughing Child of Antonio Rossellino, which I have reproduced for this edition. (Herr Bode, I may say, attributes it to Desiderio da Settignano.)

Some beautiful examples of Mino da Fiesole are also here; several Verrocchios, among them a youthful John the Baptist, illustrating the Leonardo type, as we call it, perfectly—Leonardo having studied in Verrocchio's workshop. The great and rare master himself has a relief here entitled an " Allegory of Discord ".

The next room is given to the Della Robbias—look particularly at the Child in No. 5633 by Andrea, and also at his little bagpiper in a corner—and to Michael Angelo's Cupid or Apollo; and in the next are wax sketches that might be from Michael Angelo's hand and might have been done for his giant "David" at Florence. John of Bologna, his pupil, is also here, and at the far end are two interesting heads by a modern of genius—Bastianini. But the head of a woman attributed to the school of Michael Angelo (No. 8538) is the most fascinating thing here, with its air of mischievous disdain. Below is more sculpture—French, ecclesiastical and so forth, with one distinguished case given to our own superb Alfred Gilbert, containing his exquisite "Perseus Arming," in bronze, and his silver "Victory".

Above these galleries are those in which the Salting Bequest is now displayed. We have seen the pictures which this most generous of testators left to the National Gallery; at the British Museum are his drawings; here are his porcelain, his carvings, his miniatures. They fill five rooms and alone form a monument of one man's taste and catholic acquisitiveness. All that I can say here is that everything is worth study, and that for those visitors who do not care so much for beauty as for human interest the miniatures offer a feast of delight, for not only are they very exceptional specimens but several are portraits of exceedingly pretty women. In a side case is an early painting by

Nicholas Hilliard of a courtly gentleman leaning against a tree, which has great charm, and here too are a couple of very entertaining leaves from a book of hours by Simon Benninck. The bronze medal portraits in other cases of the same room are also profoundly interesting, and it is worth mentioning here that elsewhere in the Museum are many hundreds of the best of these reproduced faithfully in electrotype as well as original. George Salting, I might say, was an Australian of great wealth who settled in London and devoted his life—he was unmarried—to the pursuit of the beautiful in art. He left all his treasures to the nation.

Other neighbouring galleries are devoted to carpets, including a prayer carpet from the mosque at Ardabil, dated 1540. That would be the date of completion; for these carpets take many families many years to weave. Here too is much lovely tapestry. Close by are fine specimens of architecture, including wonderful slate doorways from Genoa, re-erected here; the pretty brick doorway of Keats's school at Enfield; the façade of Paul Pindar's house in Bishopsgate Without; a chimney piece from North Italy by Tullio Lombardi, with the chase in full swing carved upon it; and many other exciting and suggestive examples for the young architect of the day, who, however, judging by ordinary results, does not come to South Kensington as he should, any more than the modern carpet weavers come here, or ironsmiths, or sculptors, or any other of those craftsmen and artists for whose inspiration and impulse the Museum exists.

Other ground-floor galleries contain examples of the best furniture of all times, with a few reconstructed rooms —one in white pine from Great George Street, Westminster; one from a farm-house near Alençon, with painted

15

panelling ; one in old oak from Sizergh Castle, Westmore-land, with a lovely plaster ceiling ; and one from the old palace at Bromley-by-Bow.   And everything makes one wonder what happened to English taste before English taste was sporadically born again.

In the great galleries of casts, as I have said, work of the finest Renaissance sculpture of the world is repro-duced, including not only statues but tombs, monuments, statues, altars and ciboria.   Elsewhere are the reproduc-tions of classical statuary.   Ghiberti's Baptistery gates are reproduced in painted plaster, but the wonderful earlier gates from Hildesheim Cathedral, done early in the eleventh century, are reproduced in electrotype precisely like bronze.

I say no more here, for at the catalogue desk a sixpenny book can be obtained which gives a complete bird's-eye view of all the collections, and one has but to study this for a little while before beginning the tour to understand one's way about and rightly appreciate the extent of the riches gathered here.   This catalogue desk is indeed a place to examine very thoroughly, since for a few shillings one may acquire there a valuable library.

Lastly let me say that in so far as it is definitely arranged, I know of no Museum better arranged or less tiring than are the new galleries at South Kensington, which have free lifts to every floor.

South Kensington, in addition to its own water colour collection and its Raphael cartoons, has had many valuable bequests, chief among them being the Dyce and Forster books, MSS. and pictures, the Sheepshanks collection of British paintings, the Jones bequest, the Ionides bequest, and the Constable sketches given by Miss Isabel Constable. These, with its wonderful Art Library (which is open to

HAMPSTEAD HEATH

AFTER THE PICTURE BY JOHN CONSTABLE IN THE SOUTH KENSINGTON MUSEUM

the public), its representative water colours, and its collections of etchings and Japanese prints, make it a Mecca of the art student and connoisseur of painting.

When it comes to value I suppose that the Raphael cartoons are worth all the rest of the Museum put together. To me as I have said, they are finer than anything of his at the National Gallery, and by the possession of them London, for all its dirt, can defy Rome and Florence and Paris. They have the Laocöon and the David and the Venus of Milo: we have the Elgin marbles, and Leonardo's "Holy Family," and the Raphael cartoons.

It is to South Kensington pre-eminently that one must go to study the history of English water colour painting; but I must confess to some sadness in the proceeding. The transitoriness of water colour has a depressing effect. Standing before a great oil painting of the remote past, a Velasquez, for example, a Rembrandt, or a Leonardo, one thinks only of the picture. But an old water colour painting makes me think of the dead artist. Velasquez might be living now for all the impression of decay that his work brings: but David Cox is beyond question in the grave. To pass from room to room at South Kensington among these fading pictures is to become very gloomy, very tired. Better to look at the work only of one or two men and then pass something else—Bonington for example. There is no sense of decay about Bonington's water colours. His "Verona" is one of the great things here. Nor is there any sense of decay about William James Müller, another great artist who died young and whose "Eastern Burial Ground" and "Venice" no one should miss. The harvesting scenes of Peter de Wint, a few David Coxes, John Varley's "Moel

Hebog," Callow's "Leaning Tower of Bologna" and a view of the South Downs by Copley Fielding—these also stand out in one's memory as great feats. Many Turners are here too, but for Turner's water colours the basement of the National Gallery is the place.

The Constable room is another of South Kensington's unique treasures. I would not say that his best work is here: but he never painted anything, however hurriedly, that had not greatness in it, and some of these sketches are Titanic. It is necessary to visit South Kensington if one would know this painter thoroughly—his power over weather, his mileage, his trees and valleys, his clouds and light. There is a little sketch here called "Spring" which I associate in my mind with the "Printemps" of Rousseau at the Thomy-Thierry collection in the Louvre: they are wholly different, yet each is final. There is a fishing boat here on Brighton Beach which could not be finer. And the many sketches of Dedham Vale (Constable's Fontaine-bleau) are all wonderful. You may see here his gift of finding beauty where he was. He did not need to travel over land and sea: while other painters were seeking Spain and Italy, Constable was extracting divinity from Hampstead Heath, compelling the Vale of Health to tell him its secret.

The Sheepshanks Collection of works by late Georgian and Victorian painters is interesting for its fine examples of less known masters as well as its famous works. In addition to Turner's "Royal Yacht Squadron at Cowes," a scene of golden splendour, five lovely Wilsons, two spacious and glorious landscapes by Peter de Wint, among the finest landscapes ever painted in England, three excellent Mor-lands, another divine view of Mousehold Heath by Old Crome, Gainsborough's beautiful "Queen Charlotte," and representative examples of the anecdotal school, Leslie and Webster and Landseer, the collection has an exquisite view of the Thames from Somerset House by Paul Sandby, three very interesting Ibbetsons, a good David Roberts, a Henry Dawson, very Wilsonic, a George Smith of Chichester, two William Collins and a Joshua Shaw.

The Jones Bequest, which fills a long gallery, is a kind of minor Wallace Collection—pictures, minatures and furniture, with a florid French tendency. Among the pictures are water colours by Turner and Copley Fielding, two beautiful Guardis opposite a rather similar Wilson, who in his turn is brought to one's mind by a George Smith of Chichester, a rich autumnal John Linnell, a Reynolds, a Gainsborough, a charming Vanloo—children playing musical instruments—and some interesting Tudor portraits, including Henry VIII, probably by Holbein, and Mary Queen of Scots.

To get the full value of the Dyce and Forster pictures one must be more interested in the history of the stage than I am; but here and there among them is something great with a more general appeal, such as Sir Joshua's portrait of himself. In one of the cases are some very human relics in the shape of the original MSS. of *Dombey and Son*, *Bleak House*, *Oliver Twist* and other of Dickens' novels, including *Edwin Drood*, which is open at the last page as his hand left it on the day he was stricken down to write no more. In another case is a sonnet of Keats, and in a further room is Joseph Severn's charcoal drawing of the poet's head, in Rome, just before his death.

The very interesting collection of oil paintings, drawings and etchings formed by the late Constantine Alex-

ander Ionides, one of England's wealthy Greek residents,
is to be seen at South Kensington. A small collection
representing the good taste of one humane connoisseur
offers perhaps the perfect conditions to the lover of art :
and these we have in the Ionides Bequest. The paintings are in one room, the drawings and engravings in the
other, in the centre of which is a screen wholly given to
the burin and needle of Rembrandt of the Rhine, the
greatest master that ever forced copper to his will. A
visitor to London bent upon the study of Rembrandt's
etchings would go naturally to the Print Room of the
British Museum ; but they have there no better impressions
than some of these that Mr. Ionides brought together.
The record of one of the most astonishing achievements in
the history of man is unfolded as one turns the pages of
this central screen, for, after Shakespeare (who died when
the great artist was ten), no human imagination has created
so much of human character as Rembrandt of the Rhine.
Here we are looking at only a portion of his work—his
etchings : but words fail one to put the right epithets even
to these. And there remains the work with the brush !
Here is a second state of the "Hundred Guelder piece,"
"Christ Healing the Sick," and close by it a fourth state of
that amazing work "Our Lord Before Pilate": here too in
perfect condition are the portraits of gentlemen by a gentleman—the "Young Haaring," the "Ephraim Bonus," the
"John Asselyn," the "Burgomaster Jan Six" at his window, and the etcher himself at work with a pencil. Mr.
Ionides' interest in etching extended to living masters too—
here are Whistler and Legros, Strang and Rodin. Particularly here is Millet, with his "Gleaners," his "Shepher-
dess Knitting," and other examples of simplicity and sincerity

and power.   And though the *locus classicus* for Flaxman is
University College in Gower Street, the Ionides' Flaxmans
should be asked for particularly, and also his collection of
drawings by Alphonse Legros, one of the most illustrious
of our French adopted sons, whose home has been in
England for many years, but whose genius is still far too
much a matter of the coterie.

The first painting to take the eye as one enters the
second Ionides room is Bonington's "Quay" on the screen
—an exquisite thing.   Of Bonington one can never see
too much, and here also is his oil painting of "La Place
des Molards, Geneva," injured by its very common gilt
frame.   (Like so many of the best pictures, it does not
want gilt at all.)   On other screens, which are given up
to water colours, are drawings by that great master Henri
Daumier, too little of whose work is accessible to the
English picture lover.   There are thirteen in all, of which
the "Wayside Railway Station" is perhaps the greatest,
and "The Print Collector," which it is amusing to compare
with Meissonier's at the Wallace Collection, the most
finished.   Another fascinating drawing is a sketch of
Antwerp by Hervier, a French artist of much accomplishment and charm who is also too little known in England.
I mention the oil paintings as they occur in the rather
confusing catalogue, where the advantages both of alpha-
betical and numerical arrangement are equally disdained
in favour of a labyrinthine scheme of division into nation-
alities and sub-divisions into oil and water colour and
engravings.   Guardi, whom we saw to such advantage at
the Wallace Collection, has here a decorative treatment
of a fair in the Piazza of St. Mark at Venice (No. 101),
with a sky above it of profound blue.   One of the most

charming of the old Dutch pictures is a landscape by Philip de Koninck (No. 86) which is, I think, the best work by him that I have seen; while of the new Dutch examples there is a beautiful little hay wagon by Matthew Maris (No. 90). The brothers Antoine and Louis Le Nain, of whom very few examples are to be found in England, have two pictures here, very curious and modern when one realises that they are nearly three hundred years old (Nos. 17 and 18). Corot is not quite at his best in either of his two pictures, although both are beautiful, but Courbet's "Immensité" (No. 59)—sea and sand at sunset—is wonderful. Courbet was always great. Diaz' "Baigneuse" (No. 60) is as he alone could have painted it, and Georges Michel, another French painter whose appearance on English walls is too infrequent, has a beautiful "Mill" (No. 67) that might have been derived direct from Constable and Linnell, yet is individual too. Millet's great picture here, "The Wood Sawyers" (No. 47), I do not much like: it has the air of being painted to be sold; but the other three are very interesting, especially perhaps the "Landscape" (No. 172) in the manner of Corot. Rousseau's spreading Fontainebleau tree (No. 54) is perhaps the flower of the Barbizon contribution.

Before leaving the Victoria and Albert Museum I should like to mention its admirable library of books on art which anyone may consult on paying sixpence.

The Natural History Museum, the great building to the West, in the Cromwell Road, is a Museum in the fullest sense of the word: almost everything in it is stuffed. But its interest cannot be exaggerated. Life was never so tactfully, prettily and successfully counterfeited as it is in the galleries on the ground floor, just to the left of the entrance, which contain the cases of British birds with their nests. It needs no learning in ornithology, no scientific taste, to appreciate these beautiful cases, where everything that can be done has been done to ensure realism—even to the sawing down of a tree to obtain a titmouse's nest in one of its branches. Here you may see how sand martins arrange their colonies, and here peep into the nest of the swallows beneath the eaves; but as to whether Mr. Barrie is right in thinking that they build there in order to hear fairy stories, or Hans Andersen is right in holding that their intention is to tell them, the catalogue says nothing. The Museum takes all nature for its province—from whales to humming birds, a case of which occurs charmingly at every turn: from extinct mammoths to gnats, which it enlarges in wax twenty-eight times—to the size of a creature in one of Mr. Wells' terrible books—in order that the student may make no mistake.

Perhaps the most interesting gallery in the whole building is that on the third floor devoted to men and apes, which illustrates not only the Darwinian theory (there is a statue of Darwin on the stairs) but also the indecency of science, for surely it is something worse than bad manners thus to expose the skulls of gentlemen and monkeys. The gentlemen it is true are for the most part foreigners and heathen; but none the less I came away with a disagreeable feeling that the godhead had been tarnished. The most interesting single case in the Museum is perhaps that in the great hall illustrating " Mimicry," where you may see butterflies so like leaves that you do not see them: caterpillars like twigs: and moths like lichen. Between these and the extinct monster, the Diplodocus-Carnegii—which is as long as an excursion train and seems to have been equally compounded of giraffe, elephant and crocodile, all stretched to breaking point—one can acquire, in the Cromwell Road Museum, some faint idea of the resource, ingenuity and insoluble purposes of Nature.

CHAPTER XIX

CHELSEA AND THE RIVER

Beautiful Chelsea—Turner's Last Days—St. Luke's—Church Street—
Cheyne Row's Philosopher—The Carlyles and an Intrusion—Don
Saltero's—The Publican and the Museum—Rossetti's breakfast—
The Physick Garden—The Royal Hospital—The Pensioners' coats—
London's disregard of its river—The Gulls—Speed—Whistler and
the Thames again—The National Gallery of British Art—"Every
picture tells a Story"—Old Favourites—Great English Painters—
The New Turners—Watts and Millais—The Chantrey Bequest—A
Sea-piece—Lambeth Palace.

CHELSEA has not allowed progress to injure it essentially. Although huge blocks of flats have arisen, and
Rossetti's house at No. 16 Cheyne Walk has been rebuilt
and refaced, and some very strange architectural freaks may
be observed in the neighbourhood of No. 73 (fantastic
challenges to the good taste of the older houses in the
Walk), the Embankment still retains much of its old
character and charm. London has no more attractive
sight than Cheyne Walk in Spring, when the leaves are a
tender green and through them you see the grave red bricks
and white window frames of these Anne and Georgian
houses, as satisfactory and restful as those of the Keizers-
gracht in Amsterdam.

The Walk has had famous inhabitants. To the far
western end (at No. 119) Turner retreated in his old age;
and here he lived alone as Mr. Booth,—or, as the neighbours

called him, Admiral Booth, deeming him a retired sailor—
hoping never to be found by his friends again, and it is
here that, huddled in a dressing-gown, he would climb to
the roof at day-break to watch the sun rise. And here he
died in 1851, aged nearly eighty. Sir Thomas More, whose
house stood where Beaufort Row now is—to the west of
Battersea Bridge—still lends his name to the neighbourhood; while his body rests in Chelsea Old Church, as St.
Luke's is called—a grave solid building of red brick and
stone, with a noble square tower on which a sundial and a
clock dwell side by side, not perhaps in perfect agreement
but certainly in amity. More's wife Joan is also buried
here; and here lie the mother of Fletcher the dramatist,
and the mother of George Herbert the divine poet, whose
funeral sermon was preached in the church by Dr. Donne,
and listened to by the biographer both of her son and of
her celebrant—Izaak Walton.

Church Street, Chelsea, should be explored by any one
who is interested in quaint small houses, beginning with a
fine piece of square Anne work in the shape of a free school
that appears now to be deserted and decaying. Swift,
Arbuthnot and Atterbury all lived in Church Street for a
while.

Cheyne Row, close by on the east, is made famous by
the house—No. 5—in which Carlyle lived from 1834 until
1881, there writing his *French Revolution* and *Frederick
the Great*, and there smoking with Tennyson and Fitz-
Gerald. Private piety has preserved this house as a place
of pilgrimage. It is certainly very interesting to see the
double-walled study where the philosopher wrote, and to
realise that it was by this kitchen fire that he sat with
Tennyson; to look over his books and peer at his pipes
and letters and portraits; and yet I had a feeling of in-

discretion the while. If there is any man's wash-hand-stand and bath, any woman's bed and chair, that I feel there is no need for me or the public generally to see, they are Mr. and Mrs. Carlyle's. I seemed to hear both of them distilling suitable epithets. It is not as if one could read the books or examine the letters : everything is under lock and key. There the house is, however, exactly as it was left, and better a thousand times that it should be a show for the curious than that it should be pulled down. And at any rate it contains Carlyle's death mask and a cast of his hands after death—very characteristic hands ; and his walking stick is on the wall.

The famous Don Saltero's Museum was at 18 Cheyne Walk. It is now no more ; and where are its curiosities ? Where ? Saltero was one Salter, a barber, who opened a coffee house here in 1695 and relied on his collection of oddities to draw custom. It was a sound device and should be followed. (All innkeepers should display a few curiosities · and indeed a few do. I know of one at Feltham in Sussex, and another in Camden Town ; while it was in an East Grinstead hostel that I saw Dr. Johnson's chair from the Essex Head. At Dirty Dick's in Bishopsgate Street are a few ancient relics, and Henekey's, by Gray's Inn, has an old lantern or so. But the innkeeper is not as a rule alive to his opportunities.) At the end of the eighteenth century Don Saltero's collection was dispersed. Chelsea in those days was famous also for its buns and its china. It makes neither now. Why is it that these industries decay ? Why is it that one seems to be always too late ?

It was at No. 16 Cheyne Walk that Rossetti lived, and it was here that Mr. Meredith was to have joined him, and would have done so but for that dreadful vision, on a bright May morning at noon, of the poet's breakfast—rashers cold and stiff, and two poached eggs "slowly bleeding to death" on them. In the garden at the back Rossetti kept his wild beasts. At No. 4 died Daniel Maclise, and, later, George Eliot. Passing the row of wealthy houses of which old Swan House and Clock House are the most desirable, we come to the Botanic Garden of the Royal Society of Apothecaries, with its trim walks and bewigged statue of Sir Hans Sloane in the midst. Here Linnaeus himself once strolled; but we cannot do the same, for the Physick Garden, as it used to be called, is private: yet one may peep through its gate in Swan Walk for another view of it—Swan Walk, whose square houses of an earlier day are among the most attractive in London.

Close by, however, are the Royal Hospital's gardens, which are free to all and constitute Chelsea and Pimlico's public park, filled, whenever the sun is out, with children at play. The Hospital itself, which a pleasant tradition ascribes to Nell Gwynn's kindly impulse but history credits to Charles the Second (his one wise deed perhaps), is Wren's most considerable non-ecclesiastical building in London. One would not ask it to be altered in any respect, such dignity and good sense has it; while the subsidiary buildings—officers' quarters and so forth—have charm too, with their satisfying proportions and pretty dormer windows. To be taken round the great hall by an old Irish sergeant is a very interesting experience : past the rows of tables where little groups of veterans, nearly all of them bearded, and all, without exception, smoking, are playing cards or bagatelle or reading, one of them now and then rising to hobble to the fire for a light for his pipe, over their heads hanging the flags won from a hundred battle-fields, and all around the walls portraits of great commanders. It is a noble hall. On the raised

MRS. COLMANN
AFTER THE PICTURE BY ALFRED STEVENS IN THE TATE GALLERY

platform at the end is a collection of medals belonging to old Hospitallers who left no kin to claim these trophies, and portraits, among them one of the Iron Duke, who lay here in state after his death, on a table which is still held sacred. In the chapel are more flags. The old soldiers are a more picturesque sight in summer than winter, for in winter their coats are dark blue, but in summer bright scarlet, and these very cheerfully light up the neighbouring streets and the grave precincts of their home.

In an earlier chapter I have said something of Whistler's discovery of the river at Chelsea. Certainly it is here that the urban Thames has most character. By London Bridge it is busier and more important and pretentious; by the Embankment it is more formal and well behaved; but at Chelsea it is at its best: without the fuss and the many bridges of its city course; without the prettiness and flannels of its country course: open, mysterious, and always beautiful with the beauty of gravity.

The Thames never seems to me to belong to London as it should. It is in London, but it is not part of London's life. We walk beside it as little as possible; we cross it hurriedly without throwing it more than a glance; we rarely venture on it. London in fact takes the Thames for granted, just as it takes its great men. If it led anywhere it might be more popular; but it does not. It can carry but few people home, and those are in too much of a hurry to use it; nor can it take us to the theatre or the music hall. That is why a service of Thames steamers will never pay. No one fishes in it from the sides, as Parisian idlers fish in the Seine; no one rows on it for pleasure; no one, as I have already said, haunts its banks in the search for old books and prints. Our river is not interesting to us: its Strand, one of our most crowded streets, has to be a hundred yards inland to become popular. We do not even with any frequency jump into the Thames to end our woes. Living and dying we avoid it.

The only non-utilitarian purpose to which we put the river is to feed the gulls from its bridges. During the past few years the feeding of these strange visitants has become quite a cult, so much so that on Sundays the boys do a roaring trade with penny bags of sprats. There is a fascination in watching these strong wilful birds with the cruel predatory eye and the divinely pure plumage as they swoop and soar, dart and leap, after a crumb or a fish. Every moment more gulls come and more, materialised out of nowhere, until the air just seethes with beating wings and snapping beaks. In summer they find food enough on the sea shore: it is only in winter that they come up the Thames in any numbers for London's refuse and charity.

When walking from Chelsea towards Westminster one day in the early spring of this year I saw these gulls at rest. They were on the shore of the Battersea side (somewhere near the spot where Colonel Blood hid in the rushes to shoot Charles II. as he bathed)—hundreds strong, beautiful white things against the grey mud. It was a fine afternoon and the sun made their whiteness still more radiant.

While I was standing watching them, and realising how beautiful the Chelsea river is, I was once again struck by the impression of great speed which one can get from river traffic moving at really quite a low rate. A tug came by drawing three or four empty barges. Until this invasion of unrest set in the river had been a perfect calm—not a movement on the surface, nothing but green water and blue sky, and the gulls, and Battersea Park's silent and naked trees. Suddenly this irruption. The tug was

making perhaps twelve knots (I have no means of judging)
but the effect was of terrific swiftness. She seemed with
her attendant barges to flash past. I imagine the narrowness of the river to have something to do with this illusion,
because at sea, where a much higher rate is attained, there
is no sense of speed at all. (It is true that steamers which
were as far apart as the eye could reach a few minutes ago
will meet and leave each other in an incredibly short space
of time; but the impression then filling the mind is not so
much of the speed of the boats as of the mysterious defeat
of distance.) And the quality of the speed of this tug
boat had nothing of brutality or insolence in it, as a motor-
car has: it had gaiety, mirth, a kind of cheery impudence.
It soothed as well as astonished.

On the same afternoon I was minded to enter the Tate
Gallery just to look at Whistler's exquisite nocturne of old
Battersea Bridge, which is the perfect adaptation to an
English subject of the methods of the Japanese print and
conveys the blue mystery of a London night on the river
as no other painter has ever done. I have seen all Whistler's
work: I have seen his portrait of his mother, and his
portrait of Carlyle, and his portrait of Miss Alexander.
I have seen his wonderful waves and his decorations for the
Peacock Room. I have seen his Princesse du Pays de
la Porcelaine and his Connie Gilchrist; his etchings (the
Black Lion Wharf stands before me as I write) and his
Songs on Stone; and masterly as it all is, I believe that his
London river pictures are his finest work—are the work he
was born to do above all other men. In his portraits
artifice is visible as well as art; in his best river scenes art
conquers artifice.

The Tate Gallery is in forlorn and depressing Pimlico, on
the river boundary of that decayed district, just beyond
16

Vauxhall Bridge, which for so long has been closed, and hard by that yard of ruined ships whose logs warm so many Londoners and whose historic figure-heads thrill so many boys. It is a fortunate thing—although embarrassing to the historian (but a form of embarrassment that one cannot resent)—that the Tate Gallery and the National Gallery are continually receiving additions. I write here of the Tate as it is in the spring of 1913, without reference to the loans with which it is constantly being enriched.

Built as the home of modern British art, and nobly fulfilling that destiny, the Tate has become in particular a monument to the genius of Turner, Sir Henry Tate's generosity having been supplemented by that of the late Joseph Duveen, the art dealer, to which we owe the new and superb Turner wing. How art dealers normally dispose of their wealth I know not; but undoubtedly Sir Joseph set them an example in symmetrical public benefaction.

Let us walk through the Tate Gallery in the order of its many rooms.

In No. I we find certain of the great landscape painters some of whom are also to be seen to better advantage in Trafalgar Square—Crome and his pupil Stark, Linnell, and above all Constable, in whose work we are so rich not only here and in Trafalgar Square, but also at South Kensington, where he has a room all to himself, and Burlington House. No. 1236 and 1245, notable for its Barbizon qualities, before Barbizon, are especially fine. We pass on in Room II to the old subject painters with so many of whose pictures the engravers have already made us familiar. Here are Wilkie and Webster, Mulready and Landseer, and here also is Bonington, for whose best, however, one must go to Hertford House. Room III belongs to the pre-

Raphaelites, and, since it often has valuable examples on
loan, one should make a point of visiting it periodically.
Millais, Rossetti and Burne-Jones are its giants; but
here also are Holman Hunt, who has been called the
greatest force of the School, and that powerful uncom-
promising man of genius Madox Brown, and the curiously
minute Dyce, and the exquisite William Hunt, and, out
of place here but none the less splendid, Cecil Lawson,
who painted "The Harvest Moon," that superb English
landscape over which one can see both Rembrandt and
Rubens displaying enthusiasm. Room IV is more miscellaneous. It has both Albert Moore, the delicate and
dreamy, and the direct and vigorous Sam Bough; Fred
Walker's very English tenderness, Frith's metallic "Derby
Day," a flaming sunset by Linnell, and Mason's beautiful
"Cast Shoe," wherein the sunset behaves more as it
should. Here also is that fine colourist Müller, in whose
watercolours this Gallery is elsewhere so rich, many of
them being in Room V, where the lovely Whistler nocturne
hangs, together with choice recent acquisitions, including
a superb Callow, Muirhead Bone's "Great Gantry," that
marvellous pencil drawing, and examples of Swan and
Brabazon. And so we come to the nine Turner rooms.

Of Turner my pen can say little. Before his variety
and grandeur words seem very trivial. Enough to state
that in Room V my favourites are 462, 485, 496 and 524,
and that I think 1991 in Room VII the most beautiful
thing in the whole Gallery. The Tate possesses sufficient
Turner paintings and drawings to occupy 140 pages of its
catalogue, and since from time to time those on view are
changed or interchanged with Trafalgar Square it is un-
profitable to say more of them here. Of the extraordinary
value of this collection there can be no question; and it

is peculiarly interesting to come to it, as I have done, direct from Turner's house in Cheyne Walk, where I had been thinking of the old man's last days and his passionate rapture in the rising of the sun over the river. Most of these pictures embody his attempts to translate some of that rapture into paint—once again to celebrate the orb whose light to him was life, religion, all.

With Room XV we come to the greater moderns—Mr. Sargent, Legros, Charles Furse, Mr. Sargent's "Carnation, Lily, Lily, Rose," still holding its own in spite of all its imitators. Room XVI is a very charming little hall of bronzes, with Onslow Ford's adorable "Folly" as its chief treasure, and in Room XVII we find the remarkable collection of the works of G. F. Watts given by him to the nation, of which "Love and Life" and "Love and Death" always please me most. The opposite room, XVIII, is similarly given to another great and various artist, Alfred Stevens, painter, sculptor and masterly draughtsman, who died in 1875, for further examples of whose diverse and vigorous genius one must go to South Kensington and also to St. Paul's, where his monument to Wellington, as completed by Mr. Tweed, now stands. Everything done by Stevens has the impress of a strong personality, but for me his most engaging works are his portrait of Mrs. Collmann and his lion for the British Museum railing, which may be seen in modern reproduction, fulfilling its true purpose, in Chancery Lane, opposite the Record Office.

Rooms XIX to XXV are given to purchases under the Chantrey Bequest, and it is as though a procession of old Academies had filed through, three or four pictures dropping out of each and remaining prisoners. There are a few very fine things here and many that are only mediocre   Orchardson's "Napoleon on the 'Bellerophon'" remains in the mind, and both of Mr. Arnesby Brown's landscapes, but particularly 2738, and Mr. Shannon's "Flower Girl," and Mr. Tuke's "August Blue". Upstairs is a room of odds and ends from the windows of which one may again see how true to his river was Whistler; and in various passages are good old water colours, among which I particularly like one of Müller's Avon sketches.

And so, following the river at its dreariest along Grosvenor Road, we come to Westminster; but I would like first to cross over and look at Lambeth Palace, secure in its serene antiquity, where the Archbishop of Canterbury lives. This one may do by inquiring for permission by letter to the Primate's chaplain. There is a little early English chapel here, dating from the thirteenth century, which is one of the most beautiful things in London; and the cicerone is full of kindly interest in his visitors, and of a very attractive naïve pleasure, ever being renewed, in his work as the exhibitor. The great names here are Boniface, who built the chapel, Chicheley, who built the tower, Howley, who built the residential portion and did much restoring, and such moderns as Tait and Benson, who beautified where they could. It was Archbishop Tait, for example, who set up the present windows, which follow in design those which Laud erected or amended, and which the Puritans broke on seeing, as they thought, popery in them. Laud also gave the screen, and from this Palace he went by barge—in the old stately manner of the primates—to his death. It seems to be a point of honour with the archbishops to leave some impress of their own personality on the Palace. Archbishop Benson's window in the little ante-room, or vestry, to the chapel could hardly be more charming; and the inlaid marble floor to the altar with which the present

Archbishop's name is associated is a very magnificent addition.

Long rows of Archbishops painted by the best portrait painters of their day—Holbein, Van Dyck, Lely, Hogarth, Reynolds, Romney, Gainsborough—hang on the walls of the dining hall ; but the German tourist who was making the tour of the rooms at the time that I was would not look at them. All his eyes were for the Archbishop's silver, and in particular a crumb-scoop in the form of a trowel.

CHAPTER XX AND LAST

WESTMINSTER AND WHITEHALL

Queen Anne's Gate and Mansions—The new Cathedral—The Inverted Footstool—Origins of street names—The Abbey—Writing on the Tombs—The Guides—Henry VII's Chapel—Cromwell's body—Wax-works—A window's vicissitudes—The Houses of Parliament—London's Police—Extinct Humour—London's street wit—Whitehall—Relics of Napoleon and Nelson—The Deadly Maxims—The End.

DESPITE the rebuilder Westminster is still very good to wander in, for it has the Abbey and the little old streets behind the Abbey, and St. James's Park, and Queen Anne's Gate, that most beautiful stronghold of eighteenth century antiquity—while close by it, to emphasise its beauty and good taste, are Queen Anne's Mansions. I always think that one gets a sufficiently raw idea of the human rabbit-warren from the squares of paper and marks of stairs and floors and partitions that are revealed on the walls when a house is in course of demolition: a sight very common in London ; but I doubt if the impression of man's minuteness and gregariousness is so vivid as that conveyed by the spectacle of Queen Anne's Mansions by St. James's Park station—surely the ugliest block of buildings out of America, and beyond doubt the most aggressively populous.

Westminster's architectural variety is by no means exhausted in the buildings I have named, for between the Army and Navy Stores and Victoria station (which I fancy is Pimlico) is the wonderful new Byzantine Roman

Catholic Cathedral, a gigantic mass of elaborate brickwork which within is now merely the largest barn in England but will one day be lustrous with marble. It is characteristic of London methods that a building so ambitious and remarkable as this should have been packed into an enclosed space from which a sight of it as a whole from any point of view is impossible. Its presence here, in the very heart of flat-land, would be hardly less amazing to the simple intelligence of George III than was that of the apple within the dumpling. One is conscious that it is vast and domineering and intensely un-English, but of its total effect and of its proportions, whether good or bad, one knows nothing. The lofty tower is of course visible from all points. Sometimes it has mystery and sometimes not, the effect depending upon the amount of it that is disclosed. From Victoria station I have seen it through a slight haze wearing an unearthly magical beauty; and again from another point it has been merely a factory chimney with a desire for sublimity.

Whatever opinion one may hold as to the architectural scheme of the new cathedral, there can be no doubt as to its nobility as sheer building, and no question of the splendid courage behind its dimensions. It appears to me to conquer by vastness alone, and I seem to discern a certain grim humour in these people setting as near their old time Westminster cathedral as might be this new and flauntingly foreign temple, in which the Abbey and St. Margaret's could both be packed, still leaving interstices to be filled by a padding of city churches.

For one of London's oddest freaks of ecclesiastical architecture you have only to seek Smith Square, just behind the Abbey, and study the church of St. John the Evangelist, the peculiar oddity of which is its four belfries, one at each corner. I used to be told when I lived within sound of its voice that the shape of this church was due to a passionate kick on the part of the wealthy lady who endowed it, and who, in disgust at the plans submitted by her architect, projected the footstool across the room. "There," said she, pointing to it as it lay upside down, "build it like that"; and the architect did. That is the Westminster legend, and it is probably false—a derivative from the church's shape rather than the cause of it. St. John's, however, has something more interesting to offer than its design, for it was here that the scathing author of *The Rosciad* and other satires—Charles Churchill, who was born close by in Vine Street (now Romney Street) and educated close by at Westminster School—held for a while the position of curate and lecturer, in succession to his gentle old father. Churchill's name is forgotten now, but during the four years in which he blazed it was a menace and a power.

Smith Square still contains two or three of Westminster's true Georgian houses, of which there were so many when I lived in Cowley Street twelve years ago. New roads and new buildings, including the towering pile of offices and flats which the Ecclesiastical Commissioners have just erected, as reckless of the proportions of this neighbourhood as of its traditions, have ruined Westminster. Barton Street still holds out; but for how long? Either Dean's Yard must go soon or the flat-projectors will die of broken hearts.

Barton Street took its name from Barton Booth, the actor, who invested his savings in property at Westminster. Cowley Street is named after Barton's native village in Middlesex, and has no association with Cowley the poet, although when I lived there I used to be told that it was from him that it took its style. Such is oral tradition! There is indeed no need to invent any origin for London's street names: their real origin is interesting enough. Why Mount Street? Because Oliver's Mount, a point in the fortification lines round London made by the Parliamentarians in 1643, stood here. Why Golden Square? Because in the neighbourhood was an inn called "The Gelding," which gave its name to the square and was then modified by the inhabitants because they did not like it. Why Hay Hill? Because the Aye or Eye brook once ran there: hence also the two Brook Streets. But the local tradition probably involves a load of dried grass. Why Westbourne Grove? Because of the West Bourne, another stream, now flowing underground into the Serpentine.

Why Covent Garden? Because it was the garden, not for the sale but for the culture of vegetables, belonging to the Convent: that is, the Abbey of Westminster. Why Chelsea? Because the river used to cast up a "chesel" of sand and pebbles. Selsey in Sussex is the same word. Why Cheapside? Because at the east end of it was a market place called Cheaping. Why the Hummums? Merely a Londonisation of Hammam, or Turkish Bath, which it was before it became a hotel. Why the Isle of Dogs? Because when Greenwich was a royal resort the kennels were here. Why the Strand? Because it was on the shore of the Thames. Why Bayswater? Because one of William the Conqueror's officers, Bainardus of Normandy, became possessed of the land hereabout (as of Baynard's Castle in Sussex) and one of his fields at Paddington was called Baynard's Water or Watering. Why Pall Mall? Because the old game of Pall Mall was played there. Why Birdcage Walk? Because Charles II had an aviary there. Why Storey's Gate? Because Edward Storey, keeper of the aviary, lived hard by. Why Millbank? Because a water mill stood where St. Peter's wharf now is turned by the stream that ran through the Abbey orchard (the Abbey orchard!) down Great College Street. This was one of the streams that made Thorney Island, on which Westminster Abbey and the Houses of Parliament stand. It is an island no longer, because the streams which divided it from the main land have been dammed and built over ; but an island it was, its enisling waters being the Mill Bank stream, the Thames, a brook which ran down Gardiner's Lane, and, on the east, the Long Ditch in Prince's Street. Why was Westminster so called ? Because St. Paul's was the parent and the Abbey was its western dependency—the west minster.

And here, by way of Dean's Yard, we enter the Abbey, which really needs a volume to itself. Indeed the more I think about it the more reluctant my pen is to behave at all. An old children's book which I happen to have been glancing at this morning, called *Instructive Rambles in London and the adjacent Villages*, 1800, puts the case in a nutshell. "On entering the Abbey the grandeur and solemnity of the whole struck them forcibly ; and Charles, addressing his father, said, 'By the little I already see, sir, I should think that instead of a single morning it would take many days, nay even weeks, to explore and examine into all the curious antiquities of this building'." His father agreed with him, and so do I. Equally true is it that it would take many weeks to record one's impressions. To say nothing would perhaps be better : merely to re- mark "And here we enter the Abbey" and pass on. But I must, I think, say a little.

So much has it been restored, and so crowded is it (to the exclusion of long views), that one may say that the interest of the more public part of the Abbey resides rather in its associations with the dead than in its architecture.

To see it as a thing of beauty one must go east of the altar—to the exquisite chapel of Henry VII. The Abbey proper has nothing to show so beautiful as this, grave and vast and impressive as it is; but even with this its real wonderfulness comes from its dead. For if we except the great soldiers and sailors and painters who lie at St. Paul's, and the great poet at Stratford on Avon, almost all that is most august and illustrious in English history and literature reposes here.

Entering by the north transept you come instantly upon the great statesmen, the monument to Chatham, at first only a white blur in the dim religious light, being so close to the door. Palmerston, Canning and Gladstone are near by. The younger Pitt and Fox lie here too, but their monuments are elsewhere. We have seen so many of Fox's London residences: this is the last. Beneath the north aisle of the nave lie also men of science—Newton and Darwin and Herschel. In the south aisle of the nave are the graves or monuments of various generals and governors, Kneller,[1] the painter, Isaac Watts, who wrote the hymns, John and Charles Wesley and Major André.

Poets' Corner, which is a portion of the south transept, loses something of its impressiveness by being such a huddle and also by reason of certain trespassers there: a fault due to lax standards of taste in the past. Had it been realised that the space of Westminster Abbey was limited, the right of burial there would long ago have been recognised as too high an honour to be given indiscriminately to all to whom the label of poet was applied. We now use the word with more care. The Rev. William Mason and Nicholas Rowe, John Phillips and St. Evremond, even

---

[1] Kneller refused to be buried in the Abbey: "They do bury such fools there," he said.

WESTMINSTER ABBEY

Gay and Prior, strike one in the light of interlopers. Only by dying when they did could they have found their way hither. And certain of the monuments are far too large, particularly that to John, Duke of Argyll and Greenwich, by the exuberant Roubilliac,—no matter how Canova may have admired it. The plain slabs that cover Johnson and Dickens, Browning and Tennyson, are more to one's liking; or such simple medallions as that to Jenny Lind. Shakespeare and Milton are only commemorated here; but Chaucer and Spenser, Jonson ("O rare Ben Jonson" runs his epitaph) and Dryden, Gray and Cowley—all these and many others lie at Westminster. Ben Jonson was buried standing, near the north wall of the nave, in eighteen inches of ground square. His inscription cost eighteen-pence.

So far all has been free; but the choir is not free (except on Mondays), and you must be conducted there officially. The Abbey guides are good and not impatient men, with quite enough history for ordinary purposes and an amusing pride in their powers of elocution. They lead their little flock from chapel to chapel, like shepherds in the East, treading as familiarly among the dust of kings as if it were the open street.

The first chapel, St. Benedict's, has only one queen, and she a poor unhappy slighted creature—Anne of Cleves; the second chapel, St. Edmund's, has none, the Jane Seymour that lies here being the daughter of the Protector Somerset. Yet here are many noble bodies, notably the Earl and Countess of Shrewsbury; and Eleanor de Bohun beneath a fine brass; and the little sister and brother of the Black Prince, with tiny alabaster figures of themselves atop, who died as long ago as 1340. Here also, a modern among these medievalists, lies the author of *Zanoni*

and *My Novel*. A crusader by the doorway testifies to the
old laxity of rules regarding visitors, for he is cut all over
with names and initials and dates—just as the backs of the
figures in the Laocöon group beneath the Vatican are
scribbled by Italian sightseers. How many persons know
who it was that first scratched his initials on an Abbey
tomb? Of all men, Izaak Walton, who cut his monogram
on Casaubon's stone in the south transept in 1658.

The next chapel, St. Nicholas's, is the burial place of
the Percys, a family which still has the right to lie here.
Here also are the parents of the great Duke of Buckingham, in marble on the lid of their tomb, and in dust
below it; and here lies the great Burleigh. Both this
chapel and that of St. Edmund call for coloured glass.

We come now to the south aisle of Henry VII's chapel
and get a foretaste of the glories of that shrine. A very
piteous queen lies here, Mary Queen of Scots, brought
hither from Peterboro' by her son James I, and placed
within this tomb. Charles the Second lies here also, and
William and Mary and Anne and General Monk, and
here is a beautiful bronze of the mother of Henry VII.
In the north aisle is dust still more august, for here is the
tomb of Elizabeth, erected by James I with splendid im-
partiality. Her sister, Queen Mary, lies here too, but
the guide is himself more interested, and takes care that
you are more interested, in the marble cradle containing
the marble figure of the little Sophia, the three-day-old
daughter of James I; in the tomb of the little Lady Mary;
and in the casket containing the remains of the murdered
princes, brought hither from the Tower. A slab in the
floor marks the grave of Joseph Addison, the creator of
Sir Roger de Coverley, who wrote in the *Spectator* a passage
on the Abbey and its mighty dead which should be in

every one's mind as they pass from chapel to chapel of this wonderful choir.

And so we come to the Abbey's most beautiful part— Henry VII's chapel, which is London's Sainte Chapelle. It is perhaps the most beautiful chapel in England, and beyond question the most wonderful, since not only is it an architectural jewel but it holds the dust of some of our greatest monarchs. If Henry VII had done nothing else he would live by this. Woodwork and stonework are alike marvellous, but the ceiling is the extraordinary thing —as light almost as lace, and as delicate. Not the least beautiful things here are the two stone pillars supporting the altar above the grave of Edward VI. Henry VII's tomb is in the chantry at the back of the altar, and in the same vault lies James I. George II and the Guelphs who are buried here have no monuments, but the blackguard Duke of Buckingham whom Fenton stabbed is celebrated by one of the most ambitious tombs in the Abbey, with every circumstance of artificial glory and a row of children to pray for him and women to weep. The Duke of Richmond, another friend of James I, is hardly less floridly commemor- ated—close to the tomb of Dean Stanley.

A slab in the next chapel or bay marks the grave where Cromwell lay. After the Restoration, however, when the country entered upon a new age of gold under Charles II, one of the first duties of the Londoner was to remove the Protector's body and treat it as of course it so richly deserved. It was therefore decapitated : the trunk was thrown into a pit at Tyburn and the head was set up on Westminster Hall so firmly that it was more than twenty years before it fell during a high wind. Charles the Second having reigned quite long enough, it was perhaps felt that justice had been done ; so the skull was not returned to its pinnacle but allowed to pass into reverent keeping. Cromwell's statue may now be seen, with a lion at his feet, in the shadow of Westminster Hall. The wheel has come full circle : he is there.

Compared with the chapel of Edward the Confessor behind the high altar, to which we now come, that of Henry VII is in age a mere child. Here we pass at once to the thirteenth century, Edward I being the ruling spirit. His tomb is here—the largest and plainest in the Abbey—and here lies his wife Eleanor, for whom the Crosses were built —one of the prettiest thoughts that a King ever had—a cross at every place where her body rested on its way from the North to London, Charing's Cross being the last. Edward the Confessor lies in the shrine in the midst : Henry V in that to the north of it, and preserved above are the saddle, the sword and helmet that he used at Agincourt. But popular interest in this chapel centres in the coronation chair that is kept here, in which every king and queen has sat since Edward I.

We come lastly to the chapel of St. John the Evangelist, crowded with tombs, of which by far the most beautiful, and in some ways the most beautiful in the Abbey, is that of Sir Francis Vere, copied from Michael Angelo : four warriors holding a slab on which are the dead knight's accoutrements. A cast of this tomb is in South Kensington. The guide, however, draws attention rather to Roubilliac's masterpiece—in which Death, emerging from a vault, thrusts a dart at Mrs. Nightingale, while Mr. Nightingale interposes to prevent the catastrophe. At Père la Chaise this would seem exceedingly happy and appropriate ; but it suits not our austere Valhalla. Hidden away behind the great tomb of Lord Norris are statues of John Philip Kemble and his illustrious sister Mrs. Siddons.

NOON

FROM THE PAINTING BY COROT IN THE NATIONAL GALLERY

With the possible exception of the Voltaire and one or two of the heads from the Reign of Terror, there is nothing at Madame Tussaud's so interesting as the waxworks belonging to the Dean and Chapter of Westminster, hidden away up a winding stair over the next chapel—Abbot Islip's. These one should certainly make an effort to see, for they are very quaint and they probably approximate very closely to life. The Charles the Second one can believe in absolutely, and Elizabeth too. Nelson ought not to be there at all, since he was buried at St. Paul's and these figures were originally made to rest upon the Abbey graves until the permanent memorial was ready; but all the sightseers being diverted from Westminster to St. Paul's, after Nelson's funeral, the wise Minor Canons and lay vicars (who took the waxwork profits) set up a rival Nelson of their own. It is a beautiful figure anyway.

In the cloisters, which to my mind are more alluring to wander in than the Abbey itself, are other tombs, for never were the dead so packed as they are here. Among those that lie here, chiefly clerical, are a few Thespians: Foote and Betterton and Mrs. Bracegirdle and Aphra Behn, and here lies Milton's friend who wrote a sweet book of airs, Mr. Henry Lawes, and the prettiest of short epitaphs is here too: "Jane Lister, dear childe, 1688". The cloisters lead to the ancient Chapter House, an octagonal room dating from the thirteenth century, which once was all the Parliament house England had, and to the Chamber of the Pyx, where the royal jewels were kept before they went to the Tower; and from the cloisters you gain the residences of the Canons of the Abbey, where all live in the odour and harmony of sanctity. The Deanery hides round the corner to the left as you enter from Dean's Yard, from which you also gain Westminster School, where Ben Jonson

17

and George Herbert, Dryden and Prior, Sir Christopher Wren and Gibbon, Warren Hastings and Cowper, were educated—the only historic public school left in London.

St. Margaret's, the little church under the shadow of the Abbey, like its infant child, must be visited for one of the finest windows in England, so rich and grave—a window with a very curious history. It was given by the magistrates of Dordrecht to Henry VII for his Chapel in the Abbey, but as he died before it could be erected, Henry VIII presented it to Waltham Abbey, little thinking how soon he was going to dissolve that establishment. The last Abbot transferred it to New Hall in Essex, which passed through many hands—Sir Thomas Boleyn's, Queen Elizabeth's, the Earl of Sussex's, the great Duke of Buckingham's, Oliver Cromwell's and General Monk's. It was during General Monk's ownership of New Hall that the window was taken from its place and buried in the ground for fear it should be broken by Roundheads, who had a special grudge against glass and the noses of stone saints It was disinterred when all was safe, but did not reach St. Margaret's until 1758. In this church Sir Walter Raleigh is buried, and here was married Samuel Pepys and (for the second time) John Milton. Latimer preached Lenten sermons here before Edward VI; and it was in the churchyard that Cowper, a boy at Westminster School, was standing when a sexton digging a grave threw out a skull which hit him on the leg and began that alarm of his conscience which the sinister eloquence of John Newton was to maintain with such dire results.

Of the Houses of Parliament I find myself with nothing to say. They are, I often think, beautiful; and then I wonder if they are, or are merely clever. Certainly if the Victoria Tower is the right size the Clock Tower is too slender. The best view is from the embankment walk by

St. Thomas's hospital: seen across the water the long low line of delicate stone is very happy and the central spire could not be more charming. And yet should there be so much ornament, so much daintiness? Should not our senate, should not our law courts, be plain honest buildings innocent of fantastic masonry and architectural whimsies? Somerset House, Hampton Court, Chelsea Hospital, St. James's Palace, the old Admiralty—should we not adhere to their simplicity, their directness? Yet the Houses of Parliament lighted up make a fascinating picture postcard for the young.

Years ago, when I lived in Cowley Street and still reverenced men and senators, I used on my way home at night to loiter a little in Parliament Square in the hope of seeing the demigods whom our caricaturists had made it so easy to recognise: Sir William Harcourt with a thousand chins; Mr. Gladstone submerged in his collar; Mr. Bowles with his wooden legs and iron hooks. Those were great days, when a Member of Parliament was something exalted and awful. But now all is changed. I am older and the House is transformed. Members of Parliament are three a penny, and knowing quite a number personally, I loiter in Parliament Square no more.

The whole British Empire is administered between Parliament Square and Trafalgar Square. All the Government offices are here; and whatever Parliament may be doing, their work goes on just the same.

New Scotland Yard is here too: on the right, a huge square red building which was planned for an opera house, abandoned when its foundations were all built, and then was bought by the Government for a central police station. (The two other new opera houses which have been erected in London in recent times are now music halls.) Having need for larger premises, the authorities have just built a second block, which is joined to the parent edifice by one of the most massive bridges in London—a very fine arch indeed, as impressive as the little Venetian flying passage between the Grand Hotel and its annexe at Charing Cross is delicate and fanciful.

Without its police London could not be London. They are as much landmarks as its public buildings, and are almost as permanent and venerable. The Londoner has a deep respect for his police, and not a little fear too; it is only on the Music Hall stage that they are ridiculed. A policeman on duty is often assaulted in a rage, but he is never made fun of. Probably no public servant so quickly assumes dignity and importance. I suppose that before they are policemen they are ordinary, impulsive, even foolish, country youths of large stature (the only London policeman I ever knew in the chrysalis stage was a high-spirited fast bowler); but instantly the uniform and the boots are donned they become wise and staid, deliberate and solid, breathing law and order. It is one of the best examples of the triumph of clothes. I am not sure but that a policeman's helmet is not a better symbol of London than the dome of St. Paul's: they are indeed rather similar.

The policeman as a preserver of order is less noticeable in London than as a friend, a counsellor, a preserver of the amenities. He regulates the traffic, and from his glove there is no appeal. He takes old ladies and nursemaids across the road, he writes in his book the particulars of collisions, he conveys the victims of motor-cars to the hospital, he tells strangers the way to the Abbey. The London policeman is indeed the best friend of the foreigner and the provincial. They need never be at a loss if a

VIRGIN AND CHILD

AFTER THE PICTURE BY ANDREA DEL SARTO IN THE WALLACE COLLECTION

policeman is in sight, and they will not do amiss if they address him as "Inspector".

London, as I have said, fears its policemen. Drink now and then brings a man into open defiance, and on Boat Race night the young barbarians of Oxford and Cambridge import into the West End a certain exuberance foreign to this grey city; but for the most part the policeman's life is uneventful, and his authority is unchallenged. The practical joker who used to overturn the Charleys in their boxes (that thin and tedious jest) is extinct. We have no high spirits any more: they have gone out, they are not good form. Theodore Hook, who stands for the highest of all, would die of ennui could he visit again glimpses of a London moon: Theodore Hook, some of whose "ordinary habits," I read in a work on the London of his day, "were to hang pieces of meat on the bell-handles of suburban villas, in the evening, so that during the night every stray dog that happened to pass would give a tug; by this means the bell would be set ringing five times an hour to the consternation of the family, who, with candles in hand, might in vain search the garden, or peep into the road for the cause. He would cut signboards in half, and affix the odd pieces to each other, so that the signboard owners next day would have the pleasure of witnessing their various occupations interpreted by the most ridiculous announcements in the world. He would stitch his friend's clothes up in such a fashion that when, on the following morning, the friend got into them, the conclusion that he would at once jump to was that he had from some extraordinary and unaccountable cause become fearfully swelled during the night—a conclusion which Hook would take care to confirm by expressing his great concern at his friend's appearance, and entreating him to be allowed to call a doctor."

These were some of his "ordinary habits." What a man! He would also "carry a Highlander from a tobacconist's shop, after dark, and stagger with it towards a cab, in which he would deposit the painted figure, giving the cabman the address perhaps of some influential person, and bidding him drive carefully as the gentleman inside was a nobleman slightly intoxicated." But this kind of ebullient Londoner is quite extinct, as I have said, and I suppose that it is that kill-joy the policeman who has made him so. The police have come in since Hook's time : perhaps he made them imperative. Nothing can so dispirit a practical joker as the large firm hand of the law. The law may to some extent have become a respecter of persons, but it still has no nose for a joke. The law refers all jokers to the scrutiny of the police station, which brings to bear upon them a want of sympathy more than Caledonian.

London can still produce the wag in great numbers, but his efforts are entirely verbal and are too little his own. It is the habit to extol the street wit of London; but with the best wish in the world, I for one have heard very little of it. For the most part it consists in repeating with or without timeliness some catchword or phrase of the Music Halls. It was customary to credit the old 'bus drivers with an apt and ready tongue; but my experience was that their retorts were either old or pointless. Show me a 'bus driver, I used to say, and I will show you a man who is not witty. If he were he would not be a 'bus driver. The new chauffeur drivers are too busy for any form of speech witty or otherwise.

The drivers of London all dip into the same long-filled reservoir of sarcasm, from which no new draught has emerged these fifty years. But tradition made the 'bus driver witty, just as it made the late Herbert Campbell funny ; and it will persist.

As noticeable as the London driver's want of real wit is his want of freemasonry. Every driver's hand is turned against every other. No policy of vexatiousness is too petty for one to put in practice against another: they "bore," they impede, they mock, they abuse each other; while owing to the laxity of police supervision, the narrowness of every London street is emphasised by the selfishness with which the middle of the road is kept. It ought to be compulsory for all slow moving vehicles—all that do not want to pass others—to hug the near kerb. As it is, they keep far too near the middle and reduce the width of the roadway by nearly half.

To return for a moment to the police, if you would know them at their most charming you must leave an umbrella in a cab and then go to Scotland Yard to recover it ; for the men who have charge of this department (which is the nearest thing to the Paris Morgue that London possesses) are models of humorous urbanity. Surrounded for ever by dead umbrellas, harassed day by day by the questions of a thousand urgent incoherent ladies, they are still composed and grave and polite. A visit to the adjoining office for lost miscellaneous property will convince one in a moment that there is nothing that human beings are unable to leave behind them in a London cab.

The old Palace of Whitehall consists now only of the great banqueting hall from which Charles I walked to the scaffold on the tragic morning of January 30, 1649. It was through the second window from the north end, and the scaffold was built out into the street: old prints commemorate the event—the shameful event, may I never cease to think it. There is one such print in the hall itself, in the same case with the king's beautiful silk vest that he wore on the fatal day.

Whitehall now contains some of the most interesting

relics in the world; but it is a Museum whose interest is
now and then almost too poignant. I, for one, simply
cannot look with composure at the Napoleon relics from
Longwood, least of all at the chair in which he always sat.
The mere thought of that caged eagle at St. Helena is
almost more than one can bear: and these little intimate
tokens of his captivity are too much. Yet for stronger
eyes there they are at Whitehall, including the skeleton of
his favourite horse Marengo.

Here also are relics of Nelson—the last letter he wrote
to his dearest Emma, in his nervous modern hand, just
before Trafalgar, expressing the wish soon to be happy
with her again; the clothes he used to wear; his purse; a
portion of the Union Jack that covered him on the *Victory*,
for pieces of which his sailors fought among each other;
the telescope he put to his blind eye; the sword he was
using when his arm was wounded; the mast of the *Victory*, with a cannon ball through it; and a hundred other
souvenirs of England's most fascinating hero, the contemplation of which is lifted by the magic of his personality,
the sweetness and frailty of it, above vulgar curiosity.

To pass from Nelson to Wellington is like exchanging
summer for winter: poetry for prose: romance for science;
yet it must be done. Here among other things is Wellington's umbrella, the venerable Paul Pry gamp which he
carried in his political days in London, even as Premier,
and which is as full of character as anything of his that I
ever saw, and wears no incongruous air amid such tokens
of his military life as the flags around the gallery which he
captured from the French. No one really knows the Iron
Duke until he has seen this umbrella. Such an umbrella!
If one were confronted with it as a stranger and asked to
name its owner, Wellington would be the last man one would

think of; yet directly one is told it was Wellington's, one says, " Whose else could it be? Wellington's. Of course."

Among other treasures in this Museum are the jaws of famous or infamous sharks, one of which was thirty-seven feet long ; wonderful models of boats made under difficulties by French prisoners out of mutton bones and such unlikely material—the French prisoners vying always with the patient Chinese carver of cherry stones for the championship of the world in ingenuity ; Cromwell's sword ; Drake's snuff box and walking stick ; relics of Sir John Moore ; relics of Sir John Franklin ; relics of Collingwood ; a model of the first battleship to carry guns, the prettiest, gayest, most ingratiating junk of a boat, which put to sea to guard our shores in 1486 ; two bottles of port from the *Royal George,* no doubt intended for the refreshment of the brave Kempenfeldt ; and very interesting plans of the battles of Trafalgar and Waterloo. All these and many other objects are displayed with much pride and not a little simple eloquence by an old soldier. Certainly there is in London no more interesting room than this : not only for its history but its present possessions.

Beneath, in the vaults, is a museum of artillery. Old guns and modern guns, naval guns and field guns, models of forts, shells and grenades, and all the paraphernalia of licensed killing may be studied here under the guidance of another old soldier, whose interest in his work never flags, and who shows you with much gusto how to work a Maxim gun which fires 670 rounds a minute, and at 2000 yards can be kept playing backwards and forwards on a line of men four hundred yards long. " Acts like a mowing machine," says the smiling custodian. " Beautiful ! Cuts 'em down like grass. Goes through three at once sometimes, one behind the other." It was with the unique and perplexing capabilities of this machine, perfected A.D. 1904, in my mind, that I emerged into Whitehall again, and was conscious instantly on the other side of the way of the Horse Guard sentries, each motionless on his steed. "I know what's in store for you," I thought to myself "Cut's 'em down like grass. . . . Goes through three at once sometimes." Such things make it almost a work of supererogation to be born: reduce a mother's pangs to a travesty; at least when she is the mother of a soldier. How odd it all is!—Nature on the one hand building us up so patiently, so exquisitely, cell on cell, and on the other Sir Hiram Maxim arranging for his bullets to go through three at once! It is too complicated for me. I give it up.

And so, through the obvious and comparatively unperplexing traffic of Whitehall, we come to Charing Cross again and to the end of these rambles, not because there is no more to say (for I have hardly begun yet) but because one must not go on too long. As a Londoner of Londoners, whose knowledge of the town, it has been put on record, was extensive and peculiar—far more so than mine will ever be—once remarked, the art of writing a letter is to leave off at such a point as will "make them wish there was more". And when one is writing a book one would like to do the same.

THE VICTORIA TOWER, HOUSE OF LORDS

INDEX

The names of painters are omitted from this Index

A

Abernethy, 183
Ackermann, and his *Repository*, 104
Adam, the Brothers, 91
Addison, death of, 219
— on the Abbey tombs, 254
Adelphi, the, 90, 91, 93
Ainsworth's *The Tower of London*, 152, 153
Albert Memorial, 62, 215, 221
— Hall, 215, 221
Aldersgate Street, 129
Aldgate, 168, 171, 172
Alien, a princely, in Bloomsbury, 191
Ambassadors' Yard, 45
Americans, 112, 189
Anarchists, 198
Apsley House, 2-4
Archbishops at Lambeth Palace, 245, 246
Architecture in London, 4-8, 18, 48, 56, 91, 99, 103, 104, 109, 110, 113, 123, 125-127, 141, 152, 169, 181, 183, 187, 188, 190, 216, 221, 235, 236, 245, 247-249, 255, 259, 260
Astor Estate Office, 7, 11, 90, 91
Aubrey House, 14, 214
— Walk, 12
" Auld Robin Gray," 38

B

Babies, Kensington, 215
Bacon, Francis, and Gray's Inn, 182
Bartholomew Close, 126

Bartholomew Fair, 127
Beardsley, Aubrey, 190
Bedford, Duke of, and Bloomsbury, 190
Beggars' Opera, The, 111
Bentham, Jeremy, embalmed, 190
Berkeley Square, 33, 38, 39
Beverages of the past, 130, 131
Billingsgate, 123
Birkbeck Bank, its bas-reliefs, 62
Bishop's Wood, 130
Blenheim, battle of, relics of, at the Tower, 155
Blood, Colonel, 154, 240
Bloomsbury, 181, 184-191
Blücher in London, 45
Bohemia, Queen of, portrait of, 64
Booth, Barton, 249
Borough, 172, 175
Botanical Gardens, 209
Boyer, James, and Coleridge, 186
Bracegirdle, Mrs., 111
Brick Court, Temple, 108
British Museum—
    Roman Emperors, 193
    Graeco-Roman sculptures, 193. 194
    Greek ante-room, 194
    Ephesus Room, 194
    Elgin Marbles, 195
    Terra-cottas, 195
    Bronzes, 195
    Ancient Egypt, 196
    Pottery, 196
    Medieval Room, 196
    Gems, 196
    Hall of Inscriptions, 196
    Books and MSS., 197

267

PRINTED IN GREAT BRITAIN AT THE UNIVERSITY PRESS, ABERDEEN

A SELECTION OF BOOKS PUBLISHED BY METHUEN AND CO. LTD. LONDON 36 ESSEX STREET W.C. 2

CONTENTS

A SELECTION OF

MESSRS. METHUEN'S

PUBLICATIONS

IN this Catalogue the order is according to authors.

Colonial Editions are published of all Messrs. METHUEN'S Novels issued at a price above 4s. net, and similar editions are published of some works of General Literature. Colonial Editions are only for circulation in the British Colonies and India.

All books marked net are not subject to discount, and cannot be bought at less than the published price. Books not marked net are subject to the discount which the bookseller allows.

The prices in this Catalogue are liable to alteration without previous notice.

Messrs. METHUEN'S books are kept in stock by all good booksellers. If there is any difficulty in seeing copies, Messrs. Methuen will be very glad to have early information, and specimen copies of any books will be sent on receipt of the published price *plus* postage for net books, and of the published price for ordinary books.

This Catalogue contains only a selection of the more important books published by Messrs. Methuen. A complete catalogue of their publications may be obtained on application.

Andrewes (Lancelot). PRECES PRI-VATAE. Translated and edited, with Notes, by F. E. BRIGHTMAN. *Cr. 8vo.* 7s. 6d. net.

Aristotle. THE ETHICS. Edited, with an Introduction and Notes, by JOHN BURNET. *Demy 8vo.* 15s. net.

Atkinson (T. D.). ENGLISH ARCHI-TECTURE. Illustrated. *Fourth Edition. Fcap. 8vo.* 6s. net.

A GLOSSARY OF TERMS USED IN ENGLISH ARCHITECTURE. Illus-trated. *Second Edition. Fcap. 8vo.* 6s. net.

Atteridge (A. H.). FAMOUS LAND FIGHTS. Illustrated. *Cr. 8vo.* 7s. 6d. net.

Baggally (W. Wortley). TELEPATHY: GENUINE AND FRAUDULENT. *Cr. 8vo.* 3s. 6d. net.

Bain (F. W.). A DIGIT OF THE MOON: A HINDOO LOVE STORY. *Twelfth Edition. Fcap. 8vo.* 5s. net.

THE DESCENT OF THE SUN : A CYCLE OF BIRTH. *Seventh Edition. Fcap. 8vo.* 5s. net.

A HEIFER OF THE DAWN. *Ninth Edition. Fcap. 8vo.* 5s. net.

IN THE GREAT GOD'S HAIR. *Sixth Edition. Fcap. 8vo.* 5s. net.

A DRAUGHT OF THE BLUE. *Sixth Edition. Fcap. 8vo.* 5s. net.

AN ESSENCE OF THE DUSK. *Fourth Edition. Fcap. 8vo.* 5s. net.

AN INCARNATION OF THE SNOW. *Fourth Edition. Fcap. 8vo.* 5s. net.

A MINE OF FAULTS. *Fourth Edition. Fcap. 8vo.* 5s. net.

THE ASHES OF A GOD. *Second Edition. Fcap. 8vo.* 5s. net.

BUBBLES OF THE FOAM. *Second Edition. Fcap. 4to.* 7s. 6d. net. Also *Fcap. 8vo.* 5s. net.

A SYRUP OF THE BEES. *Fcap. 4to.* 7s. 6d. net. Also *Fcap. 8vo.* 5s. net.

THE LIVERY OF EVE. *Second Edition. Fcap. 4to.* 7s. 6d. net. Also *Fcap 8vo.* 5s. net.

AN ECHO OF THE SPHERES. Rescued from Oblivion by F. W. BAIN. *Wide Demy 8vo.* 10s. 6d. net.

Balfour (Graham). THE LIFE OF ROBERT LOUIS STEVENSON. *Fif-teenth Edition. In one Volume. Cr. 8vo.* Buckram, 7s. 6d. net.

Baring (Hon. Maurice). LANDMARKS IN RUSSIAN LITERATURE. *Third Edition. Cr. 8vo.* 7s. 6d. net.

THE RUSSIAN PEOPLE. *Second Edition. Demy 8vo.* 15s. net.

A YEAR IN RUSSIA. *Cr. 8vo. 7s. 6d. net.*

Baring-Gould (S.). THE TRAGEDY OF THE CÆSARS: A STUDY OF THE CHARACTERS OF THE CÆSARS OF THE JULIAN AND CLAUDIAN HOUSES. Illustrated. *Seventh Editon. Royal 8vo. 15s. net.*

A BOOK OF CORNWALL. Illustrated. *Third Edition. Cr. 8vo. 7s. 6d. net.*

A BOOK OF DARTMOOR. Illustrated. *Third Edition. Cr. 8vo. 7s. 6d. net.*

A BOOK OF DEVON. Illustrated. *Third Edition. Cr. 8vo. 7s. 6d. net.*

Baring-Gould (S.) and Sheppard (H. F.). A GARLAND OF COUNTRY SONG. English Folk Songs with their Traditional Melodies. *Demy 4to. 7s. 6d. net.*

Baring-Gould (S.), Sheppard (H. F.), and Bussell (F. W.). SONGS OF THE WEST. Folk Songs of Devon and Cornwall. Collected from the Mouths of the People. New and Revised Edition, under the musical editorship of CECIL J. SHARP. *Second Edition. Large Imperial 8vo. 7s. 6d. net.*

Barker (E.). GREEK POLITICAL THEORY: PLATO AND HIS PREDECESSORS. *Demy 8vo. 14s. net.*

Bastable (C. F.). THE COMMERCE OF NATIONS. *Eighth Edition. Cr. 8vo. 5s. net.*

Beckford (Peter). THOUGHTS ON HUNTING. Edited by J. OTHO PAGET. Illustrated. *Third Edition. Demy 8vo. 7s. 6d. net.*

Belloc (H.). PARIS. Illustrated. *Third Edition. Cr. 8vo. 7s. 6d. net.*

HILLS AND THE SEA. *Ninth Edition. Fcap. 8vo. 6s. net.*

ON NOTHING AND KINDRED SUBJECTS. *Fourth Edition. Fcap. 8vo. 6s. net.*

ON EVERYTHING. *Fourth Edition. Fcap. 8vo. 6s. net.*

ON SOMETHING. *Third Edition. Fcap. 8vo. 6s. net.*

FIRST AND LAST. *Second Edition. Fcap. 8vo. 6s. net.*

THIS AND THAT AND THE OTHER. *Second Edition. Fcap. 8vo. 6s. net.*

MARIE ANTOINETTE. Illustrated. *Fourth Edition. Demy 8vo. 18s. net.*

THE PYRENEES. Illustrated. *Second Edition. Demy 8vo. 10s. 6d. net.*

Bennett (Arnold). THE TRUTH ABOUT AN AUTHOR. *Fcap. 8vo. 5s. net.*

Bennett (W. H.). A PRIMER OF THE BIBLE. *Fifth Edition. Cr. 8vo. 4s. net.*

Bennett (W. H.) and Adeney (W. F.). A BIBLICAL INTRODUCTION. With a concise Bibliography. *Sixth Edition. Cr. 8vo. 8s. 6d. net. Also in Two Volumes. Cr. 8vo. Each 5s. net.*

Berriman (Algernon E.). AVIATION. Illustrated. *Second Edition. Cr. 8vo. 12s. 6d. net.*

MOTORING. Illustrated. *Demy 8vo. 12s. 6d. net.*

Bicknell (Ethel E.). PARIS AND HER TREASURES. Illustrated. *Fcap. 8vo. Round corners. 6s. net.*

Blake (William). ILLUSTRATIONS OF THE BOOK OF JOB. With a General Introduction by LAURENCE BINYON. Illustrated. *Quarto. £1 1s. net.*

Bloemfontein (Bishop of). ARA CŒLI: AN ESSAY IN MYSTICAL THEOLOGY. *Seventh Edition. Cr. 8vo. 5s. net.*

FAITH AND EXPERIENCE. *Third Edition. Cr. 8vo. 5s. net.*

THE CULT OF THE PASSING MOMENT. *Fourth Edition. Cr. 8vo. 5s. net.*

THE ENGLISH CHURCH AND RE-UNION. *Cr. 8vo. 5s. net.*

Brabant (F. G.). RAMBLES IN SUSSEX. Illustrated. *Cr. 8vo. 7s. 6d. net.*

Braid (James). ADVANCED GOLF. Illustrated. *Eighth Edition. Demy 8vo. 12s. 6d. net.*

Bulley (M. H.). ANCIENT AND MEDIEVAL ART. Illustrated. *Cr. 8vo. 7s. 6d. net.*

Carlyle (Thomas). THE FRENCH REVOLUTION. Edited by C. R. L. FLETCHER. *Three Volumes. Cr. 8vo. 18s. net.*

THE LETTERS AND SPEECHES OF OLIVER CROMWELL. With an Introduction by C. H. FIRTH, and Notes and Appendices by S. C. LOMAS. *Three Volumes. Demy 8vo. 18s. net.*

Chambers (Mrs. Lambert). LAWN TENNIS FOR LADIES. Illustrated. *Second Edition. Cr. 8vo. 5s. net.*

Chesterton (G. K.). CHARLES DICKENS. With two Portraits in Photogravure. *Eighth Edition. Cr. 8vo. 7s. 6d. net.*

THE BALLAD OF THE WHITE HORSE. *Fifth Edition.* 6s. net.

ALL THINGS CONSIDERED. *Tenth Edition. Fcap. 8vo.* 6s. net.

TREMENDOUS TRIFLES. *Fifth Edition. Fcap. 8vo.* 6s. net.

ALARMS AND DISCURSIONS. *Second Edition. Fcap. 8vo.* 6s. net.

A MISCELLANY OF MEN. *Second Edition. Fcap. 8vo.* 6s. net.

WINE, WATER, AND SONG. *Ninth Edition. Fcap. 8vo.* 1s. 6d. net.

Clausen (George). ROYAL ACADEMY LECTURES ON PAINTING. Illustrated. *Cr. 8vo.* 7s. 6d. net.

Clephan (R. Coltman). THE TOURNAMENT: Its Periods and Phases. With Preface by CHAS. J. FFOULKES. Illustrated. *Royal 4to.* £2 2s. net.

Clutton-Brock (A.). THOUGHTS ON THE WAR. *Ninth Edition. Fcap. 8vo.* 1s. 6d. net.

WHAT IS THE KINGDOM OF HEAVEN? *Cr. 8vo.* 5s. net.

Conrad (Joseph). THE MIRROR OF THE SEA: Memories and Impressions. *Fcap. 8vo.* 5s. net.

Coulton (G. G.). CHAUCER AND HIS ENGLAND. Illustrated. *Second Edition. Demy 8vo.* 12s. 6d. net.

Cowper (William). POEMS. Edited, with an Introduction and Notes, by J. C. BAILEY. Illustrated. *Demy 8vo.* 12s. 6d. net.

Cox (J. C.). RAMBLES IN SURREY. Illustrated. *Second Edition. Cr. 8vo.* 7s. 6d. net.

RAMBLES IN KENT. Illustrated. *Cr. 8vo.* 7s. 6d. net.

Dalton (Hugh). WITH BRITISH GUNS IN ITALY. Illustrated. *Cr. 8vo.* 8s. 6d. net.

Davis (H. W. C.). ENGLAND UNDER THE NORMANS AND ANGEVINS: 1066-1272. *Fifth Edition. Demy 8vo.* 12s. 6d. net.

Day (Harry A.), F.R.H.S. SPADECRAFT: OR, HOW TO BE GARDENER. *Second Edition. Cr. 8vo.* 2s net.

VEGECULTURE: HOW TO GROW VEGETABLES, SALADS, AND HERBS IN TOWN AND COUNTRY. *Second Edition. Cr. 8vo.* 2s. net.

THE FOOD-PRODUCING GARDEN. *Cr. 8vo.* 2s. net.

Dearmer (Mabel). A CHILD'S LIFE OF CHRIST. Illustrated. *Fourth Edition. Large Cr. 8vo.* 6s. net.

Dickinson (Sir G. L.). THE GREEK VIEW OF LIFE. *Eleventh Edition. Cr. 8vo.* 5s. net.

Ditchfield (P. H.). THE VILLAGE CHURCH. *Second Edition.* Illustrated. *Cr. 8vo.* 6s. net.

THE ENGLAND OF SHAKESPEARE. Illustrated. *Cr. 8vo.* 6s. net.

Dowden (J.). FURTHER STUDIES IN THE PRAYER BOOK. *Cr. 8vo.* 6s. net.

Durham (The Earl of). THE REPORT ON CANADA. With an Introductory Note. *Second Edition. Demy 8vo.* 7s. 6d. net.

Egerton (H. E.). A SHORT HISTORY OF BRITISH COLONIAL POLICY. *Fifth Edition. Demy 8vo.* 10s. 6d. net.

'Etienne.' A NAVAL LIEUTENANT, 1914-1918. Illustrated. *Cr. 8vo.* 8s. 6d. net.

Fairbrother (W. H.). THE PHILOSOPHY OF T. H. GREEN. *Second Edition. Cr. 8vo.* 5s. net.

ffoulkes (Charles). THE ARMOURER AND HIS CRAFT. Illustrated. *Royal 4to.* £2 2s. net.

DECORATIVE IRONWORK. From the XIth to the XVIIIth Century. Illustrated. *Royal 4to.* £2 2s. net.

Firth (C. H.). CROMWELL'S ARMY. A History of the English Soldier during the Civil Wars, the Commonwealth, and the Protectorate. Illustrated. *Second Edition. Cr. 8vo.* 7s. 6d. net.

Fisher (H. A. L.). THE REPUBLICAN TRADITION IN EUROPE. *Cr. 8vo.* 7s. 6d. net.

FitzGerald (Edward). THE RUBÁIYÁT OF OMAR KHAYYÁM. Printed from the Fifth and last Edition. With a Commentary by H. M. BATSON, and a Biographical Introduction by E. D. ROSS. *Cr. 8vo.* 7s. 6d. net.

Fyleman (Rose). FAIRIES AND CHIMNEYS. *Fcap. 8vo. Fourth Edition.* 3s. 6d. net.

Garstin (Crosby). THE MUD-LARKS AGAIN. *Fcap. 8vo. 3s. 6d. net.*

Gibbins (H. de B.). INDUSTRY IN ENGLAND: HISTORICAL OUTLINES. With Maps and Plans. *Ninth Edition. Demy 8vo. 12s. 6d. net.*

THE INDUSTRIAL HISTORY OF ENGLAND. With 5 Maps and a Plan. *Twenty-sixth Edition. Cr. 8vo. 5s.*

Gibbon (Edward). THE DECLINE AND FALL OF THE ROMAN EMPIRE. Edited, with Notes, Appendices, and Maps, by J. B. BURY. Illustrated. *Seven Volumes. Demy 8vo. Illustrated. Each 12s. 6d. net. Also in Seven Volumes. Cr. 8vo. Each 7s. 6d. net.*

Gladstone (W. Ewart). GLADSTONE'S SPEECHES: DESCRIPTIVE INDEX AND BIBLIOGRAPHY. Edited by A. TILNEY BASSETT. With a Preface by VISCOUNT BRYCE, O.M. *Demy 8vo. 12s. 6d. net.*

Glover (T. R.). THE CONFLICT OF RELIGIONS IN THE EARLY ROMAN EMPIRE. *Seventh Edition. Demy 8vo. 10s. 6d. net.*

POETS AND PURITANS. *Second Edition. Demy 8vo. 10s. 6d. net.*

FROM PERICLES TO PHILIP. *Second Edition. Demy 8vo. 10s. 6d. net.*

VIRGIL. *Third Edition. Demy 8vo. 10s. 6d. net.*

THE CHRISTIAN TRADITION AND ITS VERIFICATION. (The Angus Lecture for 1912.) *Second Edition. Cr. 8vo. 6s. net.*

Grahame (Kenneth). THE WIND IN THE WILLOWS. *Eighth Edition. Cr. 8vo. 7s. 6d. net.*

Griffin (W. Hall) and **Minchin (H. C.).** THE LIFE OF ROBERT BROWNING. Illustrated. *Second Edition. Demy 8vo. 12s. 6d. net.*

Haig (K. G.). HEALTH THROUGH DIET. *Fourth Edition. Cr. 8vo. 6s. net.*

Hale (J. R.). FAMOUS SEA FIGHTS: FROM SALAMIS TO TSU-SHIMA. Illustrated. *Third Edition. Cr. 8vo. 7s. 6d. net.*

Hall (H. R.). THE ANCIENT HISTORY OF THE NEAR EAST FROM THE EARLIEST TIMES TO THE BATTLE OF SALAMIS. Illustrated. *Fourth Edition. Demy 8vo. 16s. net.*

Hannay (D.). A SHORT HISTORY OF THE ROYAL NAVY. Vol. I., 1217-1688. *Second Edition.* Vol. II., 1689-1815. *Demy 8vo. Each 10s. 6d. net.*

Harker (Alfred). THE NATURAL HISTORY OF IGNEOUS ROCKS. With 112 Diagrams and 2 Plates. *Demy 8vo. 15s. net.*

Harper (Charles G.). THE 'AUTOCAR' ROAD-BOOK. With Maps. *Four Volumes. Cr. 8vo. Each 8s. 6d net.*

I.—SOUTH OF THE THAMES.

II.—NORTH AND SOUTH WALES AND WEST MIDLANDS.

III.—EAST ANGLIA AND EAST MIDLANDS.

IV.—THE NORTH OF ENGLAND AND SOUTH OF SCOTLAND.

Hassall (Arthur). THE LIFE OF NAPOLEON. Illustrated *Demy 8vo. 10s. 6d. net.*

Henley (W. E.). ENGLISH LYRICS: CHAUCER TO POE. *Second Edition. Cr. 8vo. 6s. net.*

Hill (George Francis). ONE HUNDRED MASTERPIECES OF SCULPTURE. Illustrated. *Demy 8vo. 12s. 6d. net.*

Hobhouse (L. T.). THE THEORY OF KNOWLEDGE. *Second Edition. Demy 8vo. 15s. net.*

Hobson (J. A.). INTERNATIONAL TRADE: AN APPLICATION OF ECONOMIC THEORY. *Cr. 8vo. 5s. net.*

PROBLEMS OF POVERTY: AN INQUIRY INTO THE INDUSTRIAL CONDITION OF THE POOR. *Eighth Edition. Cr. 8vo. 5s. net.*

THE PROBLEM OF THE UNEMPLOYED: AN INQUIRY AND AN ECONOMIC POLICY. *Sixth Edition. Cr. 8vo. 5s. net.*

GOLD, PRICES AND WAGES: WITH AN EXAMINATION OF THE QUANTITY THEORY. *Second Edition. Cr. 8vo. 5s. net.*

Hodgson (Mrs. W.). HOW TO IDENTIFY OLD CHINESE PORCELAIN. Illustrated. *Third Edition. Post 8vo. 7s. 6d. net.*

Holdsworth (W. S.). A HISTORY OF ENGLISH LAW. *Four Volumes. Vols. I., II., III. Each Second Edition. Demy 8vo. Each 15s. net.*

Hutt (C. W.). CROWLEY'S HYGIENE OF SCHOOL LIFE. Illustrated. *Second and Revised Edition. Cr. 8vo. 6s. net.*

Hutton (Edward). THE CITIES OF UMBRIA. Illustrated. *Fifth Edition. Cr. 8vo. 7s. 6d. net.*

THE CITIES OF LOMBARDY. Illustrated. *Cr. 8vo. 7s. 6d. net.*

THE CITIES OF ROMAGNA AND THE MARCHES. Illustrated. *Cr. 8vo. 7s. 6d. net.*

FLORENCE AND NORTHERN TUSCANY, WITH GENOA. Illustrated. *Third Edition. Cr. 8vo. 7s. 6d. net.*

SIENA AND SOUTHERN TUSCANY. Illustrated. *Second Edition. Cr. 8vo. 7s. 6d. net.*

VENICE AND VENETIA. Illustrated. *Cr. 8vo. 7s. 6d. net.*

NAPLES AND SOUTHERN ITALY. Illustrated. *Cr. 8vo. 7s. 6d. net.*

ROME. Illustrated. *Third Edition. Cr. 8vo. 7s. 6d. net.*

COUNTRY WALKS ABOUT FLORENCE. Illustrated. *Second Edition. Fcap. 8vo. 6s. net.*

THE CITIES OF SPAIN. Illustrated. *Fifth Edition. Cr. 8vo. 7s. 6d. net.*

Ibsen (Henrik). BRAND. A Dramatic Poem, translated by WILLIAM WILSON. *Fourth Edition. Cr. 8vo. 5s. net.*

Inge (W. R.). CHRISTIAN MYSTICISM. (The Bampton Lectures of 1899.) *Fourth Edition. Cr. 8vo. 7s. 6d. net.*

Innes (A. D.). A HISTORY OF THE BRITISH IN INDIA. With Maps and Plans. *Second Edition. Cr. 8vo. 7s. 6d. net.*

ENGLAND UNDER THE TUDORS. With Maps. *Fifth Edition. Demy 8vo. 12s. 6d. net.*

Innes (Mary). SCHOOLS OF PAINTING. Illustrated. *Third Edition. Cr. 8vo. 8s. net.*

Jenks (E.). AN OUTLINE OF ENGLISH LOCAL GOVERNMENT. *Third Edition.* Revised by R. C. K. ENSOR. *Cr. 8vo. 5s. net.*

A SHORT HISTORY OF ENGLISH LAW: FROM THE EARLIEST TIMES TO THE END OF THE YEAR 1911. *Demy 8vo. 10s. 6d. net.*

Johnston (Sir H. H.). BRITISH CENTRAL AFRICA. Illustrated. *Third Edition. Cr. 4to. 18s. net.*

THE NEGRO IN THE NEW WORLD. Illustrated. *Crown 4to. £1 1s. net.*

Julian (Lady) of Norwich. REVELATIONS OF DIVINE LOVE. Edited by GRACE WARRACK. *Sixth Edition. Cr. 8vo. 5s. net.*

Keats (John). POEMS. Edited, with Introduction and Notes, by E. de SÉLINCOURT. With a Frontispiece in Photogravure. *Third Edition. Demy 8vo. 10s. 6d. net.*

Keble (John). THE CHRISTIAN YEAR. With an Introduction and Notes by W. LOCK. Illustrated. *Third Edition. Fcap. 8vo. 5s. net.*

Kelynack (T. N.), M.D., M.R.C.P. THE DRINK PROBLEM OF TO-DAY IN ITS MEDICO-SOCIOLOGICAL ASPECTS. *Second and Revised Edition. Demy 8vo. 10s. 6d. net.*

Kidd (Benjamin). THE SCIENCE OF POWER. *Eighth Edition. Cr. 8vo. 7s. 6d. net.*

Kipling (Rudyard). BARRACK-ROOM BALLADS. 189th Thousand. *Cr. 8vo. Buckram, 7s. 6d. net. Also Fcap. 8vo. Cloth, 6s. net; leather, 7s. 6d. net.*
Also a Service Edition. *Two Volumes. Square fcap. 8vo. Each 3s. net.*

THE SEVEN SEAS. 140th Thousand. *Cr. 8vo. Buckram, 7s. 6d. net. Also Fcap. 8vo. Cloth, 6s. net; leather, 7s. 6d. net.*
Also a Service Edition. *Two Volumes. Square fcap. 8vo. Each 3s. net.*

THE FIVE NATIONS. 120th Thousand. *Cr. 8vo. Buckram, 7s. 6d. net. Also Fcap. 8vo. Cloth, 6s. net; leather, 7s. 6d. net.*
Also a Service Edition. *Two Volumes. Square fcap. 8vo. Each 3s. net.*

THE YEARS BETWEEN. *Cr. 8vo. Buckram, 7s. 6d. net. Also on thin paper. Fcap. 8vo. Blue cloth, 6s. net; Limp lambskin, 7s. 6d. net.*
Also a Service Edition. *Two volumes. Square fcap. 8vo. Each 3s. net.*

DEPARTMENTAL DITTIES. 84th Thousand. *Cr. 8vo. Buckram, 7s. 6d. net. Also Fcap. 8vo. Cloth, 6s. net; leather, 7s. 6d. net.*
Also a Service Edition. *Two Volumes. Square fcap. 8vo. Each 3s. net.*

HYMN BEFORE ACTION. Illuminated. *Fcap. 4to. 1s. 6d. net.*

RECESSIONAL. Illuminated. *Fcap. 4to. 1s. 6d. net.*

TWENTY POEMS FROM RUDYARD KIPLING. 360th Thousand. *Fcap. 8vo. 1s. net.*

Lamb (Charles and Mary). THE COMPLETE WORKS. Edited by E. V. LUCAS. *A New and Revised Edition in Six Volumes. With Frontispieces. Fcap. 8vo. Each 6s. net.*

The volumes are :—

I. MISCELLANEOUS PROSE. II. ELIA AND THE LAST ESSAYS OF ELIA. III. BOOKS FOR CHILDREN. IV. PLAYS AND POEMS. V. and VI. LETTERS.

Lane-Poole (Stanley). A HISTORY OF EGYPT IN THE MIDDLE AGES. Illustrated. *Second Edition, Revised. Cr. 8vo. 9s. net.*

Lankester (Sir Ray). SCIENCE FROM AN EASY CHAIR. Illustrated. *Eighth Edition. Cr. 8vo. 7s. 6d. net.*

SCIENCE FROM AN EASY CHAIR. *Second Series.* Illustrated. *First Edition. Cr. 8vo. 7s. 6d. net.*

DIVERSIONS OF A NATURALIST. Illustrated. *Second Edition. Cr. 8vo. 7s. 6d. net.*

Lewis (Edward). EDWARD CARPENTER: AN EXPOSITION AND AN APPRECIATION. *Second Edition. Cr. 8vo. 6s. net.*

Lock (Walter). ST. PAUL, THE MASTER BUILDER. *Third Edition. Cr. 8vo. 5s. net.*

THE BIBLE AND CHRISTIAN LIFE. *Cr. 8vo. 6s. net.*

Lodge (Sir Oliver). MAN AND THE UNIVERSE: A STUDY OF THE INFLUENCE OF THE ADVANCE IN SCIENTIFIC KNOWLEDGE UPON OUR UNDERSTANDING OF CHRISTIANITY. *Ninth Edition. Crown 8vo. 7s. 6d. net.*

THE SURVIVAL OF MAN: A STUDY IN UNRECOGNISED HUMAN FACULTY. *Seventh Edition. Cr. 8vo. 7s. 6d. net.*

MODERN PROBLEMS. *Cr. 8vo. 7s. 6d. net.*

RAYMOND; OR, LIFE AND DEATH. Illustrated. *Eleventh Edition. Demy 8vo. 15s. net.*

THE WAR AND AFTER: SHORT CHAPTERS ON SUBJECTS OF SERIOUS PRACTICAL IMPORT FOR THE AVERAGE CITIZEN IN A.D. 1915 ONWARDS. *Eighth Edition. Fcap. 8vo. 2s. net.*

Loreburn (Earl). CAPTURE AT SEA. *Second Edition. Cr. 8vo. 2s. 6d. net.*

HOW THE WAR CAME. With a Map. *Cr. 8vo. 7s. 6d. net.*

Lorimer (George Horace). LETTERS FROM A SELF-MADE MERCHANT TO HIS SON. Illustrated. *Twenty-fourth Edition. Cr. 8vo. 6s. net.*

OLD GORGON GRAHAM. Illustrated. *Second Edition. Cr. 8vo. 6s. net.*

Lorimer (Norma). BY THE WATERS OF EGYPT. Illustrated. *Third Edition. Cr. 8vo. 7s. 6d. net.*

Lucas (E. V.). THE LIFE OF CHARLES LAMB. Illustrated. *Sixth Edition. Demy 8vo. 10s. 6d. net.*

A WANDERER IN HOLLAND. Illustrated. *Sixteenth Edition. Cr. 8vo. 8s. 6d. net.*

A WANDERER IN LONDON. Illustrated. *Eighteenth Edition, Revised. Cr. 8vo. 8s. 6d. net.*

LONDON REVISITED. Illustrated. *Third Edition. Cr. 8vo. 8s. 6d. net.*

A WANDERER IN PARIS. Illustrated. *Thirteenth Edition. Cr. 8vo. 8s. 6d. net. Also Fcap. 8vo. 6s. net.*

A WANDERER IN FLORENCE. Illustrated. *Sixth Edition. Cr. 8vo. 8s. 6d. net.*

A WANDERER IN VENICE. Illustrated. *Second Edition. Cr. 8vo. 8s. 6d. net.*

THE OPEN ROAD: A LITTLE BOOK FOR WAYFARERS. *Twenty-seventh Edition. Fcap. 8vo. 6s. 6d. net. India Paper, 7s. 6d. net.*
Also Illustrated. Cr. 4to. 15s. net.

THE FRIENDLY TOWN: A LITTLE BOOK FOR THE URBANE. *Ninth Edition. Fcap. 8vo. 6s. net.*

FIRESIDE AND SUNSHINE. *Ninth Edition. Fcap. 8vo. 6s. net.*

CHARACTER AND COMEDY. *Eighth Edition. Fcap. 8vo. 6s. net.*

THE GENTLEST ART: A CHOICE OF LETTERS BY ENTERTAINING HANDS. *Tenth Edition. Fcap. 8vo. 6s. net.*

THE SECOND POST. *Fifth Edition. Fcap. 8vo. 6s. net.*

HER INFINITE VARIETY: A FEMININE PORTRAIT GALLERY. *Eighth Edition. Fcap. 8vo. 6s. net.*

GOOD COMPANY: A RALLY OF MEN. *Fourth Edition. Fcap. 8vo. 6s. net.*

ONE DAY AND ANOTHER. *Seventh Edition. Fcap. 8vo. 6s. net.*

OLD LAMPS FOR NEW. *Sixth Edition. Fcap. 8vo. 6s. net.*

LOITERER'S HARVEST. *Third Edition. Fcap. 8vo. 6s. net.*

CLOUD AND SILVER. *Third Edition. Fcap. 8vo. 6s. net.*

LISTENER'S LURE: AN OBLIQUE NARRATION. *Twelfth Edition. Fcap. 8vo. 6s. net.*

OVER BEMERTON'S: AN EASY-GOING CHRONICLE. *Sixteenth Edition. Fcap. 8vo. 6s. net.*

MR. INGLESIDE. *Twelfth Edition. Fcap. 8vo. 6s. net.*

LONDON LAVENDER. *Twelfth Edition. Fcap. 8vo. 6s. net.*

LANDMARKS. *Fifth Edition. Fcap. 8vo. 6s. net.*

THE BRITISH SCHOOL : AN ANECDOTAL GUIDE TO THE BRITISH PAINTERS AND PAINTINGS IN THE NATIONAL GALLERY. *Fcap. 8vo. 6s. net.*

A BOSWELL OF BAGHDAD, AND OTHER ESSAYS. *Third Edition. Fcap. 8vo. 6s. net.*

'TWIXT EAGLE AND DOVE. *Third Edition. Fcap. 8vo. 6s. net.*

Lydekker (R.). THE OX AND ITS KINDRED. Illustrated. *Cr. 8vo. 7s. 6d. net.*

Macaulay (Lord). CRITICAL AND HISTORICAL ESSAYS. Edited by F. C. MONTAGUE. *Three Volumes. Cr. 8vo. 18s. net.*

Macdonald (J. R. M.). A HISTORY OF FRANCE. *Three Volumes. Cr. 8vo. Each 10s. 6d. net.*

McDougall (William). AN INTRODUCTION TO SOCIAL PSYCHOLOGY. *Twelfth Edition. Cr. 8vo. 7s. 6d. net.*

BODY AND MIND : A HISTORY AND A DEFENCE OF ANIMISM. *Fourth Edition. Demy 8vo. 12s. 6d. net.*

Maeterlinck (Maurice). THE BLUE BIRD : A FAIRY PLAY IN SIX ACTS. Translated by ALEXANDER TEIXEIRA DE MATTOS. *Fcap. 8vo. 6s. net. Also Fcap. 8vo. 2s. net.* Of the above book Forty-one Editions in all have been issued.

MARY MAGDALENE : A PLAY IN THREE ACTS. Translated by ALEXANDER TEIXEIRA DE MATTOS. *Third Edition. Fcap. 8vo. 5s. net. Also Fcap. 8vo. 2s. net.*

DEATH. Translated by ALEXANDER TEIXEIRA DE MATTOS. *Fourth Edition. Fcap. 8vo. 3s. 6d. net.*

OUR ETERNITY. Translated by ALEXANDER TEIXEIRA DE MATTOS. *Second Edition. Fcap. 8vo. 6s. net.*

THE UNKNOWN GUEST. Translated by ALEXANDER TEIXEIRA DE MATTOS. *Third Edition. Cr. 8vo. 6s. net.*

POEMS. Done into English Verse by BERNARD MIALL. *Second Edition. Cr. 8vo. 5s. net.*

THE WRACK OF THE STORM. *Third Edition. Cr. 8vo. 6s. net.*

THE MIRACLE OF ST. ANTHONY : A PLAY IN ONE ACT. Translated by ALEXANDER TEIXEIRA DE MATTOS. *Fcap. 8vo. 3s. 6d. net.*

THE BURGOMASTER OF STILE-MONDE : A PLAY IN THREE ACTS. Translated by ALEXANDER TEIXEIRA DE MATTOS. *Fcap. 8vo. 5s. net.*

THE BETROTHAL; OR, THE BLUE BIRD CHOOSES. Translated by ALEXANDER TEIXEIRA DE MATTOS. *Fcap. 8vo. 6s. net.*

MOUNTAIN PATHS. Translated by ALEXANDER TEIXEIRA DE MATTOS. *Fcap. 8vo. 6s. net.*

Mahaffy (J. P.). A HISTORY OF EGYPT UNDER THE PTOLEMAIC DYNASTY. Illustrated. *Second Edition. Cr. 8vo. 9s. net.*

Maitland (F. W.). ROMAN CANON LAW IN THE CHURCH OF ENGLAND. *Royal 8vo. 10s. 6d. net.*

Marett (R. R.). THE THRESHOLD OF RELIGION. *Third Edition. Cr. 8vo. 7s. 6d. net.*

Marriott (J. A. R.). ENGLAND SINCE WATERLOO. With Maps. *Second Edition, Revised. Demy 8vo. 12s. 6d. net.*

Masefield (John). A SAILOR'S GARLAND. Selected and Edited. *Second Edition. Cr. 8vo. 6s. net.*

Masterman (C. F. G.). TENNYSON AS A RELIGIOUS TEACHER. *Second Edition. Cr. 8vo. 7s. 6d. net.*

Medley (D. J.). ORIGINAL ILLUSTRATIONS OF ENGLISH CONSTITUTIONAL HISTORY. *Cr. 8vo. 8s. 6d. net.*

Miles (Eustace). LIFE AFTER LIFE; OR, THE THEORY OF REINCARNATION. *Cr. 8vo. 3s. 6d. net.*

THE POWER OF CONCENTRATION : How TO ACQUIRE IT. *Fifth Edition. Cr. 8vo. 6s. net.*

PREVENTION AND CURE. *Second Edition. Crown 8vo. 5s. net.*

Miles (Mrs. Eustace). HEALTH WITHOUT MEAT. *Sixth Edition. Fcap. 8vo. 1s. 6d. net.*

Millais (J. G.). THE LIFE AND LETTERS OF SIR JOHN EVERETT MILLAIS. Illustrated. *Third Edition. Demy 8vo. 12s. 6d. net.*

Milne (J. G.). A HISTORY OF EGYPT UNDER ROMAN RULE. Illustrated. *Second Edition. Cr. 8vo. 9s. net.*

Money (Sir Leo Chiozza). RICHES AND POVERTY, 1910. *Eleventh Edition. Demy 8vo. 5s. net.*

Montague (C. E.). DRAMATIC VALUES. *Second Edition. Fcap. 8vo. 5s. net.*

Myers (Charles S.). PRESENT-DAY APPLICATIONS OF PSYCHOLOGY. *Third Edition. Fcap. 8vo. 1s. 3d. net.*

Noyes (Alfred). A SALUTE FROM THE FLEET, AND OTHER POEMS. *Third Edition. Cr. 8vo. 7s. 6d. net.*

RADA: A BELGIAN CHRISTMAS EVE. Illustrated. *Fcap. 8vo. 5s. net.*

Oman (C. W. C.). A HISTORY OF THE ART OF WAR IN THE MIDDLE AGES. Illustrated. *Demy 8vo. 15s. net.*

ENGLAND BEFORE THE NORMAN CONQUEST. With Maps. *Third Edition, Revised. Demy 8vo. 12s. 6d. net.*

Oxenham (John). BEES IN AMBER: A LITTLE BOOK OF THOUGHTFUL VERSE. *228th Thousand. Small Pott 8vo. Paper 1s. 3d. net; Cloth Boards, 2s. net. Also Illustrated. Fcap. 8vo. 3s. 6d. net.*

ALL'S WELL: A COLLECTION OF WAR POEMS. *175th Thousand. Small Pott 8vo. Paper, 1s. 3d. net; Cloth Boards, 2s. net.*

THE KING'S HIGH WAY. *120th Thousand. Small Pott 8vo. 1s. 3d. net; Cloth Boards, 2s. net.*

THE VISION SPLENDID. *100th Thousand. Small Pott 8vo. Paper, 1s. 3d. net; Cloth Boards, 2s. net.*

THE FIERY CROSS. *80th Thousand. Small Pott 8vo. Paper, 1s. 3d. net; Cloth Boards, 2s. net.*

HIGH ALTARS: THE RECORD OF A VISIT TO THE BATTLEFIELDS OF FRANCE AND FLANDERS. *40th Thousand. Small Pott 8vo. 1s. 3d. net; Cloth Boards, 2s. net.*

HEARTS COURAGEOUS. *Small Pott 8vo. 1s. 3d net. Cloth Boards, 2s. net.*

ALL CLEAR. *Small Pott 8vo. 1s. 3d. net. Cloth Boards, 2s. net.*

WINDS OF THE DAWN. *Small Pott 8vo. 2s. net.*

Oxford (M. N.). A HANDBOOK OF NURSING. *Seventh Edition, Revised. Cr. 8vo. 5s. net.*

Pakes (W. C. C.). THE SCIENCE OF HYGIENE. Illustrated. *Second and Cheaper Edition.* Revised by A. T. NANKIVELL. *Cr. 8vo. 6s. net.*

Petrie (W. M. Flinders.) A HISTORY OF EGYPT. Illustrated. *Six Volumes Cr. 8vo. Each 9s. net.*

VOL. I. FROM THE IST TO THE XVITH DYNASTY. *Eighth Edition.*

VOL. II. THE XVIITH AND XVIIITH DYNASTIES. *Sixth Edition.*

VOL. III. XIXTH TO XXXTH DYNASTIES. *Second Edition.*

VOL. IV. EGYPT UNDER THE PTOLEMAIC DYNASTY. J. P. MAHAFFY. *Second Edition.*

VOL. V. EGYPT UNDER ROMAN RULE. J. G. MILNE. *Second Edition.*

VOL. VI. EGYPT IN THE MIDDLE AGES. STANLEY LANE POOLE. *Second Edition.*

RELIGION AND CONSCIENCE IN ANCIENT EGYPT. Illustrated. *Cr. 8vo. 5s. net.*

SYRIA AND EGYPT, FROM THE TELL EL AMARNA LETTERS. *Cr. 8vo. 5s. net.*

EGYPTIAN TALES. Translated from the Papyri. First Series, IVth to XIIth Dynasty. Illustrated. *Third Edition. Cr. 8vo. 5s. net.*

EGYPTIAN TALES. Translated from the Papyri. Second Series, XVIIIth to XIXth Dynasty. Illustrated. *Second Edition. Cr. 8vo. 5s. net.*

Pollard (Alfred W.). SHAKESPEARE FOLIOS AND QUARTOS. A Study in the Bibliography of Shakespeare's Plays, 1594-1685. Illustrated. *Folio. £1 1s. net.*

Porter (G. R.). THE PROGRESS OF THE NATION. A New Edition. Edited by F. W. HIRST. *Demy 8vo. £1 1s. net.*

Power (J. O'Connor). THE MAKING OF AN ORATOR. *Cr. 8vo. 6s. net.*

Price (L. L.). A SHORT HISTORY OF POLITICAL ECONOMY IN ENGLAND FROM ADAM SMITH TO ARNOLD TOYNBEE. *Ninth Edition. Cr. 8vo. 5s. net.*

Rawlings (Gertrude B.). COINS AND HOW TO KNOW THEM. Illustrated. *Third Edition. Cr. 8vo. 7s. 6d. net.*

Regan (C. Tate). THE FRESHWATER FISHES OF THE BRITISH ISLES. Illustrated. *Cr. 8vo. 7s. 6d. net.*

Reid (G. Archdall). THE LAWS OF HEREDITY. *Second Edition. Demy 8vo. £1 1s. net.*

Robertson (C. Grant). SELECT STATUTES, CASES, AND DOCUMENTS, 1660-1832. *Second Edition, Revised and Enlarged. Demy 8vo. 15s. net.*

ENGLAND UNDER THE HANOVERIANS. Illustrated. *Third Edition. Demy 8vo. 12s. 6d. net.*

Rolle (Richard). THE FIRE OF LOVE AND THE MENDING OF LIFE. Edited by FRANCES M. COMPER. *Cr. 8vo. 6s. net.*

Ryley (A. Beresford). OLD PASTE. Illustrated. *Royal 4to. £2 2s. net.*

'Saki' (H. H. Munro). REGINALD. *Fourth Edition. Fcap. 8vo. 3s. 6d. net.*

2

REGINALD IN RUSSIA. *Fcap. 8vo.*
3s. 6d. net.

Schidrowitz (Philip). RUBBER. Illustrated. *Second Edition. Demy 8vo.* 15s.
net.

Selous (Edmund). TOMMY SMITH'S
ANIMALS. Illustrated. *Sixteenth Edition. Fcap. 8vo.* 3s. 6d. net.

TOMMY SMITH'S OTHER ANIMALS.
Illustrated. *Seventh Edition. Fcap. 8vo.*
3s. 6d. net.

TOMMY SMITH AT THE ZOO. Illustrated. *Second Edition. Fcap. 8vo.*
2s. 9d.

TOMMY SMITH AGAIN AT THE ZOO.
Illustrated. *Fcap. 8vo.* 2s. 9d.

JACK'S INSECTS. Illustrated. *Cr. 8vo.* 6s.
net.

Shakespeare (William).
THE FOUR FOLIOS, 1623; 1632; 1664;
1685. Each £4 4s. *net*, or a complete set,
£12 12s. net.

THE POEMS OF WILLIAM SHAKESPEARE. With an Introduction and Notes
by GEORGE WYNDHAM. *Demy 8vo. Buckram*, 12s. 6d. net.

Shelley (Percy Bysshe). POEMS. With
an Introduction by A. CLUTTON-BROCK and
notes by C. D. LOCOCK. *Two Volumes.
Demy 8vo.* £1 1s. net.

Sladen (Douglas). SICILY: THE NEW
WINTER RESORT. An Encyclopædia of
Sicily. With 234 Illustrations, a Map, and
a Table of the Railway System of Sicily.
Second Edition, Revised. Cr. 8vo. 7s. 6d.
net.

Slesser (H. H.). TRADE UNIONISM.
Cr. 8vo. 5s. net.

Smith (Adam). THE WEALTH OF
NATIONS. Edited by EDWIN CANNAN.
Two Volumes. Demy 8vo. £1 5s. net.

Smith (G. F. Herbert). GEM-STONES
AND THEIR DISTINCTIVE CHARACTERS. Illustrated. *Second Edition. Cr.
8vo.* 7s. 6d. net.

Stancliffe. GOLF DO'S AND DONT'S.
Sixth Edition. Fcap. 8vo. 2s. net.

Stevenson (R. L.). THE LETTERS OF
ROBERT LOUIS STEVENSON. Edited
by Sir SIDNEY COLVIN. *A New Rearranged Edition in four volumes. Fourth
Edition. Fcap. 8vo. Each* 6s. net. *Leather,
each* 7s. 6d. net.

Surtees (R. S.). HANDLEY CROSS.
Illustrated. *Eighth Edition. Fcap. 8vo.*
7s. 6d. net.

MR. SPONGE'S SPORTING TOUR.
Illustrated. *Fourth Edition. Fcap. 8vo.*
7s. 6d. net.

ASK MAMMA; OR, THE RICHEST
COMMONER IN ENGLAND. Illustrated. *Second Edition. Fcap. 8vo.* 7s. 6d.
net.

JORROCKS'S JAUNTS AND JOLLITIES. Illustrated. *Sixth Edition. Fcap.
8vo.* 6s. net.

MR. FACEY ROMFORD'S HOUNDS.
Illustrated. *Third Edition. Fcap. 8vo.*
7s. 6d. net.

HAWBUCK GRANGE; OR, THE SPORTING ADVENTURES OF THOMAS
SCOTT, ESQ. Illustrated. *Fcap. 8vo.*
6s. net.

PLAIN OR RINGLETS? Illustrated.
Fcap. 8vo. 7s. 6d. net.

HILLINGDON HALL. With 12 Coloured
Plates by WILDRAKE, HEATH, and JELLICOE. *Fcap. 8vo.* 7s. 6d. net.

Suso (Henry). THE LIFE OF THE
BLESSED HENRY SUSO. By HIMSELF.
Translated by T. F. KNOX. With an Introduction by DEAN INGE. *Second Edition.
Cr. 8vo.* 6s. net.

Swanton (E. W.). FUNGI AND HOW
TO KNOW THEM. Illustrated. *Cr. 8vo.*
10s. 6d. net.

BRITISH PLANT-GALLS. *Cr. 8vo.*
10s. 6d. net.

Tabor (Margaret E.). THE SAINTS IN
ART. With their Attributes and Symbols
Alphabetically Arranged. Illustrated.
Third Edition. Fcap. 8vo. 5s. net.

Taylor (A. E.). ELEMENTS OF METAPHYSICS. *Fourth Edition. Demy 8vo.*
12s. 6d. net.

Taylor (J. W.). THE COMING OF THE
SAINTS. *Second Edition. Cr. 8vo.* 6s.
net.

Thomas (Edward). MAURICE MAETERLINCK. Illustrated. *Second Edition.
Cr. 8vo.* 6s. net.

A LITERARY PILGRIM IN ENGLAND.
Illustrated. *Demy 8vo.* 12s. 6d. net.

Tileston (Mary W.). DAILY STRENGTH
FOR DAILY NEEDS. *Twenty-fifth
Edition. Medium 16mo.* 3s. 6d. net.

Toynbee (Paget). DANTE ALIGHIERI.
HIS LIFE AND WORKS. With 16 Illustrations. *Fourth and Enlarged Edition. Cr.
8vo.* 6s. net.

Trevelyan (G. M.). ENGLAND UNDER
THE STUARTS. With Maps and Plans.
Seventh Edition. Demy 8vo. 12s. 6d. net.

Triggs (H. Inigo). TOWN PLANNING:
PAST, PRESENT, AND POSSIBLE. Illustrated. *Second Edition. Wide Royal 8vo.*
16s. net.

Underhill (Evelyn). MYSTICISM. A Study in the Nature and Development of Man's Spiritual Consciousness. *Seventh Edition. Demy 8vo. 15s. net.*

Vardon (Harry). HOW TO PLAY GOLF. Illustrated. *Eleventh Edition. Cr. 8vo. 5s. net.*

Vernon (Hon. W. Warren). READINGS ON THE INFERNO OF DANTE. With an Introduction by the Rev. Dr. MOORE. *Two Volumes. Second Edition, Rewritten. Cr. 8vo. 15s. net.*

READINGS ON THE PURGATORIO OF DANTE. With an Introduction by the late DEAN CHURCH. *Two Volumes. Third Edition, Revised. Cr. 8vo. 15s. net.*

READINGS ON THE PARADISO OF DANTE. With an Introduction by the BISHOP OF RIPON. *Two Volumes. Second Edition, Revised. Cr. 8vo. 15s. net.*

Vickers (Kenneth H.). ENGLAND IN THE LATER MIDDLE AGES. With Maps. *Second Edition, Revised. Demy 8vo. 12s. 6d. net.*

Waddell (L. A.). LHASA AND ITS MYSTERIES. With a Record of the Expedition of 1903-1904. Illustrated. *Third Edition. Medium 8vo. 12s. 6d. net.*

Wade (G. W. and J. H.). RAMBLES IN SOMERSET. Illustrated. *Cr. 8vo. 7s. 6d. net.*

Wagner (Richard). RICHARD WAGNER'S MUSIC DRAMAS. Interpretations, embodying Wagner's own explanations. By ALICE LEIGHTON CLEATHER and BASIL CRUMP. *Fcap. 8vo. Each 4s. net.*

THE RING OF THE NIBELUNG. *Sixth Edition.*

LOHENGRIN AND PARSIFAL. *Third Edition.*

TRISTAN AND ISOLDE. *Second Edition.*

TANNHÄUSER AND THE MASTERSINGERS OF NUREMBURG.

Waterhouse (Elizabeth). WITH THE SIMPLE-HEARTED. Little Homilies. *Third Edition. Small Pott 8vo. 3s. 6d. net.*

THE HOUSE BY THE CHERRY TREE. A Second Series of Little Homilies. *Small Pott 8vo. 3s. 6d. net.*

COMPANIONS OF THE WAY. Being Selections for Morning and Evening Reading. *Cr. 8vo. 7s. 6d. net.*

THOUGHTS OF A TERTIARY. *Second Edition. Small Pott 8vo. 1s. 6d. net.*

VERSES. *Second Edition, Enlarged. Fcap. 8vo. 2s. net.*

A LITTLE BOOK OF LIFE AND DEATH. *Nineteenth Edition. Small Pott 8vo. Cloth, 2s. 6d. net.*

Waters (W. G.). ITALIAN SCULPTORS. Illustrated. *Cr. 8vo. 7s. 6d. net.*

Watt (Francis). CANTERBURY PILGRIMS AND THEIR WAYS. With a Frontispiece in Colour and 12 other Illustrations. *Demy 8vo. 10s. 6d. net.*

Weigall (Arthur E. P.). A GUIDE TO THE ANTIQUITIES OF UPPER EGYPT: FROM ABYDOS TO THE SUDAN FRONTIER. Illustrated. *Second Edition. Cr. 8vo. 10s. 6d. net.*

Wells (J.). A SHORT HISTORY OF ROME. *Sixteenth Edition.* With 3 Maps. *Cr. 8vo. 6s.*

Wilde (Oscar). THE WORKS OF OSCAR WILDE. *Thirteen Volumes. Fcap. 8vo. Each 6s. 6d. net.*

I. LORD ARTHUR SAVILE'S CRIME AND THE PORTRAIT OF MR. W. H. II. THE DUCHESS OF PADUA. III. POEMS. IV. LADY WINDERMERE'S FAN. V. A WOMAN OF NO IMPORTANCE. VI. AN IDEAL HUSBAND. VII. THE IMPORTANCE OF BEING EARNEST. VIII. A HOUSE OF POMEGRANATES. IX. INTENTIONS. X. DE PROFUNDIS AND PRISON LETTERS. XI. ESSAYS. XII. SALOMÉ, A FLORENTINE TRAGEDY, and LA SAINTE COURTISANE. XIV. SELECTED PROSE OF OSCAR WILDE.

A HOUSE OF POMEGRANATES. Illustrated. *Cr. 4to. 21s. net.*

Wilding (Anthony F). ON THE COURT AND OFF. With 58 Illustrations. *Seventh Edition. Cr. 8vo. 6s. net.*

Wilson (Ernest H.). A NATURALIST IN WESTERN CHINA. Illustrated. *Second Edition. 2 Vols. Demy 8vo. £1 10s. net.*

Wood (Sir Evelyn). FROM MIDSHIPMAN TO FIELD-MARSHAL. Illustrated. *Fifth Edition. Demy 8vo. 12s. 6d. net.*

THE REVOLT IN HINDUSTAN (1857-59). Illustrated. *Second Edition. Cr. 8vo. 7s. 6d. net.*

Wood (Lieut. W. B.) and Edmonds (Col. J. E.). A HISTORY OF THE CIVIL WAR IN THE UNITED STATES (1861-65). With an Introduction by SPENSER WILKINSON. With 24 Maps and Plans. *Third Edition. Demy 8vo. 15s. net.*

Wordsworth (W.). POEMS. With an Introduction and Notes by NOWELL C. SMITH. *Three Volumes. Demy 8vo. 18s. net.*

Yeats (W. B.). A BOOK OF IRISH VERSE. *Third Edition. Cr. 8vo. 6s. net.*

PART II.—A SELECTION OF SERIES

Ancient Cities

General Editor, SIR B. C. A. WINDLE

Cr. 8vo.   6s. net each volume

With Illustrations by E. H. NEW, and other Artists

BRISTOL. Alfred Harvey.	EDINBURGH. M. G. Williamson.
CANTERBURY. J. C. Cox.	LINCOLN. E. Mansel Sympson.
CHESTER. Sir B. C. A. Windle.	SHREWSBURY. T. Auden.
DUBLIN. S. A. O. Fitzpatrick.	WELLS and GLASTONBURY. T. S. Holmes.

The Antiquary's Books

General Editor, J. CHARLES COX

Demy 8vo.   10s. 6d. net each volume

With Numerous Illustrations

ANCIENT PAINTED GLASS IN ENGLAND. Philip Nelson.

ARCHÆOLOGY AND FALSE ANTIQUITIES. R. Munro.

BELLS OF ENGLAND, THE. Canon J. J. Raven. *Second Edition.*

BRASSES OF ENGLAND, THE. Herbert W. Macklin. *Third Edition.*

CASTLES AND WALLED TOWNS OF ENGLAND, THE. A. Harvey.

CELTIC ART IN PAGAN AND CHRISTIAN TIMES. J. Romilly Allen. *Second Edition.*

CHURCHWARDENS' ACCOUNTS. J. C. Cox.

DOMESDAY INQUEST, THE. Adolphus Ballard.

ENGLISH CHURCH FURNITURE. J. C. Cox and A. Harvey. *Second Edition.*

ENGLISH COSTUME. From Prehistoric Times to the End of the Eighteenth Century. George Clinch.

ENGLISH MONASTIC LIFE. Cardinal Gasquet. *Fourth Edition.*

ENGLISH SEALS. J. Harvey Bloom.

FOLK-LORE AS AN HISTORICAL SCIENCE. Sir G. L. Gomme.

GILDS AND COMPANIES OF LONDON, THE. George Unwin.

HERMITS AND ANCHORITES OF ENGLAND, THE. Rotha Mary Clay.

MANOR AND MANORIAL RECORDS, THE. Nathaniel J. Hone. *Second Edition.*

MEDIÆVAL HOSPITALS OF ENGLAND, THE. Rotha Mary Clay.

OLD ENGLISH INSTRUMENTS OF MUSIC. F. W. Galpin. *Second Edition.*

The Antiquary's Books—*continued*

OLD ENGLISH LIBRARIES. Ernest A. Savage.

OLD SERVICE BOOKS OF THE ENGLISH CHURCH. Christopher Wordsworth, and Henry Littlehales. *Second Edition.*

PARISH LIFE IN MEDIÆVAL ENGLAND. Cardinal Gasquet. *Fourth Edition.*

PARISH REGISTERS OF ENGLAND, THE. J. C. Cox.

REMAINS OF THE PREHISTORIC AGE IN ENGLAND. Sir B. C. A. Windle. *Second Edition.*

ROMAN ERA IN BRITAIN, THE. J. Ward.

ROMANO-BRITISH BUILDINGS AND EARTHWORKS. J. Ward.

ROYAL FORESTS OF ENGLAND, THE. J. C. Cox.

SCHOOLS OF MEDIEVAL ENGLAND, THE. A. F. Leach. *Second Edition.*

SHRINES OF BRITISH SAINTS. J. C. Wall.

The Arden Shakespeare

General Editor—R. H. CASE

Demy 8vo.   6s. net each volume

An edition of Shakespeare in Single Plays ; each edited with a full Introduction, Textual Notes, and a Commentary at the foot of the page

ALL'S WELL THAT ENDS WELL.
ANTONY AND CLEOPATRA. *Third Edition.*
AS YOU LIKE IT.
CYMBELINE. *Second Edition.*
COMEDY OF ERRORS, THE.
HAMLET. *Fourth Edition.*
JULIUS CAESAR. *Second Edition.*
KING HENRY IV. PT. I.
KING HENRY V. *Second Edition.*
KING HENRY VI. PT. I.
KING HENRY VI. PT. II.
KING HENRY VI. PT. III
KING HENRY VIII.
KING LEAR. *Second Edition.*
KING RICHARD II.
KING RICHARD III. *Second Edition.*
LIFE AND DEATH OF KING JOHN, THE.
LOVE'S LABOUR'S LOST. *Second Edition.*

MACBETH. *Second Edition.*
MEASURE FOR MEASURE.
MERCHANT OF VENICE, THE. *Fourth Edition.*
MERRY WIVES OF WINDSOR, THE.
MIDSUMMER NIGHT'S DREAM, A.
OTHELLO. *Second Edition.*
PERICLES.
ROMEO AND JULIET. *Second Edition.*
SONNETS AND A LOVER'S COMPLAINT.
TAMING OF THE SHREW, THE.
TEMPEST, THE. *Second Edition.*
TIMON OF ATHENS.
TITUS ANDRONICUS.
TROILUS AND CRESSIDA.
TWELFTH NIGHT. *Third Edition.*
TWO GENTLEMEN OF VERONA, THE.
VENUS AND ADONIS.
WINTER'S TALE, THE.

Classics of Art

Edited by DR. J. H. W. LAING

With numerous Illustrations.   Wide Royal 8vo

ART OF THE GREEKS, THE. H. B. Walters. 15s. *net.*

ART OF THE ROMANS, THE. H. B. Walters. 16s. *net.*

CHARDIN. H. E. A. Furst. 15s. *net.*

DONATELLO. Maud Cruttwell. 16s. *net.*

FLORENTINE SCULPTORS OF THE RENAISSANCE. Wilhelm Bode. Translated by Jessie Haynes. 15s. *net.*

GEORGE ROMNEY. Arthur B. Chamberlain. 15s. *net.*

Classics of Art—*continued*

GHIRLANDAIO. Gerald S. Davies. *Second Edition.* 15s. *net.*

LAWRENCE. Sir Walter Armstrong. 25s. *net.*

MICHELANGELO. Gerald S. Davies. 15s. *net.*

RAPHAEL. A. P. Oppé. 15s. *net.*

REMBRANDT'S ETCHINGS. A. M. Hind. Two Volumes. 25s. *net.*

RUBENS. Edward Dillon. 30s. *net.*

TINTORETTO. Evelyn March Phillipps. 16s. *net.*

TITIAN. Charles Ricketts. 16s. *net.*

TURNER'S SKETCHES AND DRAWINGS. A. J. Finberg. *Second Edition.* 15s. *net.*

VELAZQUEZ. A. de Beruete. 15s. *net.*

The 'Complete' Series

Fully Illustrated.   Demy 8vo

COMPLETE AMATEUR BOXER, THE. J. G. Bohun Lynch. 10s. 6d. *net.*

COMPLETE ASSOCIATION FOOTBALLER, THE. B. S. Evers and C. E. Hughes-Davies. 10s. 6d. *net.*

COMPLETE ATHLETIC TRAINER, THE. S. A. Mussabini. 10s. 6d. *net.*

COMPLETE BILLIARD PLAYER, THE. Charles Roberts. 12s. 6d. *net.*

COMPLETE COOK, THE. Lilian Whitling. 10s. 6d. *net.*

COMPLETE CRICKETER, THE. Albert E. KNIGHT. *Second Edition.* 10s. 6d. *net.*

COMPLETE FOXHUNTER, THE. Charles Richardson. *Second Edition.* 16s. *net.*

COMPLETE GOLFER, THE. Harry Vardon. *Fifteenth Edition, Revised.* 12s. 6d. *net.*

COMPLETE HOCKEY-PLAYER, THE. Eustace E. White. *Second Edition.* 10s. 6d. *net.*

COMPLETE HORSEMAN, THE. W. Scarth Dixon. *Second Edition.* 12s. 6d. *net.*

COMPLETE JUJITSUAN, THE. W. H. Garrud. 5s. *net.*

COMPLETE LAWN TENNIS PLAYER, THE. A. Wallis Myers. *Fourth Edition.* 12s. 6d. *net.*

COMPLETE MOTORIST, THE. Filson Young and W. G. Aston. *Revised Edition.* 10s. 6d. *net.*

COMPLETE MOUNTAINEER, THE. G. D. Abraham. *Second Edition.* 16s. *net.*

COMPLETE OARSMAN, THE. R. C. Lehmann. 12s. 6d. *net.*

COMPLETE PHOTOGRAPHER, THE. R. Child Bayley. *Fifth Edition, Revised.* 12s. 6d. *net.*

COMPLETE RUGBY FOOTBALLER, ON THE NEW ZEALAND SYSTEM, THE. D. Gallaher and W. J. Stead. *Second Edition.* 12s. 6d. *net.*

COMPLETE SHOT, THE. G. T. Teasdale-Buckell. *Third Edition.* 16s. *net.*

COMPLETE SWIMMER, THE. F. Sachs. 10s. 6d. *net.*

COMPLETE YACHTSMAN, THE. B. Heckstall-Smith and E. du Boulay. *Second Edition, Revised.* 16s. *net.*

The Connoisseur's Library

With numerous Illustrations.   Wide Royal 8vo.   25s. net each volume

ENGLISH COLOURED BOOKS. Martin Hardie.

ENGLISH FURNITURE. F. S. Robinson. *Second Edition.*

ETCHINGS. Sir F. Wedmore. *Second Edition.*

EUROPEAN ENAMELS. Henry H. Cunynghame.

FINE BOOKS. A. W. Pollard.

GLASS. Edward Dillon.

GOLDSMITHS' AND SILVERSMITHS' WORK. Nelson Dawson. *Second Edition.*

ILLUMINATED MANUSCRIPTS. J. A. Herbert. *Second Edition.*

IVORIES. Alfred Maskell.

JEWELLERY. H. Clifford Smith. *Second Edition.*

MEZZOTINTS. Cyril Davenport.

MINIATURES. Dudley Heath.

PORCELAIN. Edward Dillon.

SEALS. Walter de Gray Birch.

WOOD SCULPTURE. Alfred Maskell.

Handbooks of English Church History

Edited by J. H. BURN. *Crown 8vo.* *5s. net each volume*

FOUNDATIONS OF THE ENGLISH CHURCH, THE. J. H. Maude.

SAXON CHURCH AND THE NORMAN CONQUEST, THE. C. T. Cruttwell.

MEDIÆVAL CHURCH AND THE PAPACY, THE. A. C. Jennings.

REFORMATION PERIOD, THE. Henry Gee.

STRUGGLE WITH PURITANISM, THE. Bruce Blaxland.

CHURCH OF ENGLAND IN THE EIGHTEENTH CENTURY, THE. Alfred Plummer.

Handbooks of Theology

Demy 8vo

DOCTRINE OF THE INCARNATION, THE. R. L. Ottley. *Fifth Edition.* 15s. net.

HISTORY OF EARLY CHRISTIAN DOCTRINE, A. J. F. Bethune-Baker. 15s. net.

INTRODUCTION TO THE HISTORY OF RELIGION, AN. F. B. Jevons. *Seventh Edition.* 12s. 6d. net.

INTRODUCTION TO THE HISTORY OF THE CREEDS, AN. A. E. Burn. 12s. 6d. net.

PHILOSOPHY OF RELIGION IN ENGLAND AND AMERICA, THE. Alfred Caldecott. 12s. 6d. net.

XXXIX ARTICLES OF THE CHURCH OF ENG- LAND, THE. Edited by E. C. S. Gibson. *Ninth Edition.* 15s. net.

Health Series

Fcap. 8vo. 2s. 6d. net

BABY, THE. Arthur Saunders.

CARE OF THE BODY, THE. F. Cavanagh.

CARE OF THE TEETH, THE. A. T. Pitts.

EYES OF OUR CHILDREN, THE. N. Bishop Harman.

HEALTH FOR THE MIDDLE-AGED. Seymour Taylor. *Third Edition.*

HEALTH OF A WOMAN, THE. R. Murray Leslie.

HEALTH OF THE SKIN, THE. George Pernet.

HOW TO LIVE LONG. J. Walter Carr.

PREVENTION OF THE COMMON COLD, THE. O. K. Williamson.

STAYING THE PLAGUE. N. Bishop Harman.

THROAT AND EAR TROUBLES. Macleod Yearsley. *Third Edition.*

TUBERCULOSIS. Clive Riviere.

HEALTH OF THE CHILD, THE. O. Hilton. *Second Edition.* 2s. net.

The 'Home Life' Series

Illustrated. *Demy 8vo.*

HOME LIFE IN AMERICA. Katherine G. Busbey. *Second Edition.* 12s. 6d. net.

HOME LIFE IN CHINA. I. Taylor Headland. 12s. 6d. net.

HOME LIFE IN FRANCE. Miss Betham Edwards. *Sixth Edition.* 7s. 6d. net.

HOME LIFE IN GERMANY. Mrs. A. Sidgwick. *Third Edition.* 12. 6d. net.

HOME LIFE IN HOLLAND. D. S. Meldrum. *Second Edition.* 12s. 6d. net.

HOME LIFE IN ITALY. Lina Duff Gordon. *Third Edition.* 12s. 6d. net.

HOME LIFE IN NORWAY. H. K. Daniels. *Second Edition.* 12s. 6d. net.

HOME LIFE IN SPAIN. S. L. Bensusan. *Second Edition.* 12s. 6d. net.

BALKAN HOME LIFE. Lucy M. J. Garnett. 12s. 6d. net.

Leaders of Religion

Edited by H. C. BEECHING. *With Portraits*

Crown 8vo.   3s. net each volume

AUGUSTINE OF CANTERBURY. E. L. Cutts.

BISHOP BUTLER. W. A. Spooner.

BISHOP WILBERFORCE. G. W. Daniell.

CARDINAL MANNING. A. W. Hutton. *Second Edition.*

CARDINAL NEWMAN. R. H. Hutton.

CHARLES SIMEON. H. C. G. Moule.

GEORGE FOX, THE QUAKER. T. Hodgkin. *Third Edition.*

JOHN DONNE. Augustus Jessop.

JOHN HOWE. R. F. Horton.

JOHN KEBLE. Walter Lock. *Seventh Edition.*

JOHN KNOX. F. MacCunn. *Second Edition.*

JOHN WESLEY. J. H. Overton.

LANCELOT ANDREWES. R. L. Ottley. *Second Edition.*

LATIMER. R. M. and A. J. Carlyle.

THOMAS CHALMERS. Mrs. Oliphant. *Second Edition.*

THOMAS CRANMER. A. J. Mason.

THOMAS KEN. F. A. Clarke.

WILLIAM LAUD. W. H. Hutton. *Fourth Edition.*

The Library of Devotion

With Introductions and (where necessary) Notes

Small Pott 8vo, cloth, 3s. net ; also some volumes in leather,
3s. 6d. net each volume

BISHOP WILSON'S SACRA PRIVATA.

BOOK OF DEVOTIONS, A. *Second Edition.*

CHRISTIAN YEAR, THE. *Fifth Edition.*

CONFESSIONS OF ST. AUGUSTINE, THE. *Ninth Edition. 3s. 6d. net.*

DAY BOOK FROM THE SAINTS AND FATHERS, A.

DEATH AND IMMORTALITY.

DEVOTIONS FROM THE APOCRYPHA.

DEVOTIONS OF ST. ANSELM, THE.

DEVOTIONS FOR EVERY DAY IN THE WEEK AND THE GREAT FESTIVALS.

GRACE ABOUNDING TO THE CHIEF OF SINNERS.

GUIDE TO ETERNITY, A.

HORAE MYSTICAE. A Day Book from the Writings of Mystics of Many Nations.

IMITATION OF CHRIST, THE. *Eighth Edition.*

INNER WAY, THE. *Third Edition.*

INTRODUCTION TO THE DEVOUT LIFE, AN.

LIGHT, LIFE, and LOVE. A Selection from the German Mystics.

LITTLE BOOK OF HEAVENLY WISDOM, A. A Selection from the English Mystics.

LYRA APOSTOLICA.

LYRA INNOCENTIUM. *Third Edition.*

LYRA SACRA. A Book of Sacred Verse. *Second Edition.*

MANUAL OF CONSOLATION FROM THE SAINTS AND FATHERS, A.

ON THE LOVE OF GOD.

PRECES PRIVATAE.

PSALMS OF DAVID, THE.

SERIOUS CALL TO A DEVOUT AND HOLY LIFE, A. *Fifth Edition.*

SONG OF SONGS, THE.

SPIRITUAL COMBAT, THE.

SPIRITUAL GUIDE, THE. *Third Edition.*

TEMPLE, THE. *Second Edition.*

THOUGHTS OF PASCAL, THE. *Second Edition.*

Little Books on Art

With many Illustrations. Demy 16mo. 5s. net each volume

Each volume consists of about 200 pages, and contains from 30 to 40 Illustrations, including a Frontispiece in Photogravure

ALBRECHT DÜRER. L. J Allen.

ARTS OF JAPAN, THE. E. Dillon. *Third Edition.*

BOOKPLATES. E. Almack.

BOTTICELLI. Mary L. Bonnor.

BURNE-JONES. F. de Lisle. *Third Edition.*

CELLINI. R. H. H. Cust.

CHRISTIAN SYMBOLISM. Mrs. H. Jenner.

CHRIST IN ART. Mrs. H. Jenner.

CLAUDE. E. Dillon.

CONSTABLE. H. W. Tompkins. *Second Edition.*

COROT. A. Pollard and E. Birnstingl.

EARLY ENGLISH WATER-COLOUR. C. E. Hughes.

ENAMELS. Mrs. N. Dawson. *Second Edition.*

FREDERIC LEIGHTON. A. Corkran.

GEORGE ROMNEY. G. Paston.

GREEK ART. H. B. Walters. *Fifth Edition.*

GREUZE AND BOUCHER. E. F. Pollard.

HOLBEIN. Mrs. G. Fortescue.

JEWELLERY. C. Davenport. *Second Edition.*

JOHN HOPPNER. H. P. K. Skipton.

SIR JOSHUA REYNOLDS. J. Sime. *Second Edition.*

MILLET. N. Peacock. *Second Edition.*

MINIATURES. C. Davenport, V.D., F.S.A. *Second Edition.*

OUR LADY IN ART. Mrs. H. Jenner.

RAPHAEL. A. R. Dryhurst. *Second Edition*

RODIN. Muriel Ciolkowska.

TURNER. F. Tyrrell-Gill.

VANDYCK. M. G. Smallwood.

VELAZQUEZ. W. Wilberforce and A. R. Gilbert.

WATTS. R. E. D. Sketchley. *Second Edition.*

The Little Guides

With many Illustrations by E. H. NEW and other artists, and from photographs

Small Pott 8vo. 4s. net each volume

The main features of these Guides are (1) a handy and charming form ; (2) illustrations from photographs and by well-known artists ; (3) good plans and maps ; (4) an adequate but compact presentation of everything that is interesting in the natural features, history, archæology, and architecture of the town or district treated.

CAMBRIDGE AND ITS COLLEGES. A. H. Thompson. *Fourth Edition, Revised.*

CHANNEL ISLANDS, THE. E. E. Bicknell.

ENGLISH LAKES, THE. F. G. Brabant.

ISLE OF WIGHT, THE. G. Clinch.

LONDON. G. Clinch.

MALVERN COUNTRY, THE. Sir B.C.A.Windle. *Second Edition.*

NORTH WALES. A. T. Story.

OXFORD AND ITS COLLEGES. J. Wells. *Tenth Edition.*

ST. PAUL'S CATHEDRAL. G. Clinch.

SHAKESPEARE'S COUNTRY. Sir B. C. A. Windle. *Fifth Edition.*

SOUTH WALES. G. W. and J. H. Wade.

TEMPLE, THE. H. H. L. Bellot.

WESTMINSTER ABBEY. G. E. Troutbeck. *Second Edition.*

The Little Guides—*continued*

BEDFORDSHIRE AND HUNTINGDONSHIRE. H. W. Macklin.

BERKSHIRE. F. G. Brabant.

BUCKINGHAMSHIRE. E. S. Roscoe. *Second Edition, Revised.*

CAMBRIDGESHIRE. J. C. Cox.

CHESHIRE. W. M. Gallichan.

CORNWALL. A. L. Salmon. *Second Edition.*

DERBYSHIRE. J. C. Cox. *Second Edition.*

DEVON. S. Baring-Gould. *Fourth Edition.*

DORSET. F. R. Heath. *Fourth Edition.*

DURHAM. J. E. Hodgkin.

ESSEX. J. C. Cox. *Second Edition.*

GLOUCESTERSHIRE. J. C. Cox. *Second Edition.*

HAMPSHIRE. J. C. Cox. *Third Edition.*

HEREFORDSHIRE. G. W. and J. H. Wade.

HERTFORDSHIRE. H. W. Tompkins.

KENT. J. C. Cox. *Second Edition, Rewritten.*

KERRY. C. P. Crane. *Second Edition.*

LEICESTERSHIRE AND RUTLAND. A. Harvey and V. B. Crowther-Beynon.

LINCOLNSHIRE. J. C. Cox.

MIDDLESEX. J. B. Firth.

MONMOUTHSHIRE. G. W. and J. H. Wade.

NORFOLK. W. A. Dutt. *Fourth Edition, Revised.*

NORTHAMPTONSHIRE. W. Dry. *Second Edition, Revised.*

NORTHUMBERLAND. J. E. Morris. 5s. net.

NOTTINGHAMSHIRE. L. Guilford.

OXFORDSHIRE. F. G. Brabant. *Second Edition.*

SHROPSHIRE. J. E. Auden. *Second Edition.*

SOMERSET. G. W. and J. H. Wade. *Fourth Edition.*

STAFFORDSHIRE. C. Masefield. *Second Edition.*

SUFFOLK. W. A. Dutt. *Second Edition.*

SURREY. J. C. Cox. *Third Edition, Rewritten.*

SUSSEX. F. G. Brabant. *Fifth Edition.*

WARWICKSHIRE. J. C. Cox.

WILTSHIRE. F. R. Heath. *Third Edition.*

YORKSHIRE, THE EAST RIDING. J. F. Morris.

YORKSHIRE, THE NORTH RIDING. J. E. Morris.

YORKSHIRE, THE WEST RIDING. J. E. Morris. 5s. net.

BRITTANY. S. Baring-Gould. *Second Edition.*

NORMANDY. C. Scudamore. *Second Edition.*

ROME. C. G. Ellaby.

SICILY. F. H. Jackson.

The Little Library

With Introduction, Notes, and Photogravure Frontispieces

Small Pott 8vo.   Each Volume, cloth, 2s. 6d. net ; also some volumes in leather at 3s. 6d. net

Anon. A LITTLE BOOK OF ENGLISH LYRICS. *Second Edition.* 3s. 6d. net.

Austen (Jane). PRIDE AND PREJUDICE. *Two Volumes.*
NORTHANGER ABBEY.

Bacon (Francis). THE ESSAYS OF LORD BACON.

Barnett (Annie). A LITTLE BOOK OF ENGLISH PROSE. *Third Edition.*

Beckford (William). THE HISTORY OF THE CALIPH VATHEK.

Blake (William). SELECTIONS FROM THE WORKS OF WILLIAM BLAKE.

Browning (Robert). SELECTIONS FROM THE EARLY POEMS OF ROBERT BROWNING.

Canning (George). SELECTIONS FROM THE ANTI-JACOBIN : With some later Poems by GEORGE CANNING.

Cowley (Abraham). THE ESSAYS OF ABRAHAM COWLEY.

The Little Library—continued

Crabbe (George). SELECTIONS FROM THE POEMS OF GEORGE CRABBE.

Crashaw (Richard). THE ENGLISH POEMS OF RICHARD CRASHAW.

Dante Alighieri. PURGATORY. PARADISE.

Darley (George). SELECTIONS FROM THE POEMS OF GEORGE DARLEY.

Kinglake (A. W.). EOTHEN. *Second Edition.* 2s. 6d. net.

Locker (F.). LONDON LYRICS.

Marvell (Andrew). THE POEMS OF ANDREW MARVELL.

Milton (John). THE MINOR POEMS OF JOHN MILTON.

Moir (D. M.). MANSIE WAUCH.

Nichols (Bowyer). A LITTLE BOOK OF ENGLISH SONNETS.

Smith (Horace and James). REJECTED ADDRESSES.

Sterne (Laurence). A SENTIMENTAL JOURNEY.

Tennyson (Alfred, Lord). THE EARLY POEMS OF ALFRED, LORD TENNYSON.
IN MEMORIAM.
THE PRINCESS.
MAUD.

Vaughan (Henry). THE POEMS OF HENRY VAUGHAN.

Waterhouse (Elizabeth). A LITTLE BOOK OF LIFE AND DEATH. *Nineteenth Edition.*

Wordsworth (W.). SELECTIONS FROM THE POEMS OF WILLIAM WORDSWORTH.

Wordsworth (W.) and Coleridge (S. T.). LYRICAL BALLADS. *Third Edition.*

The Little Quarto Shakespeare

Edited by W. J. CRAIG. With Introductions and Notes

Pott 16mo. 40 *Volumes. Leather, price* 1s. 9d. *net each volume*

Miniature Library

Demy 32mo. *Leather,* 3s. 6d. *net each volume*

EUPHRANOR: A Dialogue on Youth. Edward FitzGerald.

THE RUBÁIYÁT OF OMAR KHAYYÁM. Edward FitzGerald. *Fifth Edition. Cloth,* 1s. net.

POLONIUS; or, Wise Saws and Modern Instances. Edward FitzGerald.

The New Library of Medicine

Edited by C. W. SALEEBY. *Demy* 8vo

AIR AND HEALTH. Ronald C. Macfie. *Second Edition.* 10s. 6d. net.

CARE OF THE BODY, THE. F. Cavanagh. *Second Edition.* 10s. 6d. net.

CHILDREN OF THE NATION, THE. The Right Hon. Sir John Gorst. *Second Edition.* 10s. 6d. net.

DRUGS AND THE DRUG HABIT. H. Sainsbury. 10s. 6d. net.

FUNCTIONAL NERVE DISEASES. A. T. Schofield. 10s. 6d. net.

HYGIENE OF MIND, THE. Sir T. S. Clouston. *Sixth Edition.* 10s. 6d. net.

INFANT MORTALITY. Sir George Newman. 10s. 6d. net.

PREVENTION OF TUBERCULOSIS (CONSUMPTION), THE. Arthur Newsholme. *Second Edition.* 12s. 6d. net.

The New Library of Music

Edited by ERNEST NEWMAN. *Illustrated. Demy 8vo. 10s. 6d. net*

BRAHMS. J. A. Fuller-Maitland. *Second Edition.*

HANDEL. R. A. Streatfeild. *Second Edition.*

HUGO WOLF. Ernest Newman.

Oxford Biographies

Illustrated. Fcap. 8vo. Each volume, cloth, 4s. net ; also some in leather, 5s. net

DANTE ALIGHIERI. Paget Toynbee. *Fifth Edition.*

GIROLAMO SAVONAROLA. E. L. S. Horsburgh. *Sixth Edition.*

JOHN HOWARD. E. C. S. Gibson.

SIR WALTER RALEIGH. I. A. Taylor.

CHATHAM. A. S. McDowall.

CANNING. W. Alison Phillips.

Nine Plays

Fcap. 8vo. 3s. 6d. net

ACROSS THE BORDER. Beulah Marie Dix.

HONEYMOON, THE. A Comedy in Three Acts. Arnold Bennett. *Third Edition.*

GREAT ADVENTURE, THE. A Play of Fancy in Four Acts. Arnold Bennett. *Fourth Edition.*

MILESTONES. Arnold Bennett and Edward Knoblock. *Eighth Edition.*

IDEAL HUSBAND, AN. Oscar Wilde. *Acting Edition.*

KISMET. Edward Knoblock. *Third Edition.*

TYPHOON. A Play in Four Acts. Melchior Lengyel. English Version by Laurence Irving. *Second Edition.*

WARE CASE, THE. George Pleydell.

GENERAL POST. J. E. Harold Terry. *Second Edition.*

Sport Series

Illustrated. Fcap. 8vo. 2s. net

FLYING, ALL ABOUT. Gertrude Bacon.

GOLF DO'S AND DONT'S. 'Stancliffe.' *Sixth Edition.*

GOLFING SWING, THE. Burnham Hare. *Fourth Edition.*

HOW TO SWIM. H. R. Austin.

WRESTLING. P. Longhurst.

The States of Italy

Edited by E. ARMSTRONG and R. LANGTON DOUGLAS

Illustrated. Demy 8vo

MILAN UNDER THE SFORZA, A HISTORY OF. Cecilia M. Ady. 12s. 6d. net.

PERUGIA, A HISTORY OF. W. Heywood. 15s. net.

VERONA, A HISTORY OF. A. M. Allen. 15s. net.

The Westminster Commentaries

General Editor, WALTER LOCK

Demy 8vo

ACTS OF THE APOSTLES, THE. R. B. Rackham. *Seventh Edition.* 16s. net.

AMOS. E. A. Edghill. 8s. 6d. net.

CORINTHIANS, I. H. L. Goudge. *Fourth Edition.* 8s. 6d. net.

EXODUS. A. H. M'Neile. *Second Edition.* 15s. net.

EZEKIEL. H. A. Redpath. 12s. 6d. net.

GENESIS. S. R. Driver. *Tenth Edition.* 16s. net.

HEBREWS. E. C. Wickham. 8s. 6d. net.

ISAIAH. G. W. Wade. 16s. net.

JEREMIAH. L. E. Binns. 16s. net.

JOB. E. C. S. Gibson. *Second Edition.* 8s. 6d. net.

PASTORAL EPISTLES, THE. E. F. Brown. 8s. 6d. net.

PHILIPPIANS, THE. Maurice Jones. 8s. 6d. net.

ST. JAMES. R. J. Knowling. *Second Edition.* 8s. 6d. net.

ST. MATTHEW. P. A. Micklem. 15s. net.

The 'Young' Series

Illustrated. Crown 8vo

YOUNG BOTANIST, THE. W. P. Westell and C. S. Cooper. 6s. net.

YOUNG CARPENTER, THE. Cyril Hall. 6s. net.

YOUNG ELECTRICIAN, THE. Hammond Hall. Second Edition. 6s. net.

YOUNG ENGINEER, THE. Hammond Hall. Third Edition. 6s. net.

YOUNG NATURALIST, THE. W. P. Westell. 7s. 6d. net.

YOUNG ORNITHOLOGIST, THE. W. P. Westell. 6s. net.

Methuen's Cheap Library

Fcap. 8vo. 2s. net

ALL THINGS CONSIDERED. G. K. Chesterton.

BEST OF LAMB, THE. Edited by E. V. Lucas.

BLUE BIRD, THE. Maurice Maeterlinck.

CHARLES DICKENS. G. K. Chesterton.

CHARMIDES, AND OTHER POEMS. Oscar Wilde.

CHITRÀL: The Story of a Minor Siege. Sir G. S. Robertson.

CUSTOMS OF OLD ENGLAND, THE. F. J. Snell.

DE PROFUNDIS. Oscar Wilde.

FAMOUS WITS, A BOOK OF. W. Jerrold.

FROM MIDSHIPMAN TO FIELD-MARSHAL. Sir Evelyn Wood, F.M., V.C.

HARVEST HOME. E. V. Lucas.

HILLS AND THE SEA. Hilaire Belloc.

IDEAL HUSBAND, AN. Oscar Wilde.

IMPORTANCE OF BEING EARNEST, THE. Oscar Wilde.

INTENTIONS. Oscar Wilde.

JANE AUSTEN AND HER TIMES. G. E. Mitton.

JOHN BOYES, KING OF THE WA-KIKUYU. John Boyes.

LADY WINDERMERE'S FAN. Oscar Wilde.

LETTERS FROM A SELF-MADE MERCHANT TO HIS SON. George Horace Lorimer.

LIFE OF JOHN RUSKIN, THE. W. G. Collingwood.

LIFE OF ROBERT LOUIS STEVENSON, THE. Graham Balfour.

LITTLE OF EVERYTHING, A. E. V. Lucas.

LORD ARTHUR SAVILE'S CRIME. Oscar Wilde.

LORE OF THE HONEY-BEE, THE. Tickner Edwardes.

MAN AND THE UNIVERSE. Sir Oliver Lodge.

MARY MAGDALENE. Maurice Maeterlinck.

MIRROR OF THE SEA, THE. J. Conrad.

MIXED VINTAGES. E V. Lucas.

MODERN PROBLEMS. Sir Oliver Lodge.

MY CHILDHOOD AND BOYHOOD. Leo Tolstoy.

MY YOUTH. Leo Tolstoy.

OLD COUNTRY LIFE. S. Baring-Gould.

OLD TIME PARSON, THE. P. H. Ditchfield.

ON EVERYTHING. Hilaire Belloc.

ON NOTHING. Hilaire Belloc.

OSCAR WILDE: A Critical Study. Arthur Ransome.

PICKED COMPANY, A. Hilaire Belloc.

REASON AND BELIEF. Sir Oliver Lodge.

R. L. S. Francis Watt.

SCIENCE FROM AN EASY CHAIR. Sir Ray Lankester.

SELECTED POEMS. Oscar Wilde.

SELECTED PROSE. Oscar Wilde.

SHEPHERD S LIFE, A. W. H. Hudson.

SHILLING FOR MY THOUGHTS, A. G. K. Chesterton.

SOCIAL EVILS AND THEIR REMEDY. Leo Tolstoy.

SOME LETTERS OF R. L. STEVENSON. Selected by Lloyd Osbourne.

SUBSTANCE OF FAITH, THE. Sir Oliver Lodge.

SURVIVAL OF MAN, THE. Sir Oliver Lodge.

TOWER OF LONDON, THE. R. Davey.

TWO ADMIRALS. Admiral John Moresby.

VAILIMA LETTERS. Robert Louis Stevenson.

VARIETY LANE. E. V. Lucas.

VICAR OF MORWENSTOW, THE. S. Baring-Gould.

WOMAN OF NO IMPORTANCE, A. Oscar Wilde.

A Selection only

Books for Travellers

Crown 8vo. 8s. 6d. net each

Each volume contains a number of Illustrations in Colour

AVON AND SHAKESPEARE'S COUNTRY, THE. A. G. Bradley. *Second Edition.*

BLACK FOREST, A BOOK OF THE. C. E. Hughes.

CITIES OF LOMBARDY, THE. Edward Hutton.

CITIES OF ROMAGNA AND THE MARCHES, THE. Edward Hutton.

CITIES OF SPAIN, THE. Edward Hutton. *Fifth Edition.*

CITIES OF UMBRIA, THE. Edward Hutton. *Fifth Edition.*

FLORENCE AND NORTHERN TUSCANY, WITH GENOA. Edward Hutton. *Third Edition.*

LAND OF PARDONS, THE (Brittany). Anatole Le Braz. *Fourth Edition.*

LONDON REVISITED. E. V. Lucas. *Third Edition.* 8s. 6d. net.

NAPLES. Arthur H. Norway. *Fourth Edition.* 8s. 6d. net.

NAPLES AND SOUTHERN ITALY. Edward Hutton.

NAPLES RIVIERA, THE. H. M. Vaughan. *Second Edition.*

NEW FOREST, THE. Horace G. Hutchinson. *Fourth Edition.*

NORWAY AND ITS FJORDS. M. A. Wyllie.

ROME. Edward Hutton. *Third Edition.*

ROUND ABOUT WILTSHIRE. A. G. Bradley. *Third Edition.*

SIENA AND SOUTHERN TUSCANY. Edward Hutton. *Second Edition.*

SKIRTS OF THE GREAT CITY, THE. Mrs. A. G. Bell. *Second Edition.*

VENICE AND VENETIA. Edward Hutton.

WANDERER IN FLORENCE, A. E. V. Lucas. *Sixth Edition.*

WANDERER IN PARIS, A. E. V. Lucas. *Thirteenth Edition.*

WANDERER IN HOLLAND, A. E. V. Lucas. *Sixteenth Edition.*

WANDERER IN LONDON, A. E. V. Lucas. *Eighteenth Edition.*

WANDERER IN VENICE, A. E. V. Lucas. *Second Edition.*

Some Books on Art

ART, ANCIENT AND MEDIEVAL. M. H. Bulley. Illustrated. *Crown 8vo.* 7s. 6d. net.

BRITISH SCHOOL, THE. An Anecdotal Guide to the British Painters and Paintings in the National Gallery. E. V. Lucas. Illustrated. *Fcap. 8vo.* 6s. net.

DECORATIVE IRON WORK. From the XIth to the XVIIIth Century. Charles ffoulkes. *Royal 4to.* £2 2s. net.

FRANCESCO GUARDI, 1712–1793. G. A. Simonson. Illustrated. *Imperial 4to.* £2 2s. net.

ILLUSTRATIONS OF THE BOOK OF JOB. William Blake. *Quarto.* £1 1s. net.

ITALIAN SCULPTORS. W. G. Waters. Illustrated. *Crown 8vo.* 7s. 6d. net.

OLD PASTE. A. Beresford Ryley. Illustrated. *Royal 4to.* £2 2s. net.

ONE HUNDRED MASTERPIECES OF SCULPTURE. With an Introduction by G. F. Hill. Illustrated. *Demy 8vo.* 12s. 6d. net.

ROYAL ACADEMY LECTURES ON PAINTING. George Clausen. Illustrated. *Crown 8vo.* 7s. 6d. net.

SAINTS IN ART, THE. Margaret E. Tabor. Illustrated. *Third Edition. Fcap. 8vo.* 5s. net.

SCHOOLS OF PAINTING. Mary Innes. Illustrated. *Second Edition. Cr. 8vo.* 8s. net.

CELTIC ART IN PAGAN AND CHRISTIAN TIMES. J. R. Allen. Illustrated. *Second Edition. Demy 8vo.* 10s. 6d. net.

Some Books on Italy

FLORENCE AND HER TREASURES. H. M. Vaughan. Illustrated. *Fcap. 8vo.* 6s. *net.*

FLORENCE AND THE CITIES OF NORTHERN TUSCANY, WITH GENOA. Edward Hutton. Illustrated. *Third Edition. Cr. 8vo.* 8s. 6d. *net.*

LOMBARDY, THE CITIES OF. Edward Hutton. Illustrated. *Cr. 8vo.* 8s. 6d. *net.*

MILAN UNDER THE SFORZA, A HISTORY OF. Cecilia M. Ady. Illustrated. *Demy 8vo.* 12s. 6d. *net.*

NAPLES : Past and Present. A. H. Norway. Illustrated. *Fourth Edition. Cr. 8vo.* 8s. 6d. *net.*

NAPLES RIVIERA, THE. H. M. Vaughan. Illustrated. *Second Edition. Cr. 8vo.* 8s. 6d. *net.*

NAPLES AND SOUTHERN ITALY. E. Hutton. Illustrated. *Cr. 8vo.* 8s. 6d. *net.*

PERUGIA, A HISTORY OF. William Heywood. Illustrated. *Demy 8vo.* 15s. *net.*

ROME. Edward Hutton. Illustrated. *Third Edition. Cr. 8vo.* 8s. 6d. *net.*

ROMAGNA AND THE MARCHES, THE CITIES OF. Edward Hutton. *Cr. 8vo.* 8s. 6d. *net.*

ROME. C. G. Ellaby. Illustrated. *Small Pott 8vo.* 4s. *net.*

SICILY. F. H. Jackson. Illustrated. *Small Pott 8vo.* 4s. *net.*

SICILY : The New Winter Resort. Douglas Sladen. Illustrated. *Second Edition. Cr. 8vo.* 7s. 6d. *net.*

SIENA AND SOUTHERN TUSCANY. Edward Hutton. Illustrated. *Second Edition. Cr. 8vo.* 8s. 6d. *net.*

UMBRIA, THE CITIES OF. Edward Hutton. Illustrated. *Fifth Edition. Cr. 8vo.* 8s. 6d. *net.*

VENICE AND VENETIA. Edward Hutton. Illustrated. *Cr. 8vo.* 8s. 6d. *net.*

VENICE ON FOOT. H. A. Douglas. Illustrated. *Second Edition. Fcap. 8vo.* 6s. *net.*

VENICE AND HER TREASURES. H. A. Douglas. Illustrated. *Fcap. 8vo.* 6s. *net.*

VERONA, A HISTORY OF. A. M. Allen. Illustrated. *Demy 8vo.* 15s. *net.*

DANTE ALIGHIERI : His Life and Works. Paget Toynbee. Illustrated. *Fourth Edition. Cr. 8vo.* 6s. *net.*

LAKES OF NORTHERN ITALY, THE. Richard Bagot. Illustrated. *Second Edition. Fcap. 8vo.* 6s. *net.*

SAVONAROLA, GIROLAMO. E. L. S. Horsburgh. Illustrated. *Fourth Edition. Cr. 8vo.* 6s. *net.*

SKIES ITALIAN : A Little Breviary for Travellers in Italy. Ruth S. Phelps. *Fcap. 8vo.* 5s. *net.*

PART III.—A SELECTION OF WORKS OF FICTION

Albanesi (E. Maria). I KNOW A MAIDEN. *Third Edition. Cr. 8vo. 7s. net.*

THE GLAD HEART. *Fifth Edition. Cr. 8vo. 7s. net.*

Aumonier (Stacy). OLGA BARDEL. *Cr. 8vo. 7s. net.*

Bagot (Richard). THE HOUSE OF SERRAVALLE. *Third Edition. Cr. 8vo. 7s. net.*

Bailey (H. C.). THE SEA CAPTAIN. *Third Edition. Cr. 8vo. 7s. net.*

THE HIGHWAYMAN. *Third Edition. Cr. 8vo. 7s. net.*

THE GAMESTERS. *Second Edition. Cr. 8vo. 7s. net.*

THE YOUNG LOVERS. *Second Edition. Cr. 8vo. 7s. net.*

Baring-Gould (S.). THE BROOM-SQUIRE. Illustrated. *Fifth Edition. Cr. 8vo. 7s. net.*

Barr (Robert). IN THE MIDST OF ALARMS. *Third Edition. Cr. 8vo. 7s. net.*

THE COUNTESS TEKLA. *Fifth Edition. Cr. 8vo. 7s. net.*

THE MUTABLE MANY. *Third Edition. Cr. 8vo. 7s. net.*

Begbie (Harold). THE CURIOUS AND DIVERTING ADVENTURES OF SIR JOHN SPARROW, BART.; OR, THE PROGRESS OF AN OPEN MIND. *Second Edition. Cr. 8vo. 7s. net.*

Belloc (H.). EMMANUEL BURDEN, MERCHANT. Illustrated. *Second Edition. Cr. 8vo. 7s. net.*

Bennett (Arnold). CLAYHANGER. *Twelfth Edition. Cr. 8vo. 8s. net.*

HILDA LESSWAYS. *Eighth Edition. Cr. 8vo. 7s. net.*

THESE TWAIN. *Fourth Edition. Cr. 8vo. 7s. net.*

THE CARD. *Thirteenth Edition. Cr. 8vo. 7s. net.*

THE REGENT: A FIVE TOWNS STORY OF ADVENTURE IN LONDON. *Fifth Edition. Cr. 8vo. 7s. net.*

THE PRICE OF LOVE. *Fourth Edition. Cr. 8vo. 7s. net.*

BURIED ALIVE. *Ninth Edition. Cr. 8vo. 7s. net.*

A MAN FROM THE NORTH. *Third Edition. Cr. 8vo. 7s. net.*

THE MATADOR OF THE FIVE TOWNS. *Second Edition. Cr. 8vo. 7s. net.*

WHOM GOD HATH JOINED. *A New Edition. Cr. 8vo. 7s. net.*

A GREAT MAN: A FROLIC. *Seventh Edition. Cr. 8vo. 7s. net.*

Benson (E. F.). DODO: A DETAIL OF THE DAY. *Seventeenth Edition. Cr. 8vo. 7s. net.*

Birmingham (George A.). SPANISH GOLD. *Seventeenth Edition. Cr. 8vo. 7s. net.*

THE SEARCH PARTY. *Tenth Edition. Cr. 8vo. 7s. net.*

LALAGE'S LOVERS. *Third Edition. Cr. 8vo. 7s. net.*

GOSSAMER. *Fourth Edition. Cr. 8vo. 7s. net.*

THE ISLAND MYSTERY. *Second Edition. Cr. 8vo. 7s. net.*

THE BAD TIMES. *Second Edition. Cr. 8vo 7s. net.*

Bowen (Marjorie). I WILL MAINTAIN. *Ninth Edition. Cr. 8vo. 7s. net.*

DEFENDER OF THE FAITH. *Seventh Edition. Cr. 8vo. 7s. net.*

WILLIAM, BY THE GRACE OF GOD. *Second Edition. Cr. 8vo. 7s. net.*

GOD AND THE KING. *Sixth Edition.* Cr. 8vo. 7s. net.

PRINCE AND HERETIC. *Third Edition.* Cr. 8vo. 7s. net.

A KNIGHT OF SPAIN. *Third Edition.* Cr. 8vo. 7s. net.

THE QUEST OF GLORY. *Third Edition.* Cr. 8vo. 7s. net.

THE GOVERNOR OF ENGLAND. *Third Edition.* Cr. 8vo. 7s. net.

THE CARNIVAL OF FLORENCE. *Fifth Edition.* Cr. 8vo. 7s. net.

MR. WASHINGTON. *Third Edition.* Cr. 8vo. 7s. net.

"BECAUSE OF THESE THINGS. . . ." *Third Edition.* Cr. 8vo. 7s. net.

THE THIRD ESTATE. *Second Edition.* Cr. 8vo. 7s. net.

Burroughs (Edgar Rice). THE RETURN OF TARZAN. *Fcap. 8vo.* 2s. net.

THE BEASTS OF TARZAN. *Second Edition.* Cr. 8vo. 6s. net.

THE SON OF TARZAN. Cr. 8vo. 7s. net.

A PRINCESS OF MARS. Cr. 8vo. 5s. net.

Castle (Agnes and Egerton). THE GOLDEN BARRIER. *Third Edition.* Cr. 8vo. 7s. net.

Conrad (Joseph). A SET OF SIX. *Fourth Edition.* Cr. 8vo. 7s. net.

VICTORY: AN ISLAND TALE. *Sixth Edition.* Cr. 8vo. 9s. net.

Conyers (Dorothea). SANDY MARRIED. *Fifth Edition.* Cr. 8vo. 7s. net.

OLD ANDY. *Fourth Edition.* Cr. 8vo. 7s. net.

THE BLIGHTING OF BARTRAM. *Third Edition.* Cr. 8vo. 7s. net.

B. E. N. *Cr 8vo.* 7s. net.

Corelli (Marie). A ROMANCE OF TWO WORLDS. *Thirty-fifth Edition.* Cr. 8vo. 7s. 6d. net.

VENDETTA; OR, THE STORY OF ONE FORGOTTEN. *Thirty-fifth Edition.* Cr. 8vo. 8s. net.

THELMA: A NORWEGIAN PRINCESS. *Fifty-ninth Edition.* Cr. 8vo. 8s. 6d. net.

ARDATH: THE STORY OF A DEAD SELF. *Twenty-fourth Edition.* Cr. 8vo. 7s. 6d. net.

THE SOUL OF LILITH. *Twentieth Edition.* Cr. 8vo. 7s. net.

WORMWOOD: A DRAMA OF PARIS. *Twenty-second Edition.* Cr. 8vo. 8s. net.

BARABBAS: A DREAM OF THE WORLD'S TRAGEDY. *Fiftieth Edition.* Cr. 8vo. 8s. net.

THE SORROWS OF SATAN. *Sixty-third Edition.* Cr. 8vo. 7s. net.

THE MASTER-CHRISTIAN. *Eighteenth Edition.* 184th Thousand. Cr. 8vo. 8s. 6d. net.

TEMPORAL POWER: A STUDY IN SUPREMACY. *Second Edition.* 150th Thousand. Cr. 8vo. 6s. net.

GOD'S GOOD MAN: A SIMPLE LOVE STORY. *Twentieth Edition.* 159th Thousand. Cr. 8vo. 8s. 6d. net.

HOLY ORDERS: THE TRAGEDY OF A QUIET LIFE. *Third Edition.* 121st Thousand. Cr. 8vo. 8s. 6d. net.

THE MIGHTY ATOM. *Thirty-sixth Edition.* Cr. 8vo. 7s. 6d. net.

BOY: A SKETCH. *Twentieth Edition.* Cr. 8vo. 6s. net.

CAMEOS. *Fifteenth Edition.* Cr. 8vo. 6s. net.

THE LIFE EVERLASTING. *Eighth Edition.* Cr. 8vo. 8s. 6d. net.

Crockett (S. R.). LOCHINVAR. Illustrated. *Fifth Edition.* Cr. 8vo. 7s. net.

THE STANDARD BEARER. *Second Edition.* Cr. 8vo. 7s. net.

Doyle (Sir A. Conan). ROUND THE RED LAMP. *Twelfth Edition.* Cr. 8vo. 7s. net.

Dudeney (Mrs. H.). THIS WAY OUT. Cr. 8vo. 7s. net.

Fry (B. and C. B.). A MOTHER'S SON. *Fifth Edition* Cr. 8vo. 7s. net.

Harraden (Beatrice). THE GUIDING THREAD. *Second Edition.* Cr. 8vo. 7s. net.

Hichens (Robert). THE PROPHET OF BERKELEY SQUARE. *Second Edition.* Cr. 8vo. 7s. net.

TONGUES OF CONSCIENCE. *Fourth Edition.* Cr. 8vo. 7s. net.

FELIX: THREE YEARS IN A LIFE. *Seventh Edition. Cr. 8vo. 7s. net.*

THE WOMAN WITH THE FAN. *Eighth Edition. Cr. 8vo. 7s. net.*

BYEWAYS. *Cr. 8vo. 7s. net.*

THE GARDEN OF ALLAH. *Twenty-sixth Edition. Illustrated. Cr. 8vo. 8s. 6d. net.*

THE CALL OF THE BLOOD. *Ninth Edition. Cr. 8vo. 8s. 6d. net.*

BARBARY SHEEP. *Second Edition. Cr. 8vo. 6s. net.*

THE DWELLER ON THE THRESHOLD. *Cr. 8vo. 7s. net.*

THE WAY OF AMBITION. *Fifth Edition. Cr. 8vo. 7s. net.*

IN THE WILDERNESS. *Third Edition. Cr. 8vo. 7s. net.*

Hope (Anthony). A CHANGE OF AIR. *Sixth Edition. Cr. 8vo. 7s. net.*

A MAN OF MARK. *Seventh Edition. Cr. 8vo. 7s. net.*

THE CHRONICLES OF COUNT ANTONIO. *Sixth Edition. Cr. 8vo. 7s. net.*

PHROSO. *Illustrated. Ninth Edition. Cr. 8vo. 7s. net.*

SIMON DALE. *Illustrated. Ninth Edition. Cr. 8vo. 7s. net.*

THE KING'S MIRROR. *Fifth Edition. Cr. 8vo. 7s. net.*

QUISANTE. *Fourth Edition. Cr. 8vo. 7s. net.*

THE DOLLY DIALOGUES. *Cr. 8vo. 7s. net.*

TALES OF TWO PEOPLE. *Third Edition. Cr. 8vo. 7s. net.*

A SERVANT OF THE PUBLIC. *Illustrated. Fourth Edition. Cr. 8vo. 7s. net.*

MRS. MAXON PROTESTS. *Third Edition. Cr. 8vo. 7s. net.*

A YOUNG MAN'S YEAR. *Second Edition. Cr. 8vo. 7s. net.*

Hyne (C. J. Cutcliffe). MR. HORROCKS, PURSER. *Fifth Edition. Cr. 8vo 7s. net.*

FIREMEN HOT. *Fourth Edition. Cr. 8vo. 7s. net.*

CAPTAIN KETTLE ON THE WAR-PATH. *Third Edition. Cr. 8vo. 7s. net.*

RED HERRINGS. *Cr. 8vo. 6s. net.*

Jacobs (W. W.). MANY CARGOES. *Thirty-third Edition. Cr. 8vo. 5s. net. Also Cr. 8vo. 2s. 6d. net.*

SEA URCHINS. *Nineteenth Edition. Cr. 8vo. 5s. net. Also Cr. 8vo. 3s. 6d. net.*

A MASTER OF CRAFT. *Illustrated. Eleventh Edition. Cr. 8vo. 5s. net.*

LIGHT FREIGHTS. *Illustrated. Fifteenth Edition. Cr. 8vo. 5s. net.*

THE SKIPPER'S WOOING. *Twelfth Edition. Cr. 8vo. 5s. net.*

AT SUNWICH PORT. *Illustrated. Eleventh Edition. Cr. 8vo. 5s. net.*

DIALSTONE LANE. *Illustrated. Eighth Edition. Cr. 8vo. 5s. net.*

ODD CRAFT. *Illustrated. Fifth Edition. Cr. 8vo. 5s. net.*

THE LADY OF THE BARGE. *Illustrated. Tenth Edition. Cr. 8vo. 5s. net.*

SALTHAVEN. *Illustrated. Fourth Edition. Cr. 8vo. 5s. net.*

SAILORS' KNOTS. *Illustrated. Sixth Edition. Cr. 8vo. 5s. net.*

SHORT CRUISES. *Third Edition. Cr 8vo. 5s. net.*

King (Basil). THE LIFTED VEIL. *Cr. 8vo. 7s. net.*

Lethbridge (Sybil C.). ONE WOMAN'S HERO. *Cr. 8vo. 7s. net.*

London (Jack). WHITE FANG. *Ninth Edition. Cr. 8vo. 7s. net.*

Lowndes (Mrs. Belloc). THE LODGER. *Third Edition. Cr. 8vo. 7s. net.*

Lucas (E. V.). LISTENER'S LURE: AN OBLIQUE NARRATION. *Twelfth Edition. Fcap. 8vo. 6s. net.*

OVER BEMERTON'S: AN EASY-GOING CHRONICLE. *Sixteenth Edition. Fcap. 8vo. 6s. net.*

MR. INGLESIDE. *Thirteenth Edition. Fcap. 8vo. 6s. net.*

LONDON LAVENDER. *Twelfth Edition. Fcap. 8vo. 6s. net.*

LANDMARKS. *Fifth Edition. Cr. 8vo. 7s. net.*

THE VERMILION BOX. *Fifth Edition. Cr. 8vo. 7s. net.*

Lyall (Edna). DERRICK VAUGHAN, NOVELIST. *44th Thousand. Cr. 8vo. 5s. net.*

McKenna (Stephen). SONIA : BETWEEN TWO WORLDS. *Sixteenth Edition. Cr. 8vo. 8s. net.*

NINETY-SIX HOURS' LEAVE. *Fifth Edition. Cr. 8vo. 7s. net.*

THE SIXTH SENSE. *Cr. 8vo. 6s. net.*

MIDAS & SON. *Cr. 8vo. 8s. net.*

Macnaughtan (S.). PETER AND JANE. *Fourth Edition. Cr. 8vo. 7s. net.*

Malet (Lucas). THE HISTORY OF SIR RICHARD CALMADY : A ROMANCE. *Seventh Edition. Cr. 8vo. 7s. net.*

THE WAGES OF SIN. *Sixteenth Edition. Cr. 8vo. 7s. net.*

THE CARISSIMA. *Fifth Edition. Cr. 8vo. 7s. net.*

THE GATELESS BARRIER. *Fifth Edition. Cr. 8vo. 7s. net.*

Mason (A. E. W.). CLEMENTINA. Illustrated. *Ninth Edition. Cr. 8vo. 7s. net.*

Maxwell (W. B.). VIVIEN. *Thirteenth Edition. Cr. 8vo. 7s. net.*

THE GUARDED FLAME. *Seventh Edition. Cr. 8vo. 7s. net.*

ODD LENGTHS. *Second Edition. Cr. 8vo. 7s. net.*

HILL RISE. *Fourth Edition. Cr. 8vo. 7s. net.*

THE REST CURE. *Fourth Edition. Cr. 8vo. 7s. net.*

Milne (A. A.). THE DAY'S PLAY. *Sixth Edition. Cr. 8vo. 7s. net.*

ONCE A WEEK. *Cr. 8vo. 7s. net.*

Morrison (Arthur). TALES OF MEAN STREETS. *Seventh Edition. Cr. 8vo. 7s. net.*

A CHILD OF THE JAGO. *Sixth Edition. Cr. 8vo. 7s. net.*

THE HOLE IN THE WALL. *Fourth Edition. Cr. 8vo. 7s. net.*

DIVERS VANITIES. *Cr. 8vo. 7s. net.*

Oppenheim (E. Phillips). MASTER OF MEN. *Fifth Edition. Cr. 8vo. 7s. net.*

THE MISSING DELORA. Illustrated. *Fourth Edition. Cr. 8vo. 7s. net.*

THE DOUBLE LIFE OF MR. ALFRED BURTON. *Second Edition. Cr. 8vo. 7s. net.*

A PEOPLE'S MAN. *Third Edition. Cr. 8vo. 7s. net.*

MR. GREX OF MONTE CARLO. *Third Edition. Cr. 8vo. 7s. net.*

THE VANISHED MESSENGER. *Second Edition. Cr. 8vo. 7s. net.*

THE HILLMAN. *Cr. 8vo. 7s. net.*

Oxenham (John). A WEAVER OF WEBS. Illustrated. *Fifth Edition. Cr. 8vo. 7s. net.*

PROFIT AND LOSS. *Sixth Edition. Cr. 8vo. 7s. net.*

THE SONG OF HYACINTH, AND OTHER STORIES. *Second Edition. Cr. 8vo. 7s. net.*

LAURISTONS. *Fourth Edition. Cr. 8vo. 7s. net.*

THE COIL OF CARNE. *Sixth Edition. Cr. 8vo. 7s. net.*

THE QUEST OF THE GOLDEN ROSE. *Fourth Edition. Cr. 8vo. 7s. net.*

MARY ALL-ALONE. *Third Edition. Cr. 8vo. 7s. net.*

BROKEN SHACKLES. *Fourth Edition. Cr. 8vo. 7s. net.*

"1914." *Third Edition. Cr. 8vo. 7s. net.*

Parker (Gilbert). PIERRE AND HIS PEOPLE. *Seventh Edition. Cr. 8vo. 7s. net.*

MRS. FALCHION. *Fifth Edition. Cr. 8vo. 7s. net.*

THE TRANSLATION OF A SAVAGE. *Fourth Edition. Cr. 8vo. 7s. net.*

THE TRAIL OF THE SWORD. Illustrated. *Tenth Edition. Cr. 8vo. 7s. net.*

WHEN VALMOND CAME TO PONTIAC : THE STORY OF A LOST NAPOLEON. *Seventh Edition. Cr. 8vo. 7s. net.*

AN ADVENTURER OF THE NORTH : THE LAST ADVENTURES OF 'PRETTY PIERRE.' *Fifth Edition. Cr. 8vo. 7s. net.*

THE SEATS OF THE MIGHTY. Illustrated. *Twentieth Edition. Cr. 8vo. 7s. net.*

THE BATTLE OF THE STRONG : A ROMANCE OF TWO KINGDOMS. Illustrated. *Seventh Edition. Cr. 8vo. 7s. net.*

THE POMP OF THE LAVILETTES. *Third Edition. Cr. 8vo. 6s. net.*

NORTHERN LIGHTS. *Fourth Edition. Cr. 8vo. 7s. net.*

Perrin (Alice). THE CHARM. *Fifth Edition. Cr. 8vo. 7s. net.*

Phillpotts (Eden). CHILDREN OF THE MIST. *Sixth Edition. Cr. 8vo. 7s. net.*

THE HUMAN BOY. With a Frontispiece. *Seventh Edition*. *Cr. 8vo*. *7s. net*.

SONS OF THE MORNING. *Second Edition*. *Cr. 8vo*. *7s. net*.

THE RIVER. *Fourth Edition*. *Cr. 8vo*. *7s. net*.

THE AMERICAN PRISONER. *Fourth Edition*. *Cr. 8vo*. *7s. net*.

DEMETER'S DAUGHTER. *Third Edition*. *Cr. 8vo*. *7s. net*.

THE HUMAN BOY AND THE WAR. *Third Edition*. *Cr. 8vo*. *7s. net*.

Ridge (W. Pett). A SON OF THE STATE. *Third Edition*. *Cr. 8vo*. *7s. net*.

THE REMINGTON SENTENCE. *Third Edition*. *Cr. 8vo*. *7s. net*.

MADAME PRINCE. *Second Edition*. *Cr. 8vo*. *7s. net*.

TOP SPEED. *Second Edition*. *Cr. 8vo*. *7s. net*.

SPECIAL PERFORMANCES. *Cr. 8vo*. *6s. net*.

THE BUSTLING HOURS. *Cr. 8vo*. *7s. net*.

Rohmer (Sax). THE DEVIL DOCTOR. *Third Edition*. *Cr. 8vo*. *7s. net*.

THE SI-FAN MYSTERIES. *Second Edition*. *Cr. 8vo*. *7s. net*.

TALES OF SECRET EGYPT. *Cr. 8vo*. *6s. net*.

THE ORCHARD OF TEARS. *Cr. 8vo*. *6s. net*.

Swinnerton (F.). SHOPS AND HOUSES. *Cr. 8vo*. *7s. net*.

Wells (H. G.). BEALBY. *Fifth Edition*. *Cr. 8vo*. *7s. net*.

Williamson (C. N. and A. M.). THE LIGHTNING CONDUCTOR: THE STRANGE ADVENTURES OF A MOTOR CAR. Illustrated. *Twenty-second Edition*. *Cr. 8vo*. *7s. net*.

THE PRINCESS PASSES: A ROMANCE OF A MOTOR. Illustrated. *Ninth Edition*. *Cr. 8vo*. *7s. net*.

LADY BETTY ACROSS THE WATER. *Nineteenth Edition*. *Cr. 8vo*. *7s. net*.

SCARLET RUNNER. Illustrated. *Fourth Edition*. *Cr. 8vo*. *7s. net*.

LORD LOVELAND DISCOVERS AMERICA. Illustrated. *Second Edition*. *Cr. 8vo*. *7s. net*.

THE GOLDEN SILENCE. Illustrated. *Eighth Edition*. *Cr. 8vo*. *7s. net*.

THE GUESTS OF HERCULES. Illustrated. *Fourth Edition*. *Cr. 8vo*. *7s. net*.

IT HAPPENED IN EGYPT. Illustrated. *Seventh Edition*. *Cr. 8vo*. *7s. net*.

A SOLDIER OF THE LEGION. *Second Edition*. *Cr. 8vo*. *7s. net*.

THE SHOP GIRL. *Cr. 8vo*. *7s. net*.

THE LIGHTNING CONDUCTRESS. *Third Edition*. *Cr. 8vo*. *7s. net*.

SECRET HISTORY. *Cr. 8vo*. *7s. net*.

THE LOVE PIRATE. Illustrated. *Third Edition*. *Cr. 8vo*. *7s. net*. *Also Cr. 8vo*. *3s. 6d. net*.

CRUCIFIX CORNER. *Cr. 8vo*. *6s. net*.

Wilson (Romer). MARTIN SCHULER. *Cr. 8vo*. *7s. net*.

Books for Boys and Girls

Illustrated. Crown 8vo. 5s. net.

GETTING WELL OF DOROTHY, THE. Mrs. W. K. Clifford. *6s. net*.

GIRL OF THE PEOPLE, A. L. T. Meade.

HONOURABLE MISS, THE. L. T. Meade.

MASTER ROCKAFELLAR'S VOYAGE. W. Clark Russell.

RED GRANGE, THE. Mrs. Molesworth.

THERE WAS ONCE A PRINCE. Mrs. M. E. Mann.

Methuen's Cheap Novels

Fcap. 8vo. 2s. *net.*

ABANDONED. W. Clark Russell.

ADVENTURES OF DR. WHITTY, THE. George A. Birmingham.

ANGLO-INDIANS, THE. Alice Perrin.

ANNA OF THE FIVE TOWNS. Arnold Bennett.

ANTHONY CUTHBERT. Richard Bagot.

BABES IN THE WOOD. B. M. Croker.

BAD TIMES, THE. George A. Birmingham.

BARBARY SHEEP. Robert Hichens.

BECAUSE OF THESE THINGS. . . . Marjorie Bowen.

BELOVED ENEMY, THE. E. Maria Albanesi.

BELOW STAIRS. Mrs. Alfred Sidgwick.

BOTOR CHAPERON, THE. C. N. and A. M. Williamson.

BOY. Marie Corelli.

BRANDED PRINCE, THE. Weatherby Chesney.

BROKEN SHACKLES. John Oxenham.

BROOM SQUIRE, THE. S. Baring-Gould.

BURIED ALIVE. Arnold Bennett.

BYEWAYS. Robert Hichens.

CALL OF THE BLOOD, THE. Robert Hichens.

CAMEOS. Marie Corelli.

CARD, THE. Arnold Bennett.

CARISSIMA, THE. Lucas Malet.

CEASE FIRE. J. M. Cobban.

CHANCE. Joseph Conrad.

CHANGE IN THE CABINET, A Hilaire Belloc.

CHINK IN THE ARMOUR, THE. Mrs. Belloc Lowndes.

CHRONICLES OF A GERMAN TOWN. The Author of "Mercia in Germany."

COIL OF CARNE, THE. John Oxenham.

CONVERT, THE. Elizabeth Robins.

COUNSEL OF PERFECTION, A. Lucas Malet.

CROOKED WAY, THE. William Le Queux.

DAN RUSSEL THE FOX. E. Œ. Somerville and Martin Ross.

DARNELEY PLACE. Richard Bagot.

DEAD MEN TELL NO TALES. E. W. Hornung.

DEMETER'S DAUGHTER. Eden Phillpotts.

DEMON, THE. C. N. and A. M. Williamson.

DESERT TRAIL, THE. Dane Coolidge.

DEVIL DOCTOR, THE. Sax Rohmer.

DOUBLE LIFE OF MR. ALFRED BURTON, THE. E. Phillips Oppenheim.

DUKE'S MOTTO, THE. J. H. McCarthy.

EMMANUEL BURDEN. Hilaire Belloc.

END OF HER HONEYMOON, THE. Mrs. Belloc Lowndes.

FAMILY, THE. Elinor Mordaunt.

FIRE IN STUBBLE. Baroness Orczy.

FIREMEN HOT. C. J. Cutcliffe Hyne.

FLOWER OF THE DUSK. Myrtle Reed.

GATE OF THE DESERT, THE. John Oxenham.

GATES OF WRATH, THE. Arnold Bennett.

GENTLEMAN ADVENTURER, THE. H. C. Bailey.

GOLDEN CENTIPEDE, THE. Louise Gerard.

GOLDEN SILENCE, THE. C. N. and A. M. Williamson.

GOSSAMER. George A. Birmingham.

GOVERNOR OF ENGLAND, THE. Marjorie Bowen.

GREAT LADY, A. Adeline Sergeant.

GREAT MAN, A. Arnold Bennett.

GUARDED FLAME, THE. W. B. Maxwell.

GUIDING THREAD, THE. Beatrice Harraden.

HALO, THE. Baroness von Hutten.

HAPPY HUNTING GROUND, THE. Alice Perrin.

HAPPY VALLEY, THE. B. M. Croker.

HEART OF HIS HEART. E. Maria Albanesi.

HEART OF THE ANCIENT WOOD, THE. Charles G. D. Roberts.

HEATHER MOON, THE. C. N. and A. M. Williamson.

HERITAGE OF PERIL, A. A. W. Marchmont.

HIGHWAYMAN, The. H. C. Bailey.

HILLMAN, THE. E. Phillips Oppenheim.

HILL RISE. W. B. Maxwell.

HOUSE OF SERRAVALLE, THE. Richard Bagot.

HYENA OF KALLU, THE. Louise Gerard.

ISLAND PRINCESS, HIS W. Clark Russell.

Methuen's Cheap Novels—*continued.*

JANE. Marie Corelli.

JOHANNA. B. M. Croker.

JOSEPH. Frank Danby.

JOSHUA DAVIDSON, COMMUNIST. E. Lynn Linton.

JOSS, THE. Richard Marsh.

KINSMAN, THE. Mrs. Alfred Sidgwick.

KNIGHT OF SPAIN, A. Marjorie Bowen.

LADY BETTY ACROSS THE WATER. C. N. and A. M. Williamson.

LALAGE'S LOVERS. George A. Birmingham.

LANTERN BEARERS, THE. Mrs. Alfred Sidgwick.

LAURISTONS. John Oxenham.

LAVENDER AND OLD LACE. Myrtle Reed.

LIGHT FREIGHTS. W. W. Jacobs.

LODGER, THE. Mrs. Belloc Lowndes.

LONG ROAD, THE. John Oxenham.

LOVE AND LOUISA. E. Maria Albanesi.

LOVE PIRATE, THE. C. N. and A. M. Williamson.

MARY ALL-ALONE. John Oxenham.

MASTER OF THE VINEYARD. Myrtle Reed.

MASTER'S VIOLIN, THE. Myrtle Reed.

MAX CARRADOS. Ernest Bramah.

MAYOR OF TROY, THE. "Q."

MESS DECK, THE. W. F. Shannon.

MIGHTY ATOM, THE. Marie Corelli.

MIRAGE. E. Temple Thurston.

MISSING DELORA, THE. E. Phillips Oppenheim.

MR. GREX OF MONTE CARLO. E. Phillips Oppenheim.

MR. WASHINGTON. Marjorie Bowen.

MRS. MAXON PROTESTS. Anthony Hope.

MRS. PETER HOWARD. Mary E. Mann.

MY DANISH SWEETHEART. W. Clark Russell.

MY FRIEND THE CHAUFFEUR. C. N. and A. M. Williamson.

MY HUSBAND AND I. Leo Tolstoy.

MY LADY OF SHADOWS. John Oxenham.

MYSTERY OF DR. FU-MANCHU, THE. Sax Rohmer.

MYSTERY OF THE GREEN HEART, THE. Max Pemberton.

NINE DAYS' WONDER, A. B. M. Croker.

NINE TO SIX-THIRTY. W. Pett Ridge.

OCEAN SLEUTH, THE. Maurice Drake.

OLD ROSE AND SILVER. Myrtle Reed.

PATHS OF THE PRUDENT, THE. J. S. Fletcher.

PATHWAY OF THE PIONEER, THE. Dolf Wyllarde.

PEGGY OF THE BARTONS. B. M. Croker.

PEOPLE'S MAN, A. E. Phillips Oppenheim.

PETER AND JANE. S. Macnaughtan.

POMP OF THE LAVILETTES, THE. Sir Gilbert Parker.

QUEST OF GLORY, THE. Marjorie Bowen.

QUEST OF THE GOLDEN ROSE, THE. John Oxenham.

REGENT, THE. Arnold Bennett.

REMINGTON SENTENCE, THE. W. Pett Ridge.

REST CURE, THE. W. B. Maxwell.

RETURN OF TARZAN, THE. Edgar Rice Burroughs.

ROUND THE RED LAMP. Sir A. Conan Doyle.

ROYAL GEORGIE. S. Baring-Gould.

SAÏD, THE FISHERMAN. Marmaduke Pickthall.

SALLY. Dorothea Conyers.

SALVING OF A DERELICT, THE. Maurice Drake.

SANDY MARRIED. Dorothea Conyers.

SEA CAPTAIN, THE. H. C. Bailey.

SEA LADY, THE. H. G. Wells.

SEARCH PARTY, THE. George A. Birmingham.

SECRET AGENT, THE. Joseph Conrad.

SECRET HISTORY. C. N. and A. M. Williamson.

SECRET WOMAN, THE. Eden Phillpotts.

SET IN SILVER. C. N. and A. M. Williamson.

SEVASTOPOL, AND OTHER STORIES. Leo Tolstoy.

SEVERINS, THE. Mrs. Alfred Sidgwick.

SHORT CRUISES. W. W. Jacobs.

SI-FAN MYSTERIES, THE. Sax Rohmer.

SPANISH GOLD. George A. Birmingham.

SPINNER IN THE SUN, A. Myrtle Reed.

STREET CALLED STRAIGHT, THE. Basil King.

SUPREME CRIME, THE. Dorothea Gerard.

TALES OF MEAN STREETS. Arthur Morrison.

TARZAN OF THE APES. Edgar Rice Burroughs.

Methuen's Cheap Novels—*continued*.

TERESA OF WATLING STREET. Arnold Bennett.

THERE WAS A CROOKED MAN. Dolf Wyllarde.

TYRANT, THE. Mrs. Henry de la Pasture.

UNDER WESTERN EYES. Joseph Conrad.

UNOFFICIAL HONEYMOON, THE. Dolf Wyllarde.

VALLEY OF THE SHADOW, THE. William Le Queux.

VIRGINIA PERFECT. Peggy Webling.

WALLET OF KAI LUNG. Ernest Bramah.

WAR WEDDING, THE. C. N. and A. M. Williamson.

WARE CASE, THE. George Pleydell.

WAY HOME, THE. Basil King.

WAY OF THESE WOMEN, THE. E. Phillips Oppenheim.

WEAVER OF DREAMS, A. Myrtle Reed.

WEAVER OF WEBS, A. John Oxenham.

WEDDING DAY, THE. C. N. and A. M. Williamson.

WHITE FANG. Jack London.

WILD OLIVE, THE. Basil King.

WILLIAM, BY THE GRACE OF GOD. Marjorie Bowen.

WOMAN WITH THE FAN, THE. Robert Hichens.

WO₂. Maurice Drake.

WONDER OF LOVE, THE. E. Maria Albanesi.

YELLOW CLAW, THE. Sax Rohmer.

YELLOW DIAMOND, THE. Adeline Sergeant.

Methuen's One and Threepenny Novels

Fcap. 8vo. 1*s.* 3*d. net*

BARBARA REBELL. Mrs. Belloc Lowndes.

BY STROKE OF SWORD. Andrew Balfour.

DERRICK VAUGHAN, NOVELIST. Edna Lyall.

HOUSE OF WHISPERS, THE. William Le Queux.

INCA'S TREASURE, THE E. Glanville.

KATHERINE THE ARROGANT. Mrs. B. M. Croker.

MOTHER'S SON, A. B. and C. B. Fry.

PROFIT AND LOSS. John Oxenham.

RED DERELICT, THE. Bertram Mitford.

SIGN OF THE SPIDER, THE. Bertram Mitford.

PRINTED BY MORRISON AND GIBB LIMITED, EDINBURGH

27/6/19.